URBAN DESIGN DOWNTOWN

URBAN DESIGN DOWNTOWN

POETICS AND POLITICS OF FORM

ANASTASIA LOUKAITOU-SIDERIS

AND

TRIDIB BANERJEE

UNIVERSITY OF CALIFORNIA PRESS

BERKELEY   LOS ANGELES   LONDON

University of California Press
Berkeley and Los Angeles, California

University of California Press, Ltd.
London, England

Library of Congress Cataloging-in-Publication
Data

Loukaitou-Sideris, Anastasia, 1958–
    Urban Design Downtown: poetics and
politics of form / Anastasia Loukaitou-Sideris
and Tridib Banerjee.
        p.   cm.
    Includes bibliographic references and
    index.
    ISBN 0–520–20930–3 (cloth: alk. paper)
    1. City planning—California—Case
studies.   2. Central business districts—California—Case studies.   3. Urban policy—California—Case studies.
I. Banerjee, Tridib.   II. Title.
HT167.5.C2L68   1998
307.1'216'09794—dc 21   97–10758
                                 CIP

Printed in the United States of America

9 8 7 6 5 4 3 2 1

The paper used in this publication meets the
minimum requirements of American National
Standard for Information Sciences—Perma-
nence of Paper for Printed Library Materials,
ANSI Z39.48–1984.

TO OUR FAMILIES ■

CONTENTS

List of Illustrations   ix

Acknowledgments   xiv

Introduction: The New Downtown   xviii

Part One   **The Evolution of Downtown Form**

1   The Changing Face of Downtown   3

2   Models of Downtown Design   35

3   Corporate Production of Downtown Space   73

Part Two   **The Politics of Development**

4   The Politics of Place Making   103

5   The Two Faces of Downtown   151

6   Public Life and Space in Transition   175

Part Three   **The Poetics of Form**

7   The Poetics of Corporate Open Spaces   199

8   One Percent Aesthetics   233

9 Theming and Stage Setting: The Story of Production

and Promotion   255

10 Postmodern Urban Form   277

Epilogue: Challenges for Downtown Urban Design   299

Notes   309

Bibliography   322

Index   345

LIST OF ILLUSTRATIONS

1. New York City, 1888
2. Chicago, 1895
3. Los Angeles, 1885
4. Los Angeles, ca. 1910
5. New York City, ca. 1915
6. New York City, ca. 1908
7. Rockefeller Center, New York, 1934
8. Los Angeles, 1923
9. Los Angeles, Bunker Hill, 1967
10. Los Angeles, Bunker Hill, 1990s
11. Renaissance Center, Detroit, 1995
12. Los Angeles, Bunker Hill, 1890s
13. Bunker Hill in transition
14. Los Angeles, Bunker Hill, 1971
15. Bunker Hill, 1960s
16. Pueblo Plaza, ca. 1877
17. Pueblo Plaza, 1883
18. Plan of the Pueblo of San Fernando de Bexar, ca. 1730
19. Jackson Square, New Orleans, 1903
20. New York City, 1910–1930
21. Pershing Square, 1923
22. Burnham plan for Chicago, 1909
23. Burnham plan for central Chicago, 1909
24. New York City, setback zoning, 1916
25. New York City, possible building forms, 1916

26. New York City, "setback style"

27. Hugh Ferriss's "The Business Zone," 1929

28. Le Corbusier's *La Ville Contemporaine*

29. E. Maxwell Fry's "The Future Tower City," 1931

30. A. J. Frappier's proposed Chrystie-Forsyth Parkway, 1931

31. Houston, Texas, 1960s

32. Downtown Forth Worth, Texas, 1956

33. Revitalization plan for Philadelphia, Pennsylvania, 1973

34. Aerial view of Market Street design, Philadelphia, 1973

35. The access tree diagram for midtown Manhattan, 1969

36. Urban design proposal for Manhattan, 1960

37. People mover system in downtown Detroit, 1995

38. New York City, 1960s

39. Cleveland, Ohio, 1960s

40. Fulton Mall, Fresno, California, 1960s

41. Revitalization of downtown district, Seattle, 1974

42. Harborplace, Baltimore, 1996

43. Faneuil Hall Market, Boston, 1990

44. Downtown Los Angeles districts

45. Security Pacific Plaza: Site plan

46. Security Pacific Plaza, 1996

47. Security Pacific Plaza, 1996

48. Noguchi Plaza: Site plan

49. Noguchi Plaza, 1996

50. Noguchi Plaza, 1996

51. Citicorp Plaza: Seventh Street–level site plan

52. Citicorp Plaza, 1991

53. Crocker Center: Site plan

54. Crocker Galleria, 1991

55. Crocker Center: Sketch of roof garden

56. Crocker Center, 1991

57. Grabhorn Park, 1991

58.   Rincon Center: Site plan

59.   Rincon Center, 1992: Old post office building

60.   Rincon Center, 1992: Outdoor space

61.   Rincon Center, 1992: The atrium

62.   One Hundred First Plaza: Site plan

63.   One Hundred First, 1991

64.   One Hundred First, 1992: The sun terrace

65.   One Hundred First, 1991: Stairs leading to the plaza

66.   Citicorp Plaza: Section and elevation

67.   Citicorp Plaza, 1996

68.   Citicorp Plaza, 1996

69.   California Plaza: Site plan

70.   California Plaza, 1996: The Watercourt

71.   California Plaza, 1996

72.   Bunker Hill Steps, 1996

73.   Figueroa at Wilshire: Site plan

74.   Figueroa at Wilshire, 1996

75.   Figueroa at Wilshire Plaza, 1996

76.   Pershing Square: Mapped activities

77.   Pershing Square, 1986

78.   Pershing Square, 1986

79.   Downtown Los Angeles: Pedestrian activity

80.   Downtown San Francisco: Pedestrian activity

81.   Pershing Square Competition, 1986: Winning design by SITE

82.   Pershing Square, 1996

83.   Pershing Square, 1996

84.   Pershing Square, 1996

85.   Los Angeles, Broadway Street, 1996

86.   Los Angeles, mural on Broadway Street, 1996

87.   Los Angeles, mural on Spring Street, 1996

88.   Los Angeles, vendor in Pueblo Plaza on El Grito Day, 1996

89.   Distance traveled to Los Angeles plazas

90.   Distance traveled to San Francisco plazas

91.   Age of users in Los Angeles plazas

92.   Age of users in San Francisco plazas

93.   Occupancy pattern in Los Angeles plazas

94.   Occupancy pattern in San Francisco plazas

95.   Frequency of visits in Los Angeles plazas

96.   Frequency of visits in San Francisco plazas

97.   Time spent in Los Angeles plazas

98.   Time spent in San Francisco plazas

99.   Grabhorn Park, 1992

100. San Francisco, sketch of Commercial Street

101. Sketch of Grabhorn Park

102. One Hundred First Plaza, 1991

103. Bunker Hill Steps, 1996

104. Figueroa at Wilshire Plaza, 1996

105. Rincon Center, 1992: Atrium

106. Conceptual sketch of Rincon Center by Scott Johnson

107. Crocker Center, 1992

108. Crocker Center, 1992

109. Crocker Center roof garden, 1992

110. Crocker Center roof garden, 1992

111. Sketch of Crocker Galleria

112. Citicorp Plaza, 1996

113. Citicorp Plaza, property line on Seventh Street, 1996

114. California Plaza, 1996: The Watercourt

115. Axonometric sketch of Horton Plaza

116. Conceptual sketch of Horton Plaza by Jon Jerde

117. Horton Plaza, 1995

118. Sculpture by Isamo Noguchi, Little Tokyo, Los Angeles, 1996

119. Monument in downtown Detroit, 1995

120. Museum of Contemporary Art in Los Angeles, 1996

121. Museum of Contemporary Art in Los Angeles, 1996: Outdoor art

122.   *Corporate Head*, Citicorp Plaza, 1996

123.   *Pigeons Acquire Philosophy*, Citicorp Plaza, 1996

124.   Water and fire sculpture by Eric Orr, 1996

125.   Rincon Center, 1992: The rain column

126.   California Plaza, 1996: Amphitheater in the Watercourt

127.   Map of public art in downtown Los Angeles

128.   Public art in downtown Los Angeles, 1996

129.   Horton Plaza, 1995

130.   Horton Plaza, 1995

131.   Model of the Metropolis project

132.   Sketch of proposed Crocker Center

133.   Sketch of proposed Crocker Center

134.   Sketch of proposed Crocker Center

135.   Promotional map of downtown Los Angeles

136.   Bunker Hill urban renewal project, 1968

137.   Los Angeles, 1993: Map of catalytic projects

138.   Los Angeles, 1993: Map of civic open spaces and avenidas

139.   Downtown Los Angeles public and private open spaces

140.   Downtown San Francisco public and private open spaces

141.   Building footprints in Bunker Hill, 1953 and 1993

ACKNOWLEDGMENTS

■ We must begin by thanking the National Endowment for the Arts (NEA), which in recent years has been the target of significant, politically motivated federal budget cuts. We want to acknowledge that in large measure this book has been made possible by grants from the NEA, which funded the studies from which we derived our essential insights. An NEA grant is more than just a source of funding; it is also a recognition of the worth of our proposed venture, a venture that was not likely to interest a more mission-oriented government agency or corporate foundation. An NEA grant is an honor and an affirmation of our interest in advancing the understanding of the social intentions and consequences of urban design. We are deeply grateful for that. Long live the National Endowment for the Arts!

We want to extend a note of special thanks to Amit Ghosh, currently the chief of comprehensive planning at the San Francisco Department of City Planning, who enthusiastically supported our study from the beginning and encouraged us to look at San Francisco downtown spaces. Amit and his colleague Eva Lieberman were instrumental in our selection of specific case studies in San Francisco.

Our narratives of the evolution and implementation of various projects are based on interviews with many professionals from the fields of planning, architecture, urban design, and real estate development. For background information on San Francisco's downtown planning and urban design, we are fortunate to have had discussions with five past planning directors—Allan Jacobs, Rai Okamoto, Dean Macris, Lou Blajez, and Amit Ghosh—and also Peter Bosselman and George Williams. For information regarding Los Angeles' efforts to create downtown open space, we thank Mickey Gustin, Ed Helfeld, Yukio Kawaratani, John Spalding, Jeff Skorneck, and Allyne Winderman. For information on specific San Francisco downtown projects, we thank

xiv

Rai Okamoto and David Larson for Crocker Center; Martin Brown, Andrew Butler, and Oki Komada for Grabhorn Park; Frank Cannizzaro, Scott Johnson, and Jay Mancini for Rincon Center; and Michael Barker, Jeffrey Heller, and Richard Keating for One Hundred First. For insights on the Los Angeles developments, we thank Jon Jerde, Yukio Kawaratani, and Rolf Kleinhans for Citicorp Plaza; Don Cosgrove, Arthur Erickson, Greg Schultz, and Tim Vreeland for California Plaza; Jim Anderson, Lawrence Halprin, and Jeff Skorneck for the Bunker Hill Steps; Oki Komada, David Martin, and Colin Shepard for Figueroa at Wilshire; John Vallance and Helene Frieds for the Metropolis project. For information on San Diego's Horton Plaza, we thank Jon Jerde, Richard Orne, John Gilchrist, Craig Pettit, Max Schmitt, and Michael Stepner.

We also owe our thanks to several individuals who were willing to share their insights about various projects and to review initial drafts of individual chapters and even the whole manuscript. In particular we would like to thank Professors William C. Baer, Marc Francis, John Friedman, Richard Lai, Michael Southworth, and Anne Vernez Moudon, who offered us invaluable suggestions and comments for the improvement of this book.

The empirical work on Los Angeles' downtown spaces began in 1986 as part of the dissertation research of Anastasia Loukaitou-Sideris (1988), which examined the effects of privatization on the function, use, and design of urban open spaces. The initial empirical work was followed by a 1988 study—conducted by a planning laboratory/workshop at USC under the direction of Tridib Banerjee—of several public and corporate open spaces in downtown Los Angeles. In addition, our students at UCLA and USC have studied as part of their course work many of the Los Angeles open spaces, thus contributing to our understanding of the issues. We cannot mention all of these students here, but we thank them collectively.

The initial empirical study of Los Angeles' downtown spaces was extended in 1991 to include San Francisco, and the extended study involved a comparison of the policies and politics that have guided development in these two California cities. The extended study was made possible by an organizational grant from the NEA and matching support received from the School of Urban Planning and Development of USC. We would like to thank Mr. Randolph McAusland, the then director of the Design Arts Program of the NEA, for his special interest in this study and for his encouragement at the beginning of the project. The case study of Horton Plaza was taken from a study, also funded by the NEA, undertaken by Tridib Banerjee that focused on "invented streets" and the emerging phenomenon of public life in privatized spaces.

For the empirical research and fieldwork, we wish to acknowledge the significant contributions of several graduate students who helped us conceptualize the study, collect data, and conduct user surveys. Our graduate research assistants at USC (Balaji Parthasarathy, now a doctoral planning student at the University of California, Berkeley, and Kanishka Goonawardena, now a doctoral planning student at Cornell and a Getty scholar) did most of the field observations, photo sweeps, and user interviews. Jay Simon, another USC graduate research assistant, helped us set up and conduct various expert interviews. Jyoti Hosagraher, then a doctoral student at the University of California, Berkeley, and now an assistant professor at the University of Oregon, helped us conduct the photo sweeps and user surveys in San Francisco. She also did all the archival research at the San Francisco Department of City Planning. Kevin Maher, also a USC graduate research assistant, joined the project in fall of 1991 and completed the coding of photo sweeps and user interviews. Joel Hendrickson, who was a graduate planning student at UCLA at the time of the fieldwork, and Rongsheng Luo, a doctoral planning student at USC, helped us with the computer analysis of user surveys and photo-sweep data. Several graduate students at USC School of Urban Planning and Development helped collect data on Horton Plaza. We thank Caroline Lavoie, now an assistant professor at Utah State University, and doctoral candidates at USC James Forsher (now an assistant professor at Florida State University) and Amer Moustafa (now an assistant professor at California Polytechnic State University, San Luis Obispo), for their help.

In the later stage of information synthesis and literature review, it was very important to have the help of Gail Sansbury, a doctoral student in the Department of Urban Planning at UCLA, who identified many of the relevant bibliographical sources. Gail has also collaborated with Anastasia Loukaitou-Sideris in the historical research of the Bunker Hill area of Los Angeles. Finally, the last stage of this book's production would not have been possible without the invaluable work of Liette Gilbert, also a doctoral student in the Department of Urban Planning at UCLA, who helped compile the references, identify and compile illustrations, assure copyright releases from publishers, libraries, and individuals, and index the book. Liette also photographed most of the Los Angeles spaces. She and Rebecca Liu, a dual-degree student in the joint program in urban design at the School of Urban Planning and Development and the School of Architecture at USC, drew some of the maps and site plans that accompany the text.

Finally, our deepest appreciation to our institutions, the Department of Urban Planning in the School of Public Policy and Social Research at UCLA and the School of Urban Planning and Development at USC, for providing resources and sabbatical time for this intellectual pursuit, and to our editors at the University of California Press, Stan Holwitz, Harry Asforis, Scott Norton, Mary Severance, and Carlotta Shearson for their support and wise counsel.

INTRODUCTION: THE NEW DOWNTOWN

■ The American downtown has undergone major transformations in this century. The downtown skyline has become more vertical and prominent as the skyscrapers of corporate America have competed with one another to assert their presence in the urban panorama. Yet, the visual dominance of the downtown skyline belies the growing threats to its traditional roles and functions. Underneath the physical changes lie more profound transitions. Downtown's primacy as a center of commerce and employment has been challenged for some time as outlying commercial centers have attracted new offices and retail businesses. Its public realm has begun to atrophy as activities of business and commerce have become increasingly isolated and insular and are being conducted within the enclosed and protected spaces of privatized atriums, gallerias, skywalks, lobbies, and plazas. The result is a polarized urbanism characterized by the exclusive regime of the "private" downtown of corporate America and its white-collar workers, on the one hand, and the "public" downtown of the blue-collar workers, the denizens, and the destitute, on the other. These two worlds coexist side by side but rarely cross boundaries. Contacts between these two worlds are obviated by architectural and urban design, and this obviation is augmented by continual surveillance by closed-circuit cameras and security guards.

Downtown stakeholders—businesses, property owners, financial institutions, city councils, and the media—have toiled hard over the years to maintain the preeminence of the downtown and to promote its image. Indeed, if we ask the resident of a major American city today the question that Kevin Lynch (1960) asked his subjects nearly forty years ago—"What comes to your mind when you think of downtown?"—we will probably get a range of answers. The downtown skyline of glittering skyscrapers bearing logos of multinational and transnational corporations symbolizes many things to many people: the accumulation of capital, the concentration of power and influence, the glory of corporate America, the essence of a postindustrial economy, the unfettered spirit of free enterprise and entrepreneurship, and so on.

The contemporary American downtown still remains the dominant center of the metropolitan area, even after decades of decentralization and sprawl. As aptly captured in the title of the book *Downtown Inc.*, by Bernard Frieden and Lynn Sagalyn (1989), downtown is not just a business district; it is an enterprise that is run by the city government and corporate interests. We take this analogy a step further. We propose that American downtowns are more than just an enterprise; they can indeed be seen as an industry. American downtowns today represent an industry devoted to managing the affairs of the economy—local, state, national, and even international. This industry (1) processes, protects, and manages capital; (2) packages ideas and information; (3) brokers influence and power; and (4) produces decisions affecting the accumulation of wealth, the circulation of capital, and the jobs and welfare of people throughout the land and in other lands as well.

The workers are mostly white-collar professionals and managers, with a support staff of white-collar clerical and secretarial workers. As a case in point, 76 percent of all workers in downtown Los Angeles today can be categorized as professionals, managers, salespeople, or clerical workers (Community Redevelopment Agency 1991). These workers and their work milieu are serviced by a very thin layer of blue-collar labor force comprising food service, janitorial, maintenance, and delivery workers. Many of these white-collar workers—those who use computers, process and retrieve data, or rely on communication technologies for their daily work—are increasingly being classified as a part of the information sector of the economy (Freeman 1996).

Like individual firms within an industry, American downtowns now compete with each other to attract businesses, corporate headquarters, shopping complexes, convention centers, sports arenas, and the like. In addition to this external competition, American downtowns also face considerable internal competition. Downtowns of major metropolitan cities no longer enjoy the unrivaled primacy they used to command with respect to secondary districts or suburban centers. As the suburbs have matured, they have created their own downtowns to service the new industries and middle- and upper-class workers they have attracted. The "edge city" phenomenon (Garreau 1991) has created many smaller downtowns at the edge of the metropolitan urban core. By collectively luring a sizable chunk of the jobs and retail activities generated in the metropolitan economy, they have taken a major toll on the downtown office market. Most American downtowns find themselves saddled with a large inventory of office space. With high vacancy rates and slower absorption of the current inventory of new office buildings, downtowns are now overbuilt (Dowall 1986).[1] A report published by Grubb and Ellis (1992), a real estate and property management company, reveals that of 31.4 million square feet of office space available in downtown Los Angeles almost 7 million, or 21.4 percent, are vacant. Although the case of downtown Los Angeles may be extreme, it is by no means unique; other major American downtowns face similar problems with many completely vacant older office buildings. Leasing rates have dropped in this buyer's market. Public agencies like school district headquarters, which used to occupy older office buildings at the edge of the downtown, can now afford to lease spaces in new office towers with concierge services. Similarly, having lost the competition for retail activities to outlying shopping malls accessible by freeway, downtowns are constantly struggling to maintain their dominance as the primary business and employment centers. Holding the center together in the face of centrifugal market forces, which are aided and abetted by a public policy of suburbanization, is a major challenge for American downtowns today.[2]

Meanwhile, conventional shopping malls have become larger, more complex, and much more inclusive in use and function. While the original shopping malls—because of their exclusive emphasis on the middle-class consumer market—represented precisely what downtowns were not, today's malls have become major urban centers, a viable alternative to the traditional Main Street. The script of the contemporary malls is much more deliberate. They now include post offices, art galleries, hotels, counseling centers, extension programs of major universities, and even amusement parks. Witold Rybczynski (1993) calls them "new downtowns" while acknowledging that some observers like Kenneth Jackson (1985) may still disagree. The point made by Rybczynski, is nevertheless relevant because centers like City Walk or the Mall of America pose new challenges to the retail and entertainment functions of traditional downtowns.

This challenge has been further exacerbated in recent years by the dramatic changes in communication technology, which have significantly increased not only home-based work—especially for the professional workforce—but also home-based shopping and entertainment. Nonterritorial offices may make conventional offices obsolete. This possibility has no doubt increased the potential for further decentralization and for further obviation of the functions of the traditional Main Street.

Indeed the public purpose of the traditional downtown—the *civitas*—is also threatened. People still go to downtown to fight a traffic ticket or take out a building permit, or even for an occasional art show or a concert, but how often do people congregate in front of the city hall for a public address or a campaign speech these days? In recent history, significant numbers of Los Angelenos congregated in downtown to celebrate only when the Dodgers won the World Series or the Lakers won the NBA championship. Periodically some downtowns become a focus of public congregation: for an annual parade, like Macy's Thanksgiving parade in New York, the celebration of the Chinese New Year in San Francisco, the ceremonial arrival of Santa Claus in Hollywood, or a public event, like Cinco de Mayo in Los Angeles or the Boston Marathon.

Political rallies rarely happen in downtown civic forums these days, and public discourse is even less common. Thirty years ago when the new Boston City Hall was constructed in historic Scollay Square, the adjacent large open space was expected to serve the democratic purpose of political rallies or protest meetings. Yet, even during the Vietnam protest years, when public rallies were commonplace, the people of Boston chose to congregate in the Boston Common—a historic open space—rather than the city hall plaza. Celebrating a Celtics' victory or a pennant by the Red Sox was deemed a more appropriate occasion for an assembly at City Hall.

There used to be a time when a campaign appearance with a mayor in a city hall plaza was a must for a presidential candidate. Today downtown civic plazas are not always a popular venue even for a presidential or gubernatorial campaign rally. Candidate Ford and candidate Clinton chose Glendale Galleria—an enclosed, upscale shopping mall in the city of Glendale, twelve miles from downtown Los Angeles—for their presidential campaign appearances in southern California.[3] During the 1992 presidential campaign, when candidate

Ross Perot—who made his fortune in electronics and computers—introduced his electronic town hall meetings, Gerald Marzorati (1992) of the *New York Times* wondered if this was indeed the dawn of what he called "cyber-civitas." Recalling de Tocqueville's commentary on the American democracy some 150 years ago, in which he spoke of the tension between the autonomous tendencies of individualism and the participatory and communitarian instincts of public citizenship, Marzorati hoped that the emergence of "Perotville" did not mean a decline of the body politic and public life. The imminent decline in the American public life remains a recurring theme in the literature on urbanism. There are certainly indications that the public life of American downtowns is under considerable stress. And Marzorati's commentary in itself is a sign of the tension that the public downtowns of American cities are experiencing today.

It is no wonder then that today, more than ever before, downtown corporate interests want the middle- and upper-class population to live and shop downtown. This goal can be achieved if the built environment is appealing, attractive, and furnished with amenities for workers and visitors. Urban design, therefore, is an important part of packaging and promoting the new downtown.

In the following chapters we will argue that while the imperative of design is well established, its tenet has changed significantly in American downtowns. For one, design initiative has shifted from the public to the private sector as a direct result of the declining fiscal resources of local governments. As a consequence, public institutions are becoming increasingly dependent on private investments for shaping the built environment and are at the same time relying heavily on regulations and the entitlement process to negotiate the outcome of design.[4]

According to Frieden and Sagalyn (1989), more than one hundred new retail centers opened in American downtowns between 1970 and 1988: "Developers built where cities greased the way" (172). They note that cities were major coinvestors for three of every four projects built from 1970 to 1985. While in the early seventies private capital bankrolled half of the downtown malls, in later years cities themselves became major financiers. Although coinvestment has accounted for four out of every five new projects and has ranged from raising cash through municipal bonds to land assembly, land write-down, and infrastructure improvements, the design concepts have largely been dictated by the designers hired by the private sector. The role of public design for the downtown built form has steadily shrunk in the new partnership that Frieden and Sagalyn refer to as "Downtown Inc." Public domain plazas, museums, civic buildings, open spaces, broad avenues, and civic sculptures have long since faded. The visions that shaped the historical design of cities like Buffalo, Cincinnati, Kansas City, New York, Philadelphia, San Francisco, Washington, and the like have also been abandoned, seemingly for good.

The contemporary urban design of downtown is linked primarily to the redevelopment process and is guided by opportunity or exigency rather than by consideration of the whole. There is not even a vision of how the incremental changes will add up. Downtown urban design is like a jigsaw puzzle in which the pieces are isolated from one another. The specific features of the new urban design can be summarized as follows. First, it is mainly dependent on private initiatives, philanthropy, or outright exaction for creating public amenities, which would have been created through public investment in earlier times. Second, since the private sector response to these demands has been motivated by the desire to maximize and protect the return on the investment, these amenities have been designed for tenants who lease space in these buildings and for their clients and workers, rather than for the public at large. Third, design circumstances are mainly opportunistic and are often a response to public policy that is reactive than proactive. Fourth, such responses are ad hoc, disjointed, episodic, incrementalist, and, in the larger scheme of things, a non sequitur. Fifth, this new urban design has consequently lost the larger public purpose or vision that guided earlier urban design proposals. Sixth, the privatization process has exacerbated the polarization of the downtown form into a public but derelict downtown of the indigents, on the one hand, and a private and glamorous downtown of corporate America, on the other. Finally, this new urban design philosophy is very different from the earlier one that relied on the strategic location of and investment in public projects and improvements to stimulate private developments in a desired pattern.

We believe that the above changes signify a major "paradigm shift," to borrow Thomas Kuhn's (1970) all-too popular term. They represent profound transformation in the practice and purpose of urban design. To the extent that these changes have occurred gradually over time, there has been little time to pause and take stock. Here we propose to examine the process that has led to this transformation. It is now time to evaluate the process that has emerged and been legitimized by evolving urban design. What are the causes and consequences of this new downtown urban design? What is the nature of design episodes—for design has indeed become episodic—within the changing circumstance of downtown development and redevelopment? What are the challenges for future urban design? These are the principal questions we explore in this book.

AIMS AND THEMES

The aim of this book is in part to document this profound shift in the attitudes, institutions, and processes involved in the reshaping of contemporary downtown space and form. Our intent is to focus on the political economy of this shift and on urban design's role as an agent of this shift. Our work consists of several case studies of recently completed projects in the downtowns of three major California cities: Los Angeles, San Diego, and San Francisco. The aim of these studies was initially to examine the trend toward privatization of urban open spaces and to examine the nature of public life in these privatized domains. Although the specific focus was on open spaces and public places, the case studies incorporated detailed documentation of the overall project complex of which these spaces are an integral part.

In choosing these case studies we do not mean to create an impression that urban design is all about creating open spaces between buildings. Certainly there are examples in the literature that give that impression. But urban design—or city design, as Kevin Lynch (1984) preferred to call this enterprise—encompasses much more than the design of any one component of the urban form (see also Kostof 1992 and Bacon 1974). Of course there are many different interpretations of the importance of the various elements of urban form in defining the public life and urbanism of cities. Authors like Anne Vernez Moudon (1987) and Allan Jacobs (1993) have emphasized the design of city streets as a critical aspect of urban design. We too feel that the larger organization of the spatial structure of cities was often defined by critical street elements, and this approach was very much a part of the synoptic and public tradition of urban design we will discuss elsewhere in this book. Our focus on corporate open spaces is not an artifact of our personal predilections but simply a result of the very nature of downtown transformation currently underway. Our coverage of corporate open spaces as examples of urban design is not a reflection of a de facto acceptance of their scope but precisely the basis of the argument we make in this book—that in the making of the new downtown we have witnessed a shift from streets and spaces belonging to the public at large to the more discrete, enclosed, isolated, and private open spaces of corporate America.

Before we present the overall scheme of this book we should briefly discuss how our work can be placed within the literature on postmodern urbanism, urban planning, and design. As should be apparent from the title of this book, our work is defined by the intersection of two principal themes: the downtown area and urban design. Our first theme is the downtown area, perhaps the most important and sui generis district of American cities. In particular we are interested in the downtowns of core cities of large metropolitan regions—like Boston, New York, Chicago, Los Angeles, and San Francisco—rather than the downtowns of smaller cities or suburban communities. In establishing this focus we see our work linked to the literature on the spatial structure and organization of cities, especially that based in social sciences. Human ecology, regional economics, and urban geography are the fields that typically offer empirical insights about the structure, organization, and dynamics of the central business district (CBD) in the context of the larger city. While this literature is helpful in describing and explaining the dynamics of spatial change mainly as a market outcome, we are more interested in aspects of the deliberate decisions and processes—by both the public and the private sectors—that lead to piecemeal changes in the built form. Our interest in the political economy of development decisions connects us to the rich literature on the urban history and historiography of American cities. Although our interests lie mainly in interpreting the current trends in downtown urban design, the period histories of individual cities and historiographic accounts of American city development provide the necessary foundation for our work.

Our second theme is of course urban design—the particular creative aspects of conceiving and putting together large-scale development projects, as shaped by contemporary institutions and the inevitable political processes that surround such events. Our aim here is to explain the current transformations of the built form of the downtown districts from this urban design perspective. In presenting this account we also describe the nature of the design outcome, and the social and political implications of the emerging built form. Doing so takes us to the ongoing discussions on the changing nature of public and private domains, the future of civil society, and the effects of global economic order on local places. We are thus connected to the larger orbit of crossdisciplinary and critical thinking on the postmodern condition (Lyotard 1984) and the condition of postmodernity (Harvey 1989). These are critical perspectives, and in recent years we have seen a rich accumulation of literature focusing on contemporary urbanism and the built environment. These writings have essentially analyzed the built environment as a mirror of the contemporary material culture, deconstructed either as a part of the global culture of consumption (Harvey 1988) or as the "cultural logic" of late capitalism (Jameson 1991). We have depended on this literature for theoretical constructs and critical perspectives. It has helped us to articulate the conflicts and contradictions inherent in the contemporary downtown environment.

But this interpretation of form, as an outcome of historical, cultural, political, and economic processes, is but one explanation, albeit an important one, of the contemporary condition. It is a synoptic, macroscopic, and global interpretation. It does not examine how each increment of change in form is conceived and produced. Thus, unfortunately, it does not inform us about the practice and conduct of the profession in creating these discrete changes in urban form. Yet, it is this behind-the-scenes story that is also critical from the perspective of practice and professional conduct. Since we see our book as an attempt to make the practice of urban design more socially responsible, this inside story is equally important. If the postmodern theoretical frame offers a top-down view, our inside story based on in-depth case studies offers a bottom-up view. These stories add faces, personalities, and agencies—and their aspirations, visions, and uncertainties—to this otherwise anonymous metaprocess implicit in the critical perspectives on postmodern urbanism.

We want to present the story not just of the designer's vision but also of how that vision is formed and how projects are conceived, scripted, produced, and eventually packaged. Here our work connects with the design literature, and while there is again a rich legacy of literature on historic city design, there is relatively little that discusses the process behind the production of the built environment. There have been some recent journalistic accounts of how single buildings have been "produced," but these accounts lack a theoretical or conceptual frame of reference. Here we expect that our work will advance the understanding of the nature of urban design and how it has changed in recent years.

Because our enterprise lies in the intersection of several streams of intellectual thought and tradition, methodologically we are less committed to any one field and, consequently, less constrained by the rigors and predilections of any one tradition than we might be otherwise.[5] While this free-form approach is perhaps more risky intellectually, it allows us to be synoptic in our overview and creative in our interpretation. Since one of our principal aims is to understand and explain the nature of contemporary urban design practice, such a free-form approach is unavoidable. We expect that the following chapters will present a coherent story of urban design downtown today, a story that covers its historical antecedents, its changing economic and political context, its negotiated processes, and the actual production of the built environment.

A GUIDE TO CHAPTERS TO FOLLOW

In the following chapters we present the story of the changing faces of American downtown: its history, its politics, and its poetics. The chapters are organized in three parts.

In the first part we present a historical overview of the evolution of the form and the organization of the structure of major American downtowns and CBDs (as they are called elsewhere in the Western world).[6] We trace this evolution as it was influenced by economic forces, technological developments, public policy, immigration, and urbanization. We also review the major urban design plans and proposals that were developed during this evolution. Our point in this review is to show the shifting roles of the corporate, philanthropic, and public sectors in shaping the appearance and design of the downtown. In chapter 1, we give a historical overview of the changing faces of downtown, tracing the transformations of downtown's built form and social activities going back to the early nineteenth-century. In chapter 2, we review the major urban design paradigms and the specific plans and proposals for American downtowns during different historic periods. This review shows not only the changing ideologies for downtown but also the shifting roles of the public and private sectors in downtown development. In chapter 3, we analyze the political economy of privatization and its effects on American downtowns. We examine three spaces in downtown Los Angeles and illustrate the ramifications of the privatization process on the production and physical representation of downtown space.

In the second part, we examine the current downtown condition from a critical perspective. We focus on the politics of deal-making in project development and the disturbing trend toward a polarized downtown and a declining public realm. In chapter 4, we review the politics of place making in the contemporary downtown. Using eight case studies from two cities, we discuss and compare the negotiation and deal-making that underlie the creation of new downtown space. We argue that the last twenty years of redevelopment efforts have generated two distinct worlds in American downtowns: the rich, flashy, corporate downtown of today and the poor, derelict, abandoned historic core of yesterday. In chapter 5, we analyze these two faces of downtown and their human dimensions. We argue that downtown's urban form can be interpreted as a reflection of broader social changes and the political economy of such changes. In chapter 6, we discuss the forces that have caused a decline of public life and analyze the impact of these forces on contemporary downtowns and their uses. This chapter utilizes case study data to profile downtown users and their activities, perceptions, and feelings.

Finally, in the third part we focus on the behind-the-scenes stories of how various projects were designed, how they were shaped by personal visions and the dictates of public policy or by the imperative of market success. In chapter 7, we use examples from three California cities (Los Angeles, San Francisco, and San Diego) to analyze the poetics of design and to illustrate how it shapes the organization of space and the visual form of the new urban centers. In chapter 8 we look into another important component of downtown's physical environment: public art. Using selected examples from Los Angeles and San Francisco, we document a sense of diminished "publicness" in art pieces whose primary objective is to increase the marketability of downtown corporate spaces. In chapter 9 we examine the ways that contemporary downtown settings are "packaged" and promoted to prospective users. In some ways, downtown's urban form resembles a collection of fragmented pieces—stage sets and theme parks to attract and entertain a specific clientele. In the final chapter we present the major themes that capture the dynamics of postmodern urbanism and urban design, which are amply illustrated in the form of American downtown. We conclude by addressing some of the critical challenges for downtown urban design.

Throughout the book we try to bring in examples from various American downtowns. Here we depend mainly on secondary sources—accounts like those of Frieden and Sagalyn (1989), Robert Beauregard (1989), Susan Fainstein (1994), Michael Sorkin (1992), Deyan Sudjic (1992), Carl Abbott (1993), and Larry Ford (1994). For our case study research, however, we focus on the experiences of Los Angeles, San Francisco, and San Diego. Our geographic proximity to and familiarity with the settings of these cities are two reasons for this preference. Also there is considerably less literature on West Coast cities than on the older cities of the East Coast, a fact that made our examination of the former more tempting. Finally, California has witnessed tremendous growth over the last few decades. Its major urban settings have experienced social, political, economic, and cultural upheavals, enough to qualify them as exemplary products of postindustrial society. It can be argued that Los Angeles, San Francisco, and San Diego resemble windows to the new urbanism of American cities in these waning years of the twentieth century. Through these cities we can see processes and patterns that are happening, or are likely to happen, in other downtown developments. Thus, the examination of development in these cities can help us understand the broader trends that are afoot in other American downtowns.

PART ONE

THE

EVOLUTION

OF

DOWNTOWN

FORM

1

The evolution of the American downtown and its core area, the central business district (CBD), has been influenced by several forces: the functional, the economic, the technological, and the political (Ford 1994). The imperatives of market forces led to the concentration of high-density office space in a limited geographic area and resulted in a visually distinctive district in the urban core. The economic power of the business and corporate elite, symbolized by their monumental "cathedrals of business," gave this district its characteristic imagery and skyline. Modern technology—steel-frame construction, fast elevators, central heating and air-conditioning—was an essential precursor to the emergence of skyscrapers and the resulting vertical expansion of downtowns. Electricity for lighting turned night into day and temporally expanded the activities of the core. New transit technologies exacerbated the separation between work and home while fostering a radial urban form and the centrality of downtown. Political factors, often translated into zoning regulations, planning guidelines, and development incentives, continued to nurture and protect CBDs, keeping away undesirable and "offensive" land uses.

In an article written in the 1960s, geographer James Vance (1966) developed a six-stage model to describe the evolution of a CBD. During the *inception* stage, the CBD emerges as a distinct place, although it may not have an identifiable urban form and may have few if any special buildings. This is followed by an *exclusion* stage, in which activities (residential, industrial, and so on) that are not appropriate for the CBD are filtered out, through high rents or social pressure. Some buildings change use, while new structures are built to accommodate new needs. Then a stage of *segregation* occurs, in which uses begin to sort themselves out into coherent subdistricts (retail, financial, entertainment, government, and so on). The process of *extension* occurs when new, specialized activities require a considerable amount of new space. CBDs then grow vertically and/or horizontally. The stage of *replication and readjustment* is reached when certain central functions show up in outlying areas in the form of secondary (often suburban) centers. These CBD replicas contain shopping centers and offices and sometimes compete with the original center for the attraction of businesses. However, in the *redevelopment* stage, most CBDs rebuild continuously, so as to better compete with the outlying suburban centers and other CBDs in the nation or overseas.

In a series of earlier articles, other geographers tried to define, delimit, and analyze the internal structure of the North American CBD, which was described as the "core area in which definitive qualities reach their greatest intensity; it has zonal boundaries, and these boundaries, for the most part, are impermanent" (Murphy and Vance 1954, 191). In the 1950s, when most North American downtowns had already experienced the stages of exclusion and segregation, geographers devoted considerable research effort in delimiting the CBD as a region by analyzing its land-use variations (Murphy, Vance, and Epstein 1955). The retailing of goods and services for profit and the performing of various office functions were classified as characteristic CBD activities. But residences, storage facilities, industrial establishments, warehouses, and institutional, governmental and public establishments were considered non-CBD in character (Murphy and Vance 1954). However, a later article argued that the last three types of land occupancy "clearly contribute to both the absolute and relative centrality of a central place" and hence should be considered as part of the CBD (Bowden 1971, 123). These are examples of the changing conception of the nature of CBDs and downtowns in general.

We have chosen to use a different framework for categorizing the different phases of downtown development. Our categories are more synoptic and are based on what we consider to be some of the major epochs of the U.S. downtown. We will trace the transformations of downtown's built form from the walking center of the colonial era and the centripetal core of the turn of the century to post-Depression decay, urban renewal, and downtown renaissance of recent times.

THE WALKING DOWNTOWN (1800–1870)

The emergence of the American CBD is the spatial outcome and physical expression of a profound urban restructuring that took place between 1830 and

1850, a restructuring that converted the mercantile colonial town into the industrial capitalist center (Soja 1989). The first specialized CBD emerged in New York (ca. 1810) around Wall Street, which developed into the financial center of the region. Because of its location at the southern end of Manhattan, this new urban district was named "downtown." Soon, similar business districts developed in Boston, Philadelphia, and Chicago. By 1850, San Francisco had built its central district—consisting of seven commercial blocks around Portsmouth Plaza (Bowden 1971). While most East Coast downtowns developed through reuse and adaptation of their existing urban form to serve new needs and conditions, newer western cities established after the mid-1800s were laid out with specialized "business blocks" at the time of the initial settlement or shortly thereafter (Ford 1994).

By the 1820s new financial institutions—banks, insurance companies, trust companies—had developed, requiring their own distinctive space. Special buildings, such as the Merchants' Exchange and the Stock Exchange, appeared for the first time in downtown and provided convenient settings for businessmen to conduct their business.[1] By the 1830s, public, open-air markets, which had been a vibrant feature of colonial towns, were giving way to private business establishments and merchants' showrooms (Goldfield and Brownell 1990). In coastal cities during this period, the center of commercial activity moved from the waterfront to Main Street—the heart of the CBD. Wholesale warehouses occupied the edges of downtown, conveniently located near the waterfront. Retailers found it beneficial to locate along Main Street, where they could display their goods and attract customers. Broadway Street in New York, Market Street in Philadelphia, Canal Street in New Orleans, Seventh Street in Los Angeles, King Street in Charleston—all major commercial thoroughfares—became the commercial showcases for their downtowns (Goldfield and Brownell 1990). A variety of retail activities started appearing in the expanding downtowns during the middle of the nineteenth century: clothing and shoe stores, dry-goods shops, jewelry stores. In photographs and paintings of the period one can see storefronts and window displays of small shops bordering the yet unpaved streets. Horse-drawn omnibuses, carriages, and wagons mixed with pedestrians.

The coming of the railroad gave a further boost to Main Street commercial activity. According to Chester Liebs (1985, 7–8),

Through the downtown depot and railway freight house, goods arrived and local products were shipped out, newcomers alighted, visitors tarried, and residents set forth to explore a larger world. Fortunes were made, communities prospered, and by the late nineteenth century these developments could all be read on the frontage of a community's principal street. . . .

Main Streets were usually the first to be lit with gas and later with electricity, the first to sport a streetcar line or elevated railroad or subway, and the first to be paved. They also served as the civic and religious hubs for the communities around them. Main Street was the home not only of stores and offices, but also of imposing churches, theaters, banks, hotels, courthouses, city halls, war memorials, libraries and other banners of community well-being. The corridor formed by these varied structures, jammed tight along both sides of the sidewalk, became the ideal setting for speeches, parades and celebrations.

In the second half of the nineteenth century, the modern industrial city provided the economic incentive and building technology for a new enterprise: the department store.[2] This imposing "palace of merchandise" soared over the roofs of smaller stores, banks, hotels, and churches in downtown. The department store's immense inventory, luxurious surroundings, and trained personnel captured the imagination of downtown visitors. The appearance of the department store "heightened the illusion of shared luxury among shoppers. In the form of a marble palace, a cast-iron showplace, a sprawling grand depot, or a masonry castle, it emphasized dedication to the ideal of shopping as an endless delight" (Barth 1980, 130).

The emergence of the department store had an impact on the social uses of downtown. The CBD, previously a predominantly male realm, became increasingly open to women. Department store advertising focused mostly on the tastes of women customers, who were now acknowledged to be in charge of family consumption. Extremely popular department stores such as A. T. Stewart's and Macy's in New York, E. J. Lehman's Fair and Marshall Field's in Chicago, Wanamaker's in Philadelphia, and the Emporium in San Francisco served as focal points for downtown (Buck-Morss 1989; Friedberg 1993) and in the words of Henry James made "the enjoyment of the city as down-towny as possible" (quoted in Barth 1980, 110). While during the eighteenth century the town square, plaza, common green, or place d'armes was perceived to be

the geographic and symbolic center of cities, during the nineteenth century the department store and its surrounding commercial district became the center of urban activity. In the eighteenth century, people gathered at the town center to participate in civic functions or public events. One century later, people came to the CBD to conduct their own business. Buying, selling, trading, and window shopping became the primary activities conducted in American city centers.

The early-nineteenth-century downtown was dense and compact, and the concentration of activities in a limited geographic area produced a mixed pattern of land use. Department stores abutted train depots; warehouses stood next to offices. This was a walking downtown, since the central area rarely exceeded seven or eight blocks. Dense rows of buildings from one to ten stories high formed continuous facades along the sidewalks (see figure 1), some-

FIGURE 1
New York City, 1888: Fifth Avenue, looking north from the tower of Saint Patrick's Cathedral. United States History, Local History and Genealogy Division, The New York Public Library, Astor, Lennox and Tilden Foundations (Boyer 1985).

times interspersed with churches or noncommercial edifices (Liebs 1985). Around the downtown section, quite close in proximity, were both slums and fashionable streets. As urban historian Sam Bass Warner (1972, 84) has argued, "If the criterion of urbanity is the mixture of classes and ethnic groups, in some cases including a mixture of blacks and whites, along with dense living and crowded streets and the omnipresence of all manner of business near the homes in every quarter, then the cities of the United States in the years between 1820 and 1870 marked the zenith of our national urbanity."

THE HUB OF THE RADIAL CITY (1870–1930)

Chicago emerged as the paradigmatic American city during the late nineteenth century (see figure 2). Chicago was a miracle of the American economic system, a system that brought a second economic restructuring in the 1870s characterized by industrial decentralization, concentration of capital in the form of corporate monopolies, and intensification of land uses at the center (Soja 1989).

At the end of the nineteenth century, Chicago author C. D. Warner wrote the following about his city:

> In 1888 Chicago is a magnificent city. . . . But it is the business portion of the south side that is the miracle of the time, the solid creation of energy and capital since the fire—the square mile containing the Post Office and City Hall, the giant hotels, the opera houses and theatres, the Board of Trade Building, the many-storied offices, the great shops, the club houses, the vast retail and wholesale warehouses. This area has the advantage of some other great business centres in having broad streets at right angles, but with all this openness or movement, the throng of passengers and traffic, the intersecting street and cable railways, the loads of freight and the crush of carriages, the life and hurry of excitement are sufficient to satisfy the most eager lover of metropolitan pandemonium. Unfortunately for a clear comprehension of it the manufactories vomit dense clouds of bituminous coal smoke, which settle in a black mass in this part of town, so that one can scarcely see across the streets in a damp day, and the huge buildings loom up in the black sky in ghostly dimness. . . . No other city in the Union can show business warehouses and offices of more architectural nobility. The mind inevitably goes to Florence for comparison with the structures of the Medicean merchant princes." (quoted in Smith 1964, 164–65)[3]

FIGURE 2
Chicago, 1895: State
Street, looking north.
Courtesy of the Library
of Congress (Bluestone
1991, 111).

FIGURE 3
Los Angeles, 1885: Main
Street, looking north from
Commercial Street.
Special Collections,
University Research
Library, University of
California, Los Angeles.

New transportation technologies enabled downtown to develop as the hub
of a radial urban form. Streetcar systems laid out in a radial pattern to converge
on downtown emphasized its primacy and significance as the all-too-powerful
focus of the expanding industrial metropolis (see figures 3 and 4). As aptly
captured by Chicago sociologists Robert Park and Ernest Burgess in the 1920s,
the American city of the late nineteenth and early twentieth centuries was
extending out from its CBD with a zoned built environment of residential
rings (ghettos, immigrant settlements, apartment districts, single family neighborhoods, and upper income enclaves). Although derived from Chicago as the
prototype, the radial city with a single center was the typical pattern for almost
all industrial metropolises of the time (Warner 1972).

At the turn of the century, the consolidation of rail, oil, steel, and utility
companies was well underway. Large corporations were increasingly replacing

FIGURE 4
Los Angeles, ca. 1910:
Broadway and Seventh
streets, looking south.
Special Collections,
University Research
Library, University of
California, Los Angeles.

small businesses as the economy's principal organizational unit (Stern, Gilmartin, and Mellins 1987). Even though the factories of these corporations were being pushed toward the edges of downtown, their headquarters occupied prominent locations in the CBD. The wealth and power of business moguls would be permanently imprinted on downtown's urban form. Corporations needed an army of office workers to keep track of their ever spreading regional, national, and international operations. The downtown, as the prime metropolitan center, was the logical location for corporate offices and industrial headquarters. Corporate skyscrapers, privately financed and built, were their natural and practical home. Skyscrapers provided office space for expanding enterprises in finance, insurance, commerce, and trade and quickly became the preeminent symbols of American CBDs.

By the 1880s a series of technological, structural, and design innovations

allowed the construction of high-rise office towers (Tunnard and Reed 1956). The invention of steel-frame construction, mechanical elevators, heating and air-conditioning systems, and fire protection enabled skyscrapers to rise free of the city below them. Early skyscrapers usually had bases flush with the sidewalk and had ground-floor frontages lined with shops (see figure 5). In the second half of the twentieth century, in an effort to distinguish themselves from the surrounding buildings, and also in order to conform to floor-area-ratio (FAR) requirements, skyscrapers would retreat from the street. Office plazas would serve as forecourts to these all-important cathedrals of business and power.

Skyscraper construction brought about a dramatic transformation in downtown's urban form. For one, the profile of the downtown skyline became dramatically vertical (see figure 6). Demand for office buildings pushed residential and industrial uses out of the CBD. Owners of older low-rise structures at the center found it profitable to raze old buildings and sell the land or, if they were adequately entrepreneurial, build a new high-rise. "Tear down that old rat trap

FIGURE 5
Opposite: New York City,
ca. 1915: Union Square,
looking north along
Fourth Street. Museum of
the City of New York
(Boyer 1985, 129).

FIGURE 6
New York City, ca. 1908:
Broadway Avenue.
Courtesy of the Library
of Congress.

and erect a new building" became the slogan at the turn of the century (Hoyt
in Ruchelman 1977, 2). There was a sense of loss as the old downtown was
replaced by the new, tall buildings. In 1904, Henry James, seeing the spire of
his beloved Trinity Church lost amid tall buildings, deplored the disappearance
of the five-story Victorian New York City (in Ward and Zunz 1992, 5). By
1912, Manhattan had 1,510 buildings from nine to seventeen stories high, and
91 buildings from eighteen to fifty-five stories (Ward and Zunz 1992, 49). New
York and Chicago were at the forefront of this race to scrape the skies, but
other American downtowns followed suit with buildings that gave their downtowns similar distinctive skylines.

Because skyscraper building required a larger footprint than could be accommodated in existing small lots, the urban morphology of downtown started changing at the turn of the century. In a trend that would reach its apogee during the urban renewal era, small lots were consolidated, streets and alleys were closed, and superblocks were developed. Many small lots and small businesses gave way to a few large ones. More than any other single building, Rockefeller Center in New York (see figure 7), planned in the 1920s and built in the 1930s, epitomized the trend toward building a city within a city (Tafuri 1983). Rockefeller Center, which was initially conceived as a cultural center but was finally realized as a purely commercial development, piled more office space than ever before on one site. Such consolidation would occur again, to a much larger extent, fifty years later, during the urban-renewal era.

The new technological capability to pack an enormous amount of commercial space on one site and reap huge profits was responsible for the soaring of land values in downtown's prime locations. Land costs reflected the potential value of the land built upon to the maximum allowable FAR. As geographer Homer Hoyt explained for turn-of-the-century Chicago,

> The advent of the skyscraper was responsible for a marked increase in ground values in the CBD of Chicago from 1889 to 1891. Although the 25 or 30 buildings from 12 to 16 stories in height erected from 1889 to 1894 if bunched together would not have occupied more than three solid blocks, or 7 percent of the main business district, all land in that area was revalued on the basis of what it could produce if occupied by a 16-story building. (Hoyt in Ruchelman 1977, 2)

Franklin Head, writing about Chicago in *The New England Magazine* in July 1892, marveled,

> It is but a few years since the first sale of real estate in this favored locality, and the most hopeful of our real estate dealers conceded that the price was excessive and that it would be long before this valuation would be exceeded; but within the last two years several sales and leases have been made based upon a valuation as high as $10,000 per front foot, and even at this valuation it is claimed that the property when improved with the best style of lofty office or mercantile building will earn a reasonable interest upon its cost. High rentals would seem to be a serious drawback

FIGURE 7
New York City, 1934:
Rockefeller Center.
Courtesy of the Library
of Congress.

in lines of business open to general competition; yet merchants appear to find it to their advantage to pay the extravagant rents necessitated by the high price of central property, rather than to remove to equally commodious quarters half a mile distant at one-tenth the annual rent. One reason of this may be that all the four hundred miles of intramural lines of transportation, in the way of horse-car, cable, and elevated roads, terminate in the business centre of the city, and thus bring the customers of the merchants from all parts of the city to their very doors. (Head 1892, 558)

The value of prime commercial space in most CBDs was measured by the number of feet fronting the street. Often, the convergence of transportation lines to a particular corner of the CBD gave rise to the "peak land value intersection," where real estate values were markedly higher than in any other part of the center, or for that matter the whole city. In a trend that would intensify in the post–World War II era, a "downtown frame" of semiabandoned low-rise (four- to five-story) buildings (old warehouses and residential or commercial structures) would appear at the edges of the center just a half a mile away from the peak land value intersection (Ford 1994). Thus, it is during this period, in the late nineteenth and early twentieth centuries, that we first observe the polarization of downtown, the division between wealth and poverty, new and old, core and frame. This trend would only intensify and would come to plague cities at the century's end.

The soaring of real estate values in the CBD brought the stages of exclusion and segregation into full swing. Many businesses were unable to pay the high rents and were forced out of the center. Factories that typically required a lot of space chose to locate in cheaper areas. By 1880 few residential buildings remained downtown. The bulk of brownstones that housed the middle class were located at the periphery. The well-to-do were already residing in more distant suburbs. Meanwhile, the CBD was reorganized in a series of specialized districts. Financial institutions found it beneficial to cluster together, so the financial district occupied a premier location downtown. In 1892 Chicago had about thirty large banking establishments, "nearly all of which would be embraced in a circle with a radius of 900 feet" (Head 1892, 558). In the 1890s the prime downtown location in Atlanta, called Five Points, included more than thirteen banks and insurance companies (Goldfield and Brownell 1990).

Retail districts were another distinct entity. They included department stores, typically near major transit routes, and specialty stores with luxury goods for the most upscale clientele. In Los Angeles, Seventh Street became the "Mecca for Merchants" and assembled the most important outlets of that time.[4] The entertainment district was also an important segment of downtown. In the 1890s New York's most important theaters, hotels, and restaurants were gathered along Broadway Street. A street with the same name in Los Angeles was the home of magnificent movie theaters (see figure 8).

As we will see in the next chapter, City Beautiful plans during the early

twentieth century, sponsored by downtown corporate and commercial interests, were explicitly designed to establish a CBD of office buildings, department stores, hotels, theaters, and grand railway terminals and to push out factories, warehouses, and wholesale markets (Weiss 1992). Zoning, first initiated in New York in 1916 and widely espoused by other cities, helped to rigidly compartmentalize the industrial metropolis. As Mark Weiss (1992, 51) explains, one of the driving forces for the passing of New York's zoning ordinance was the Fifth Avenue Association, a group of merchants, hotel owners, investors, lenders, and real estate brokers who wanted to stabilize and reinforce the image of Fifth Avenue as a high-class shopping district.

Downtowns became the hub of major urban activities. By the 1920s they had reached their peak as centers of power and wealth. Now almost exclusively centers for business and shopping, downtowns hosted each day thousands of

FIGURE 8
Los Angeles, 1923:
Broadway Street.
Department of Special
Collections, University
of Southern California,
Doheny Library.

white-collar office workers, shoppers, and visitors. Contemporary photographs show busy streets with pedestrians on the sidewalks and different modes of transportation in the carriage way. By the 1920s, with the automobiles becoming more numerous, complaints about traffic congestion and noise started appearing in newspaper editorials. But for all its vibrancy and dynamism the American downtown was becoming a very anomic place. Chicago sociologists captured the transformation when they described the people in the crowds that filled downtown streets as isolated individuals, cut off from one another by a screen of thousands of impersonal commercial contacts (Park 1915).

THE DECLINING CENTER (1930–1960)

American downtowns reached their peak in the 1920s, but decline soon followed. The Depression dealt a crippling blow to private-sector construction activity. Many skyscraper owners and builders found themselves heavily in debt. After the building boom of the 1920s, an oversupply of office space was evident in the high vacancy rates for downtown office buildings. After the collapse of the economy during the Depression, the value of skyscrapers plummeted and remained stagnant for many years. In most cities the tallest building in 1929 was still the tallest three decades later (Ford 1994).

During the Depression years it was mainly the federal government that commissioned the few buildings that were built downtown.[5] In order to stimulate the economy and employ the jobless, a federal agency, the Public Works Administration, put its stamp on certain downtowns around the country by erecting various civic buildings (city halls, libraries, civic auditoriums, concert halls, and museums). The low and often unassuming structure of these buildings was in sharp contrast with the monumental city halls of the earlier City Beautiful era and the flashy corporate towers. In a way, the architecture of these New Deal buildings presaged the weakening role of the public sector in the downtown development in the coming decades.

While the sluggish economy of the Depression era contributed to the woes of downtown, other forces further exacerbated the decline of downtown's prominence and its perceived centrality. Increasingly after the 1920s, the suburbs would become the more dynamic growth areas of the American metropolis. Expanding automobile use allowed more and more people to live further and further away from the center. After World War II, a multibillion dollar program for the construction of national highways further enabled the dispersal of suburbs all over the American landscape. Federal policies encouraged home ownership for millions of aspiring middle-class families. Ironically, the increased prosperity of the late 1940s and 1950s contributed to downtown's demise by allowing millions of Americans to realize their dream: a detached house in the suburbs.

Businesses quickly followed residences in an unprecedented exodus from downtown. Department stores, specialty stores, movie theaters, hotels, and offices found a new and more profitable market in the suburbs. As early as the 1920s, a number of shop owners, disheartened by the congestion, lack of adequate parking space, and exceedingly high rents in downtown, had opted for new locations along arterial strips radiating from the center (Loukaitou-Sideris 1994). Neighborhood retail stores, as well as department stores and office buildings, started flourishing along these commercial corridors that served adjacent residential districts. For nearby residents, it became much more comfortable to patronize the neighborhood stores than to go all the way downtown to shop. Although these commercial strips appeared throughout the nation's cities, none became as prominent and well known as Wilshire Boulevard in Los Angeles. In the late 1920s and 1930s the "Miracle Mile" part of this street became the place to be for businesses and their clients.

In the post–World War II era, the mobility of Americans increased dramatically. The National Highway Trust Fund,[6] set up by Congress in 1956, was the primary financial force for the building of the interstate highway system. This new grid of highways, superimposed on the American metropolises, reduced the location advantage and the primacy previously enjoyed by the CBDs (Muller 1986). As increased mobility enabled retail and commerce to locate even further away from downtown, self-sufficient suburban centers started to form. By the 1950s it was the air-conditioned and enclosed suburban shopping mall, with ample parking, that appealed to consumers' fancy and money. In most downtowns no new department stores opened after World War II, and many existing stores closed. Downtowns continued to decline in almost every city in the post–World War II period. This decline was reflected by the numerous for rent signs on store fronts, the vacant office buildings, the neglected appearance of the establishments that were still in business, and the general deterioration of downtown's urban form. The downtown frame of abandoned commercial buildings surrounding the core expanded during this period. At the same time, skid row residential hotels and converted rooming houses around downtown provided shelter for those trapped in downtown.

In contrast to the vibrant and congested streets of the 1920s, downtown streets in the 1950s appeared empty of people and activity. From 1948 to 1954 overall sales were booming, but the downtown share of retailing fell by one-quarter in thirteen of the largest metropolitan areas in the United States (Frieden and Sagalyn 1989, 13). Victor Gruen, an Austrian architect who became very prominent in the 1960s for his urban design proposals for the redevelopment of many downtowns, described the "ailing" American city centers in a book entitled *The Heart of Our Cities*. Gruen lamented the loss of vitality of retail in downtown areas around the country. He described the "radical dying" of major department stores and smaller retail businesses in downtown Manhattan and the departure of many theaters from the Broadway district. He documented the dwindling of inhabitants in downtown Cincinnati from 11,500 in 1940 to 6,500 in 1960 and the reduction of retail establishments from 1,054 in 1948 to only 854 a decade later. Similarly, he described the downtown areas of Detroit and Boston as experiencing high vacancy rates in office and retail establishments. Real estate values were crumbling, and cultural institutions languished (Gruen 1964, 90).

The understanding that downtown was a declining center, a failing real estate market, an area in crisis, finally struck mayors, city councils, and planners in the 1950s. While master plans of the 1940s gave little attention to downtown, plans of the 1950s and 1960s called for revitalization of the "blighted" CBDs (Abbott 1993).[7] Downtown banks, corporations, and merchants' associations with significant stakes in CBD renewal lobbied for a restoration of business confidence in downtown that would enable the city center to acquire its "proper" economic, cultural, and symbolic role. Federal legislation, the Housing Acts of 1949 and 1954, gave them a mechanism to do exactly that.

THE "RENEWED" DOWNTOWN (1960s–1970s)

The very amount and character of obsolescence of underdeveloped sites and of traffic congestion which make up the principal problems of downtown, of themselves also create the opportunity for spectacular improvement and changes.

WALTER BRAUNSCHWEIGER, NOVEMBER 1, 1959

*Los Angeles has a remarkable opportunity to proceed with development of a new
downtown. There is a need for new, large structures and for investors to build buildings and for us to build a city. . . . The plan can enhance the value of the Los Angeles
central area as the headquarters for business and as a cultural and recreational center.*
WALTER BRAUNSCHWEIGER, NOVEMBER 2, 1959

Comments such as these offered by Walter Braunschweiger (quoted in the *Los
Angeles Times*), chairman of the Los Angeles Central City Committee and executive vice-president of Bank of America, at the presentation of his committee's master plan for downtown Los Angeles were typical views expressed all
over the country.[8] By the end of the 1950s, some seven hundred CBD plans
emerged (Frieden and Sagalyn 1989). They were all committed to converting
the ailing urban core to a modern and efficient business center. Their target
was the underutilized or "blighted" land at the city core. The definition of
blight, however, was often obfuscated by zealous redevelopment agencies and
politicians who wanted to make a case for redevelopment. The new vision of
modern downtown required comprehensive clearance. But few cities were capable of bearing the enormous financial costs (even with the help of corporate
executives) of such an effort (Kantor 1988). It was only with the help of the
federal urban renewal program that city governments were able to purchase
and clear huge tracts of downtown land.

Urban renewal as a concept was formally proposed in 1941, and legislation
was submitted to Congress in 1945. After prolonged and heated debates, the
legislation was passed over bitter opposition in 1949. The Housing Act of 1949
assisted renewal schemes, which were often used to enable downtown expansion. Amendments in 1954 and 1959 further transformed the Housing Act of
1949 into a downtown renewal program. The data are quite revealing. Fifty-
two percent of all urban renewal funds went for projects within one mile of the
city center, and 82 percent went for projects within two miles of it (Frieden
and Sagalyn 1989, 25).

Urban renewal efforts in American downtowns involved extensive land
clearance. Through the power of eminent domain, planning agencies were able
to acquire land, evict occupants, and demolish the existing structures in an
effort to prepare for development.[9] City government officials, private developers, and the local business community all participated in the redevelopment
activities, but, clearly, the initiative for and the power of redevelopment, at least
during the first stages of the process, were with the public sector. So many

cities saw in this period the rise of powerful redevelopment agencies: Boston Redevelopment Authority (BRA) in Boston, Community Redevelopment Agency in Los Angeles (CRA), San Francisco Redevelopment Agency (SFRA) in San Francisco, and the like. With them came the redevelopment czars—Edward Logue in Boston, Justin Herman in San Francisco, Robert Moses in New York—who became extremely influential in reshaping their city's downtown (Bennett 1986).

A typical federal urban renewal project took approximately twelve years to complete (Anderson 1964). Moreover, even cleared land offered at a cost below its real market value often did not seem to attract developers, who were con-

FIGURE 9
Opposite: Los Angeles,
1967: Bunker Hill razed.
Department of Special
Collections, University
of Southern California,
Doheny Library.

FIGURE 10
Los Angeles, Bunker Hill,
1990s: The new
corporate skyline. Chris
Morland, Community
Redevelopment Agency
of Los Angeles.

cerned with the return on their investment in depressed downtowns. For years, therefore, extensive areas of the core were graded and cleared but remained vacant, and they were often converted to parking lots (see figure 9).

Another physical impact of redevelopment on downtown's urban form was the emergence of a new urban pattern of superblocks and wide thoroughfares. While the assemblage of smaller lots for skyscraper buildings had been a familiar practice since the turn of the century, redevelopment plans now dictated consolidation of many blocks and closure of public streets and alleys (Beauregard 1986). Whole downtown blocks, once occupied by a multitude of shops and buildings, gave way to corporate megastructures (see figure 10). Land uses became lumpy as the "fine grain" fabric of downtown was progressively replaced by internally oriented mega-development projects.[10] The land uses of this new

CBD were geared exclusively toward a transactional, service economy, one focusing on banking, finance, insurance, professional services, and trade rather than manufacturing.

During the late 1950s and 1960s, the seeds of projects such as the Prudential Center in Boston, Gateway Center in Pittsburgh, the World Trade Center in New York, Renaissance Center in Detroit (see figure 11), Moscone Center in San Francisco, and Broadway and California Plazas in Los Angeles were planted in downtowns across the nation. Brochures published by redevelopment agencies projected the character of the new downtown: sleek office towers, luxury high-rise condominiums, wide boulevards, open-air plazas. But as the new downtown core was expanding vertically in the American cities, the downtown frame was encroaching horizontally into the core. The new flashy towers were attracting tenants away from older office buildings, which, because they were on the "wrong" side of downtown, were left vacant and decaying.

This new vision of the modernist city required drastic changes in downtown's urban form. The downtown grid was obliterated by new access streets, the block system was altered, and if the landmarks of the past—the city hall, the railroad terminal, the courthouse, the fire station—survived, they were dwarfed by the skyscrapers. The small shops, warehouses, and remaining dwellings were all swept away by the bulldozer. Distances between activities increased, sidewalks became narrower, and curb cuts to underground parking structures made the sidewalks unfriendly to pedestrians. White-collar pedestrians were pulled away from the street into plazas and onto skywalks (Robertson 1995). This typical process of urban form "renewal" is illustrated by the redevelopment of the Bunker Hill district in downtown Los Angeles.

The Bunker Hill story   Bunker Hill is today the premier office district of downtown Los Angeles. It is a corporate landscape of high-rise office towers and modernist plazas that has erased any memories of its previous topography, urban form, and social activities.[11] Graded, cut, and filled, the entire landscape of Bunker Hill changed dramatically after the CRA of Los Angeles, established in 1948 to oversee redevelopment efforts in downtown Los Angeles, began its renewal project in the immediate postwar period. Bunker Hill's story starts in the late 1860s, when two wealthy Anglos, Prudent Beaudry and Stephen Mott, bought the hill lands in tax sales. The subdivision of the land was re-

FIGURE 11
Detroit, 1995:
Renaissance Center.
Photograph by Tridib
Banerjee.

corded in 1869, but actual building did not begin until the 1870s. Even though the residents of Bunker Hill came for different reasons, most of them shared the desire to live in comfort and class in the unique environment of the hill. The physical layout of the hill served as a refuge from the hustle and bustle of the expanding city below (Adler 1963).

In the 1880s Bunker Hill became one of the fashionable residential districts of Los Angeles and was home to a large number of lawyers, doctors, and merchants. Novel architectural styles, such as Queen Anne and Eastlake, started appearing. Two- and three-story mansions were built with ornate balconies and verandas, corner towers, arched windows, round-ended shingles, and stained glass (see figure 12). These mansions reflected the wealth, power, and

class status of their elite residents. In the 1890s the first hotels appeared on the hill, and by 1899 visitors could find accommodations in one of the five hotels and two rooming houses of Bunker Hill (Pugsley 1977).

By the 1920s and 1930s, as the downtown area was expanding westward, Bunker Hill began to show signs of a change in population. Many longtime residents left for newer and more fashionable districts. Many of the mansions were sold to landlords, who began to subdivide them into numerous rooms to be rented mostly to single men. This era saw the building of tenement housing on the hill, and the proliferation of small retail establishments—mom-and-pop stores, cafés, restaurants, drugstores, shoe-repair shops, and dry-cleaning services—freestanding or on the ground floor of residential buildings. But construction quickly came to a halt, and no new buildings arose between 1930 and 1940. However, during that same decade, the population on the hill increased by 19 percent. The 1940 census found a low-income population, with a large share of older men, residing on the hill. Of the 1,976 dwelling units at the time of the 1940 census, only 2.2 percent were owner occupied. Bunker Hill was still a good residential environment, but for a different segment of the population. A team of experts in 1941 found that "Bunker Hill is not a detriment to the downtown area, it is an asset. It supplies excellent sites for superior types of multiple dwellings commanding a view of the entire surrounding country. Such structures would provide replenishment of the downtown tributary resident purchasing power which is urgently needed, and encourage the rehabilitation of near-by blighted areas" (Robbins and Tilton 1941).

But ten years later, in 1951, the newly established CRA of Los Angeles would condemn Bunker Hill itself as blighted and would designate it for redevelopment. The winds of change began to blow over Bunker Hill. Photographs and accounts of Bunker Hill streets in the 1950s were dominated by negative images. A series of photos commissioned by the City Housing Authority sought to document substandard housing and blight in Bunker Hill. Unlike the earlier images of well-tended front yards and entry ways, these photographs frequently showed the backs of poorly maintained, wooden, multistory residential buildings. Children played under drying laundry in these back yards and in alleys crowded with parked cars, often next to incinerators. The still images, used by both the City Housing Authority and the CRA, became symbols of decay and neglect associated with a failing social order in a period that championed urban renewal as a means of promoting economic efficiency. They acted as rhetorical devices meant to dramatize material conditions and to sway public opinion to adopt the meanings attached to these conditions (Beauregard 1993). The means of "correction" of the perceived "unfavorable environment" of Bunker Hill involved the razing of all 396 buildings and the displacement of its eleven thousand mostly low-income residents (Community Redevelopment Agency 1966).

The pressure for change came from the business and real estate sectors, as well as from nearly every public agency in the city. The police department depicted the hill as a high-crime area; the fire department stressed the difficulty of fighting fires on top of the hill; the department of health classified only 18 percent of the residential units as acceptable habitations; the Department of City Planning complained about the cost of services to Bunker Hill residents as well as the loss of tax revenues; and the CRA painted a picture of blight and dereliction.[12] Both public and private sectors agreed that Bunker Hill was an obstacle that prevented the business district's expansion westward (Davis 1991).

Redevelopment in the Los Angeles CBD started with the drafting by the CRA of the *Proposed Urban Renewal Plan*, which was adopted by the Los Angeles City Council in March 1959. The adoption of *The Redevelopment Plan* established the Bunker Hill Urban Renewal Project. In 1960 the CRA began acquisition of Bunker Hill properties, relocation of residents and business, demolition of buildings, and site-improvement work. The design for Bunker Hill proposed "a total of approximately 3,750 dwelling units, 3,000 hotel units, 12 million square feet of office and over one-half million square feet of retail space" (Community Redevelopment Agency 1968).

It took some time for the CRA to win approval for federal funds and still longer to resolve a court case brought by residents of Bunker Hill who fought to keep their neighborhood.[13] But the landscape began to change even before the case was decided in favor of the CRA in 1964. The redevelopment plan followed all the doctrines of modernist city planning: it segregated pedestrian and auto traffic, created superblocks and megastructures, and differentiated each zone of activity from the others, and in so doing, it stripped from these Bunker Hill streets the vibrancy and overlay of functions that had characterized them for almost a century.

Analysis of land ownership in the Bunker Hill area quantifies the results of the block-consolidation process. In a 1961 map, the number and location of streets were the same as they had been at the turn of the century, but by 1981, the twenty-nine blocks of Bunker Hill had been reduced to twenty-three. The comparison of the figure-ground maps of 1926 and 1956 (prior to the redevelopment) with those of one decade later is also striking. By 1964 most buildings had been razed and the dense urban fabric of previous decades has disappeared (see figure 13).

When the CRA acquired the land, it often remained undeveloped for long periods of time. One of the first acts of the Bunker Hill Urban Renewal Project

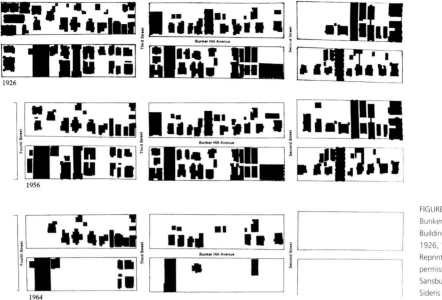

FIGURE 13
Bunker Hill in transition:
Building footprints in
1926, 1956, 1964.
Reprinted with the
permission of Gail
Sansbury (Loukaitou-
Sideris and Sansbury
1996).

was the creation of a parking lot. Until deals could be finalized with private developers, which often took decades, much of Bunker Hill became a vast sea of parked cars (see figure 14). Most photographs of the 1950s and 1960s show cars parked in every possible space. For the creation of parking lots and warehouses, buildings were demolished and the land was graded. The hill was smoothed, homogenized, graded and de-graded. The redevelopment projects created isolated corporate "monuments," which turned their back to public streets, replacing those streets with private pedestrian ways and plazas.

In a photograph of the late 1960s, we are reminded of modernist architect Le Corbusier's sketches (see figure 15). A multilane street rushes toward a group of high-rise towers. This new setting is built for speed, not pedestrian movement. The surface street shown in this photograph, Grand Street, has become wider, and its street walls have disappeared; in fact, the street appears to be suspended above the landscape of parking lots, suggesting a series of supporting columns.

Created in a period of intense land speculation, the streets of Bunker Hill enjoyed almost a hundred years of organic evolution. In each succeeding era,

the built form was added to, changed, or replaced, but the continuity of the landscape remained intact because the major points of reference—the topography, certain landmarks, and the streets themselves—remained. Then, in an episodic act, a planning intervention, this continuity was disrupted, and the many layers of its history were erased. Today, the built form of Bunker Hill reveals little about its past heritage.

The present environment of Bunker Hill lacks the qualities of complexity, diversity, and context that characterized the earlier landscape. The megablocks that now characterize Bunker Hill have been developed as disjointed and isolated projects. The episodic nature of such developments prevents them from effectively connecting with the city's larger urban tissue, or with one another.

FIGURE 15
Emergence of a new
Bunker Hill, 1960s.
Department of Special
Collections, University
of Southern California,
Doheny Library.

The "inside" private spaces are insular with little connection to the "outside" public domain. High-rise towers turn their backs to the city; corporate plazas are separated from sidewalks by high protective walls; elevated pedestrian walkways separate white-collar pedestrians from the unpredictable street life; escalators lead to sunken shopping malls and parking structures. As a result, Bunker Hill streets are presently empty of pedestrian activity at all times, with the possible exception of the weekday lunch hour. At that time one can find a few office workers venturing down the streets on their way to lunch.

Redevelopment has created exclusive corporate settings in Bunker Hill. At the same time it has contributed to a polarized development of a public, but old and derelict, downtown of indigents east and southeast of Bunker Hill (where the skid row area and the garment and flower districts are located) and the private and glamorous corporate landscape of the new downtown (see figure 10). In contrast to the integrated street environment of the earlier neighborhood, Bunker Hill today is the exclusive realm of the white-collar office worker. The poor, the homeless, the bag ladies, the immigrants, are all confined to the old downtown.

Finally, the contemporary Bunker Hill environment is an ahistorical landscape. The architecture and imagery of office buildings, plazas, and urban malls are characteristically similar to those of most North American downtowns. This similarity, combined with the absence of "urban clues"—older buildings and urban artifacts that convey the history of the site—prevents the visitor to Bunker Hill from being oriented in space and time.

Bunker Hill, like parts of other American downtowns, has witnessed dramatic changes in its urban form and social context. In each succeeding era, the built form was added to, changed, or replaced. For the most part, these changes added layers of development creating a patchwork quilt of different buildings and spaces. Then a planning intervention erased those different layers of history of the site. The new Bunker Hill and, for that matter, the new downtown display imagery and meaning very different from those displayed by the old.

2

Ludwig Mies van der Rohe, one of the prominent architects of the modern movement, once declared that the destiny of architecture and design is to translate the "will of the epoch into space." In the previous chapter we examined how the wills of different epochs, influenced by socioeconomic, technological, political, and cultural forces, produced different downtowns. In this chapter we will discuss how these circumstances were mediated on urban form through normative and visionary design. We will present different models of downtown design, which are products of different historic periods. From colonial antecedents to the City Beautiful plans to modernist schemes, these models are part of the evolving history of the deliberate design for American downtowns. In the later chapters of this book we will focus on the most current phase of this history.

THE COLONIAL MODEL: A SQUARE AT THE CORE

The urban form of colonial town centers was often inspired by the design formulas of European settlers. Colonial cities did not have specialized business districts; they did, however, have a center, a public open space that was symbolically placed at the heart of each town. This was the square, plaza, common green, or place d'armes (see figures 16 and 17). Around the square, together with major public buildings (church, customs house, hospital, town hall) were shops and dwellings for merchants.[1] For Spanish settlements the design of the square—the plaza (for an example, see figure 18)—was prescribed by the Laws of the Indies, which were proclaimed by King Philip II of Spain in 1573 (Morris 1979; Kostof 1992). The laws, inspired by Vitruvius's principles of town planning, established as the focal point of the urban settlement a rectangular plaza, with its dimensions in a recommended two to three ratio. French settlers

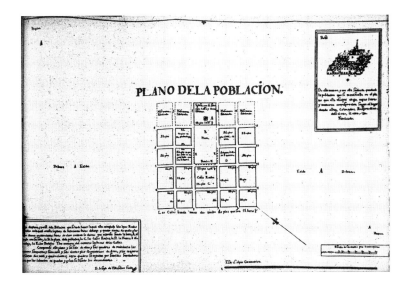

PLANO DELA POBLACION.

FIGURE 16
Opposite, top: Los
Angeles, ca. 1877: Pueblo
Plaza. Special Collections,
University Research
Library, University of
California, Los Angeles.

FIGURE 17
Opposite, bottom: Los
Angeles, 1883: Pueblo
Plaza. Special Collections,
University Research
Library, University of
California, Los Angeles.

FIGURE 18
Above: Plan of the Pueblo
of San Fernando de Bexar,
San Antonio, Texas,
ca. 1730. Reprinted
with the permission of
Princeton University Press
(Reps 1965, 37).

used the pattern of European bastide towns for their settlements. They arranged their newly founded towns of Montreal, New Orleans, St. Louis, and Mobile around an open space, the place d'armes, which as it name implies served for the training of the local militia and for parades, celebrations, and civic ceremonies. The center for Puritan communities in New England was the village green or common, a rather unpretentious space that could come in any size or shape. The green or common invariably served as the center of community life and as a setting for public gatherings, military training, and sometimes even for cattle grazing.

The common underlying purpose of these early North American town centers was their benefit to the community at large. They were "early attempts at a deliberate, self-conscious representation of community" (Torre 1981, 33). Colonial towns represented integrated wholes; their public was more or less a homogeneous, uniform entity. The town center, represented by the square, was conceived as a setting for collective action. People went there to participate in public activities that were often political and carried communal meanings (Jackson 1984b).

The square at the core would serve as the "generative space" of the entire settlement, which was laid out from the center outward (Suisman 1993). Unlike the ideal plans of the Renaissance, which envisioned towns as complete star-shaped entities, early colonial towns were never complete or fixed; their grid could extend on either side of the square as topography and need determined. But the square was always the predetermined starting point. It was designed to serve as the focus of the town that would evolve around it.[2] Jackson Square, so named in the early nineteenth century in honor of President Andrew Jackson, in New Orleans was designed by a French military engineer in 1721 as a waterfront parade ground (see figure 19). Market Square in Pittsburgh was composed to be the site of the courthouse, city hall, public market, and later a theater and a concert hall. The Plaza in Santa Fe similarly served as the heart of the city. Pioneer Square in Seattle was designed to be the focus of the city's commercial district.

As August Heckscher (1977, 145) explains, "The typical American square—a hole in the checkerboard—was derived from the prevalent grid, being a block (or occasionally a group of blocks) from which buildings were permanently excluded. In its internal organization the urban square has been plainly related to the grid, being formal and geometrical, with entrances and pathways in line with the streets and with ornamentation placed at the axes of traffic." Of course the most well-known precedent on North American soil for what Heckscher describes was William Penn's plan for the city of Philadelphia. Consistent with the doctrines of Renaissance town planning and influenced by the proposals for the reconstruction of London after the Great Fire, in 1682 Penn with the help of his surveyor, Thomas Holme, laid out a city whose center was a ten-acre square at the intersection of two principal streets. The square was designed to include "houses for public affairs" and open space for the benefit of all the city's residents (Toffey 1985).

As already discussed in the previous chapter, when towns progressively became centers of a mercantile economy, an identifiable CBD emerged, shaped

by demands for shipping, storage, distribution, and administration. The town square quickly lost its prestige as the all-important town center. Indeed, mid–nineteenth-century designers described town squares as "little squirrel cages," totally inadequate to serve contemporary needs (quoted in Schuyler 1986). Land uses around the square changed. Sometimes squares survived as downtown parks; other times they were subdivided into lots. Often the CBD shifted geographically and the square was no longer the center. In any case, by the mid-nineteenth century little remained of the colonial square's original concept and role. Traveling around New England and New York, Timothy Dwight, the president of Yale University, complained in 1821, "It is remarkable that the scheme of forming public squares, so beautiful, and in great towns so conducive to health, should have been almost universally forgotten" (quoted in Webb 1990, 126).

FIGURE 19
New Orleans, 1903: Jackson Square. Courtesy of the Library of Congress.

FIGURE 20
New York City, 1910–1930: Fifth Avenue and the Plaza. Courtesy of the Library of Congress.

FIGURE 21
Opposite: Los Angeles, 1923: Pershing Square. Special Collections, University Research Library, University of California, Los Angeles.

THE CITY BEAUTIFUL MODEL: LEGACY OF GRAND DESIGNS

Make no little plans, they have no power to stir men's blood. Make big plans; aim high in hope and work.

DANIEL BURNHAM, 1912

These words by Daniel Burnham, the architect and planner who put his imprint on many city plans during the early twentieth century, marked an era in which large-scale design proposals were initiated as a response to the chaos and disorder of the growing industrial city. The City Beautiful model was also inspired by the baroque precedents of Europe—the much admired cities of

France, Italy, Germany, and England. But now the scale was larger than in colonial times, and the architecture was grandiose. A formalistic reconstruction of the center of American cities was inspired by the principles of baroque town planning: broad tree-lined boulevards, diagonally crisscrossing a city's undifferentiated grid; monumental civic buildings, built in the neoclassical, Beaux Arts tradition; majestic vistas terminating in equestrian sculptures and ornamental fountains; and the like (see figures 20 and 21).

The City Beautiful vision of the ideal city was built upon the premise of a glorified center. The centrality and primacy of the downtown business district were underscored by the manipulation and beautification of urban form: the convergence of grand avenues on the center, the building of monumental city halls, public libraries, museums, civic auditoriums, rail terminals, and ornamental parks (see figure 22). Implied in all this was a notion that the grand design of the center would encourage civic pride and civic responsibility, that

aesthetic enhancement would result in better citizenship. Widespread support of City Beautiful plans by downtown merchants and the business elite reflected their shrewd realization that such public improvements could make downtowns more attractive and profitable.

Daniel Burnham's city plans and Frederick Law Olmsted's proposals for open space networks within cities captured the imagination of mayors, city councils, and business associations at the turn of the century. Their proposals marked the beginning of the grand civic design approach to downtown development. For almost twenty years, architects, civil engineers, and landscape architects would produce plans inspired by the City Beautiful spirit, commissioned by municipal governments, and sponsored by downtown commercial interests. These plans strove to create a thriving downtown of offices, retail establishments, hotels, and department stores—using civic design to showcase clean and attractive commercial and cultural districts—and, ultimately, to get rid of the unsightly factories and warehouses (Weiss 1992).

Historians agree that the opening of the World's Columbian Exposition in 1893 signaled the beginning of the City Beautiful movement. The fair's "White

City" was built in the best neoclassical tradition with glittering white buildings in monumental architecture, with grand courts and reflecting ponds of water in canals and lagoons. It became the celebrated precedent for the City Beautiful planning to follow (Foglesong 1986). During the first twenty years of this century, the downtowns of cities such as Washington, Boston, Cleveland, Philadelphia, Baltimore, New York, Chicago, St. Louis, and Minneapolis would get major facelifts. Countless improvement societies sprang up all over the nation. In 1917 the American Institute of Architects reported in its *City Planning Progress in the United States* that 233 cities had initiated improvement programs of various sorts (in Reps, 1965). The most influential plans and programs of the period, however, had Daniel Burnham's stamp on them.

The first important application of City Beautiful planning was in Washington, D.C. The beautification of the city with monumental architectural and landscaping improvements was seen as fitting for the capital of the American republic. In 1901 Daniel Burnham was appointed by Congress to head a commission that included Frederick Olmsted Jr. (the son of Frederick Law Olmsted, who was too ill to participate), architect Charles McKim, and sculptor Augustus Saint-Gaudens. The first action of the commission was to study an unimplemented century-old proposal by French engineer Pierre L'Enfant for the replanning of Washington. This was a grand design, inspired by the baroque plan of Versailles (where L'Enfant had spent much of his childhood), that called for a T-shaped arrangement, with the Capitol, the White House, and the Washington Monument at the three ends. The second action of the commission was to visit parks and public buildings in Paris, Rome, Budapest, Frankfurt, Berlin, and London to trace the origins of L'Enfant's inspiration. After seven weeks of travel the members of the commission made up their minds about the main elements of the plan (Reps 1965).

The committee's plan, a revival of L'Enfant's proposal, was one of monumental public facilities, buildings, and spaces, and it focused solely on the city's central area. The plan suggested a north-south axis connecting the White House to the Washington Monument and extending southward to a central point on the bank of the Potomac River, a point that would be embellished with sculptures and fountains. It prescribed a main east-west axis passing from the Washington Monument and linking the Capitol to a proposed site for a future Lincoln Memorial. This axis was in the form of a grand mall, patterned after the Champs Elysees in Paris. The Mall, a grass strip three hundred feet wide with rows of elms in columns of four, was to be lined with galleries and museums on both sides. Just off the Mall, Lafayette Square was to be surrounded by uniform public buildings. Congress opted for the grandeur, symmetry, and monumentality that characterized this urban design vision for the capital city. By the 1920s most elements of the plan had been realized.

If the plan for Washington was marked by collaboration between politicians and designers, the plan for the CBD of Cleveland, presented two years later (in 1903), was characterized by an alliance between businessmen and designers, an alliance backed by the city's mayor, Tom Johnson. The seeds for the plan were sown when a group of local businessmen, impressed by the "White City" of the World's Columbian Exposition, aspired to recreate a similar model for their downtown. Recruited for this effort was again Daniel Burnham, who suggested the redesign of Cleveland's center to the northeast of the older commercial hub known as Public Square (Hines 1974). The Cleveland Group Plan of 1903 stimulated similar "civic center" plans in other cities (Gerckens 1988). As historian Richard Foglesong (1986, 153–54) describes,

> The plan was typical of City Beautiful efforts in its emphasis on the aesthetic relationship of buildings and grounds. Covering a tract five blocks in length and two in width, the plan provided for a grouping of the designated public buildings together with a new headquarters for the Chamber of Commerce and Union Station. These buildings were to be set around a central mall patterned after the Fair's Court of Honor. Also borrowed from the Fair were the design principles governing the building group: uniformity of architecture was of primary importance, designs were to be "derived from the historic motives of the classic architecture of Rome," one material was to be used throughout, and a uniform scale (in terms of height, bulk, and cornice line) was to be utilized for all the buildings.

In the way of this beautification effort for the CBD of Cleveland were low-income residential structures of a skid row district. Without hesitation, the design committee recommended their removal because the buildings had "no great value," and the land was "less costly than that which surrounds it" (Foglesong 1986, 154). Half a century later, similar arguments would be used to justify the clearance of downtown sites for urban redevelopment.

Daniel Burnham's fame had reached the West Coast when a group of influential San Franciscans invited him in 1906 to prepare a plan for their city. After a quick survey of San Francisco, Burnham criticized the inappropriateness of the grid that covered the city's hilly topography. Therefore, his plan focused on recreating an ideal street system. A grand boulevard was to encircle the city, to which all other arteries would lead. Radial boulevards were proposed to facilitate circulation and connect the new neighborhoods with the old (Hines 1974). By reworking the city's street system, Burnham incorporated for the first time some regional thinking in his plan—a trend that was to continue in his next effort, the plan of Chicago. The major emphasis of the San Francisco plan was the city's downtown. The architect's vision included a proposal for a civic center of governmental and cultural buildings around a grand civic plaza, at the intersection of Market Street and Van Ness Avenue. Tree-lined boulevards radiated from the plaza and were occasionally widened by traffic circles. On April 18, 1906, the San Francisco earthquake and subsequent fire devastated the downtown district. What might have been an opportunity for the plan's implementation proved to be its demise, as the city's merchants opted for a quick reconstruction instead of pursuing the grand, but much slower and more costly, City Beautiful vision.

In the Chicago plan—probably Burnham's most significant contribution to American city planning—one can trace not only the legacy of the City Beautiful movement but also the seeds of a new era to follow. The plan was initiated by the Chicago Commercial Club but required the extensive involvement of city agencies for its promotion and implementation. This was the first truly metropolitan plan in that it was a proposal for the redevelopment of the whole city and beyond—an area within a sixty-mile radius of the city center. The plan called for a system of radial and concentric highways that gave better access to the hub of the city, and the construction of surface, overhead, and underground transportation loops around the CBD (see figure 23). An intra-city train system was proposed to link the center to the outlying suburbs. As we will later discuss, this emphasis on transportation links to the city center would presage planning proposals in the 1950s and 1960s.

Another major element of the plan included a regional network of parks, together with a twenty-mile scenic lakefront development, a response to the recreational needs of the modern industrial city (Condit 1973). But the presentation and drawings for Chicago's business district were far more detailed than

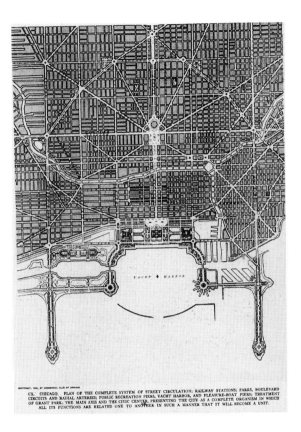

FIGURE 23
Plan of Chicago by
Burnham and Bennett,
1909. Reps, J. W.
The Making of Urban
America: A History of City
Planning in the U.S.
© 1995 by Princeton
University Press.
Reprinted/reproduced
by permission of
Princeton University Press.

CX. CHICAGO. PLAN OF THE COMPLETE SYSTEM OF STREET CIRCULATION; RAILWAY STATIONS; PARKS, BOULEVARD
CIRCUITS AND RADIAL ARTERIES; PUBLIC RECREATION PIERS, YACHT HARBOR, AND PLEASURE-BOAT PIERS; TREATMENT
OF GRANT PARK; THE MAIN AXIS AND THE CIVIC CENTER, PRESENTING THE CITY AS A COMPLETE ORGANISM IN WHICH
ALL ITS FUNCTIONS ARE RELATED ONE TO ANOTHER IN SUCH A MANNER THAT IT WILL BECOME A UNIT.

those of any other element of the plan. Renderings and drawings on various scales detailed the development of a grandiose civic center, focusing on a vast, pentagonal plaza from which ten principal avenues radiated. This was the ultimate city center, the heart of the metropolis, the climax of Daniel Burnham's baroque composition. Buildings of great uniformity and monumentality defined the center, with the domed City Hall at the center of the complex. The architectural treatment of buildings and space was clearly inspired by all the doctrines of the City Beautiful legacy. But the rhetoric of the text, which emphasized conception of the city as "a center of industry and traffic" (Burnham and Bennett 1970) and a concern for rational coordination, control, and regulation of land uses and transportation, signified the evolution of a new model of city design that would have enduring impacts on American downtowns.

City Beautiful plans emphasized aesthetics and visual order. The proponents of the movement marveled at the great Renaissance squares, the baroque town planning of the popes and the princes and kings of Europe, and the grand boulevards of Baron Haussmann's Paris. City Beautiful schemes used solely physical means—balance, axiality, hierarchical arrangements—in a quest for order on the urban landscape. Many (Mumford 1961; Foglesong 1986, Bennett 1990) have criticized these plans for their insufficient attention to pressing social needs, their naive faith in physical determinism, their obvious bias in favor of the upper classes, their lack of popular participation in decision making, their imposition of an imported order on the urban landscape, their explicit focus and investment on the CBD, and their blatant disregard for other dilapidated city neighborhoods.

These plans represented coherent urban design statements for whole downtown areas and called for a purposeful intervention and a larger public role in the achievement of their ideals. While most of the plans were initiated by private interests, they required public agencies to make them happen. This intervention entailed a rethinking of the balance between private goals and social needs in shaping the city. The need for public control and regulation of city building—a trend that would continue much more extensively during the next era—was recognized for the first time. City Beautiful planning was based on the paramountcy of the public sphere and on the parallel notions of *civitas* and the public man. It assumed that in civil society the planning and design of public facilities and spaces are a matter of public responsibility and initiative. City Beautiful plans envisaged major public works projects as the priming actions for city building. This, of course, was done in European accents and styles and reflected the tastes of the downtown business elite who patronized these plans rather than the values of the general public.

THE CITY PRACTICAL MODEL: PRELUDE TO MODERNISM

Planning consists not merely of beautiful pictures and civic centers of interesting projects for pleasure boulevards. Planning decides where things go and by what means and access. It seeks to achieve its end by both voluntary co-operation and legal compulsion.

ROBERT M. HAIG, 1927

The beautification programs enacted all over the country during the first years of the century did not, in the minds of many, solve the problems that were plaguing CBDs: congested streets, incompatible land uses, and lack of light and air exacerbated by an ever increasing stock of high-rise buildings. These concerns resulted in an abrupt switch from a paradigm that emphasized aesthetics to one that called for scientific rationality and efficiency in the planning of urban form. The City Practical model did not utilize architectonic means to shape urban form. Instead, it introduced regulatory mechanisms to bring the desired order to the American CBD: zoning of land uses, restriction of building heights, establishment of building envelopes and set backs. But if the means were different the objectives were the same: continuation of downtown primacy and enhancement of real estate assets.

The city of New York became the premier urban laboratory where the City Practical model was first applied. By 1913, Manhattan had become a city of towers, with 997 buildings of eleven to twenty stories and 51 buildings of twenty-one to sixty stories (Willis 1993). But almost side by side with the proud office towers, the high-class retail establishments, and the luxurious hotels one could still find "messy" loft buildings, warehouses, and industrial facilities. In particular, the garment industry with its mostly immigrant workforce was perceived as a threat to upscale downtown businesses. In 1907, the Fifth Avenue Association, composed of powerful businessmen, hotel owners, bankers, retail merchants, and real estate brokers, was established with the sole goal of reinforcing the image of Fifth Avenue as a high-class shopping district (Weiss 1992). The group lobbied hard to create a landmark ordinance. The New York City Building Zoning Ordinance, adopted in 1916 by the Commission on Building Districts and Restrictions, established an influential precedent of districting by use.[3] The commission promised downtown property owners that such a tactic would help stabilize (or even enhance) land values (Gilmartin 1995). New York was the nation's premier city; its zoning legislation inspired other zoning ordinances across the country. By the end of the 1920s more than 750 communities had adopted zoning resolutions as a means of controlling urban form (Hall 1989).

New York's resolution of 1916 created three categories of land use—"residential," "business," and "unrestricted"—and five classes of height districts. Building heights were limited in proportion to the width of the adjoining

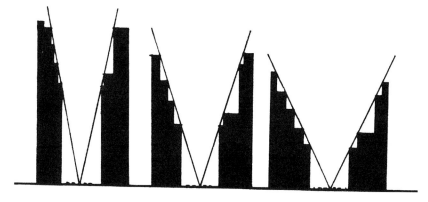

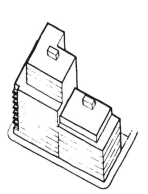

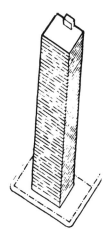

street. The ordinance also introduced the concept of zoning envelope, an imaginary spatial envelope beyond which a building could not extend. In an effort to ensure light and air at the lower floors and street level (rents at the lower floors were quite depressed at the time), the ordinance required building setbacks that started after a prescribed vertical height (see figure 24).[4] A tower of unrestricted height was allowed only over one-quarter of the lot area (see figure 25).

Zoning has had quite an impact on the visual form of downtown. For one, it encouraged lot assembly. Developers realized that it was not worth building a tall structure on a small lot; the upper floors would be very tiny because of the setbacks. Bigger sites, however, meant taller buildings. As a result, the downtown landscape took on a gargantuan appearance. The effects on downtown's real estate industry were also pronounced. In New York, where it all started, developers added 30 million square feet of office space in Manhattan between 1921 and 1929. In 1930 alone, seventeen major office towers were erected (Fitch 1993). Landmark buildings such as the Empire State Building (1931), Bankers Trust (1932), and Rockefeller Center (1933–1939) were all products of this era that witnessed the apotheosis of skyscrapers.

Downtown architecture was also defined by zoning. According to architectural historian Carol Willis (1993), architects started to treat the setback as an aesthetic element, emphasizing the edges of buildings with decorative bands and ornamental treatments. Today, we would call such treatment Art Deco style, but at the time it was called "New York style," "setback style," or simply "modern" (see figure 26). So in the 1920s a new brand of architecture appeared in the nation's downtowns, which departed considerably from the stylistic vocabulary of academic classicism. As one author put it, "the zoning resolution ushered in, quite by accident, the great experiment of Art Deco Architecture" (Gilmartin 1995, 201). A *New York Times* article of 1924 analyzed the results of zoning on downtown's urban form:

> The zoning law, enacted with strictly utilitarian intent, has resulted in an unforeseen revolution in metropolitan architecture. New York is becoming a skyscraper Babylon, a city whose streets are lined with terraced cliffs of Gothic and Renaissance workmanship, the terraces abloom with flowers and shrubs and trees; a city of a multitude of aerial gardens . . . the Hanging Gardens of Babylon translated to the uses of a generation that has devised the skyscraper. (quoted in Stern, Gilmartin, and Mellins 1987, 34–35)

The new built form of downtown, determined by the zoning envelope, was depicted in a series of drawings and renderings by architect Harvey Willey Corbett and renderer Hugh Ferriss (Ferriss 1929). These renderings showed a sea of towers rising from parking decks and surrounded by ample open space. Superhighways weaved through the skyscrapers, some on ground level, some elevated; while a heavy rail network crisscrossed downtown at a subterranean

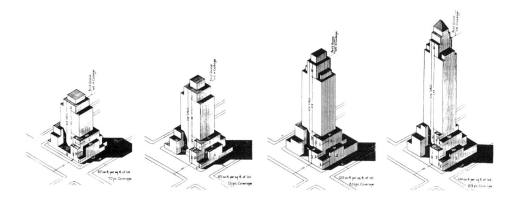

FIGURE 26
New York City: "Setback style" generated by zoning ordinance of 1916. Regional Plan Association, Inc., New York City (Regional Plan Association 1931a, 2:174–75).

FIGURE 27
Hugh Ferriss's "The Business Zone," 1929: A futuristic image (Ferris 1929).

level (see figure 27). According to Corbett the solution to downtown's congestion would come by fostering the "fast movement of traffic of all forms which was essential for healthy growth." He envisioned that "New York would become a very modernized Venice, a city of arcades, piazzas, and bridges, with canals for streets, only the canals will not be filled with water but with freely flowing motor traffic, the sun glittering on the black tops of the cars and the

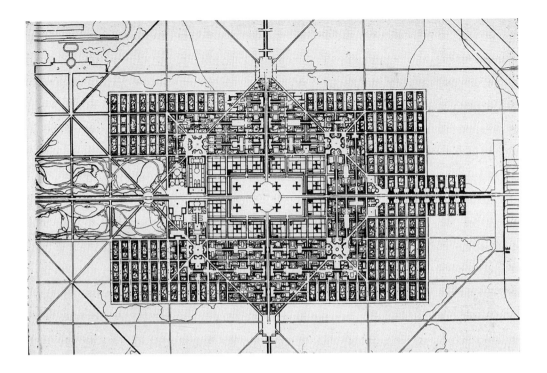

buildings reflected in the waving flood of rapidly rolling vehicles" (Stern, Gilmartin, and Mellins 1987, 38–39, n. 130).

This new vision for the center of the modern American metropolis echoed influences from Europe. The Futurists' work in Italy, in particular Antonio Sant'Elia's sketches of 1914, expressed an admiration for speed, movement, and mobility and an immense trust in the powers of modern technology to create the mechanized city. Similarly, in the early 1920s Le Corbusier's modernist vision of *La Ville Contemporaine* showed a city whose center was composed of magnificent towers surrounded by sweeping open space (Le Corbusier 1927; 1929). Multi-lane highways, railway networks, and even an airfield were all found at the hub of this "city of tomorrow" (see figure 28).

If New York's zoning resolution of 1916 opened the door to the City Practical, another planning document from the same city exemplified the era's most cherished ideals. The thousands of pages that comprised the first *Regional Plan of New York and Its Environs* attested to the growing belief of the time in scien-

FIGURE 28
Opposite: Le Corbusier's
La Ville Contemporaine,
a plan for 3 million
inhabitants. 1998 Artists
Rights Society (ARS), New
York/ADAPG, Paris/FLC
(Blake 1960, 35).

FIGURE 29
E. Maxwell Fry's "The
Future Tower City," 1931.
Regional Plan Association,
Inc., New York City
(Regional Plan Association
1931a, 2:152).

tism and rationalism and in comprehensiveness and efficiency as the means to guide the city's socioeconomic and physical development (Regional Plan Association 1929, 1931a, 1931b). Employing volumes of statistical surveys, the plan went well beyond the aesthetic orientation of the City Beautiful plans. The plan was sponsored by the Russell Sage Foundation and was initiated by a private entity, the Regional Plan Association (RPA), whose members included bankers, railroad men, executives of various philanthropic foundations, developers, large-property owners, and various professionals specializing in zoning, housing, planning, and landscape architecture (Fitch 1993).[5]

The RPA plan covered an area of 5,528 square miles but was concerned mostly with territory "within easy commuting distance" of Manhattan (Scott 1969). The plan envisioned a city of glittering skyscrapers (see figure 29). The primary goal of the plan was the expansion and preservation of the Manhattan CBD (Fitch 1993). Through the powers of zoning, the "inappropriate" industrial and residential uses were to be pushed outside of the core. Deteriorating structures at the center were to be eliminated by enacting stringent regulations. The center had to reclaim its lost order. As the plan's authors argued,

> Some of the poorest people live in conveniently located slums on high-priced land. On patrician Fifth Avenue, Tiffany and Woolworth, cheek by jowl, offer jewels and gimcracks from substantially identical sites. . . . A stone's throw from the stock exchange the air is filled with the aroma of roasting coffee; a few hundred feet from Times Square with the stench of slaughter houses. In the very heart of this "commercial" city, on Manhattan Island, south of 59th street, the inspectors in 1922 found nearly 420,000 workers employed in factories. Such a situation outrages one's sense of order. Everything seems misplaced. One yearns to rearrange things, to put things where they belong. (Haig 1929, 33)

The plan gave tremendous emphasis to stimulating transportation construction (see figure 30). It proposed highways radiating from Manhattan, metropolitan "loops," circumferential rail and road "belts" bypassing the center, and vertical separation of different modes of transportation in downtown, including a separate pedestrian system at an upper level. These were the first steps toward similar ideas that would appear in the nation's downtowns in the post–World War II era. Transportation links would help accomplish the three major directions of development:

1. Diffused re-centralization of industry with the objects of lessening the density of congested centers and of creating new centers.
2. Diffusion of residence into compact residential neighborhoods throughout the whole urban region integrated with the industrial sections so as to reduce distances between homes and places of work.
3. Sub-centralization of business so arranged as to provide the maximum of convenience to residents (Regional Plan Association 1929, 149–50).

The City Practical model of design represented a transition to planning in the modern era. It initiated paradigms that were followed and accentuated during the post–War World II era. The positivist underpinnings of the model, its

FIGURE 30
A. J. Frappier's proposed
Chrystie-Forsyth Parkway,
1931. Regional Plan
Association, Inc., New
York City (Regional
Plan Association 1931a,
2:399).

faith in scientific rationality, its belief in the liberating powers of technology, were all essentially modern. The division of downtown into functional cells defined by zoning was a rational solution meant to secure a stable and orderly development of the most prime land in the real estate market. Zoning represented the promise of scientific progress. Experts equipped with scientific data would ensure the order and functionality of downtown. Even though primarily a practical tool, zoning became also a form-defining instrument for American downtowns as the downtown skyline increasingly became defined by controls and regulations (Willis 1986).

The idea that the whole city—private property as well as public space— could be subject to public controls inspired a sense of power on the part of the public sector. Of course, it did not hurt that the planners' suggestions were in harmony with the ideas of the social, financial, philanthropic, and propertied elite of the city. Their espousal of the City Practical ideology guaranteed its success.[6]

THE MODERNIST MODEL: SYSTEMS AND NETWORKS

After World War II, as the older sections of downtown began to deteriorate, a new phase of rebuilding began under the auspices of the urban renewal program and the development of the inner-city segments of the interstate highway system (see figure 31). As the modern metropolis was transformed into a centrifugal, polycentric urban form, thanks to freeway development and suburban growth fueled by the exodus of the middle and upper classes from the central city, downtown areas started facing competition from suburban centers. Large-scale urban design plans were prepared once again for American downtowns. The plans developed during the post–World War II period were characterized by attempts, typical of the modern era, to comprehensively plan the totality of the downtown environment. After all, the spirit of modernism, as explained by Habermas (1985), was to participate in the totality of social and physical manifestations. The drafting of master plans or comprehensive plans was the result of a logical process that assured guidelines for the creation of an efficient urban form, purely determined by function. Modernism cut off the relationship between history and the city. Urban renewal tools were used to create a clear slate, a historically autonomous form liberated from past memories and experiences. The power of zoning was used to carve out segregated functional cells for housing, commerce, recreation, and cultural activities in an attempt to create efficient downtowns, where people would come for business and commerce (Boyer 1983). According to the modernist vision, land use and transportation were integrated, and pedestrian and vehicular circulation were meant to tie all activities and places together in a comprehensive and efficient manner. The suburban shopping center—modern, efficient, accessible, with everything in its place under a unifying theme—became the much admired prototype for downtown development. It was reasoned that "the shopping center mall has for many years proved to be safe, pleasant, and economically sound. This principle, if properly applied in the downtown area, can pay many dividends in attractiveness, safety, and efficiency" (Welton Becket quoted in Hebert 1959c).[7]

FIGURE 31
Houston, Texas, 1960s:
Newly constructed
freeway connecting the
downtown. Courtesy of
Redstone Tiseo Architects
(Redstone 1976, 140).

The totality of the modernist scheme for downtown was best exemplified in
Victor Gruen's 1956 scheme for downtown Fort Worth (see figure 32). In this
plan, downtown was essentially treated as a megablock shopping center, cut off
from the rest of the city by a series of freeway loops and ring roads that were
described by Gruen (1964) as "defense lines" and "fortification systems." The
"heart of the city" was surrounded by a ring of six parking garages at its periphery and was served by a highway loop. Motorists were expected to leave
their cars and walk to the center in various people-mover systems. There, the
environment was patterned after the suburban shopping mall, with courts, plazas, arcades, and skywalks.

As in every good shopping center design, circulation was an essential element of the plan. Three specific measures were recommended to increase

people's access to downtown services (Gruen 1964, 217): (1) enhancement of public transportation, (2) a system of underground roads for service traffic, and (3) an accessory pedestrian-transportation system of moving sidewalks and slow, electrically driven vehicles.

Even though Gruen's plan for Fort Worth was never implemented, his ideas sparked a series of plans around the country that envisioned multimodal transportation systems bringing people to a unified downtown. Just a couple of years later, in 1959, architect Adrian Wilson described the Los Angeles Central City Committee's vision for downtown Los Angeles:

> The whole downtown area lying within the four freeways[8] should become in effect, an isolated superblock. But it would not be isolated, to the extent that all the surface streets serving it would be blocked off or used as malls. This "loop" would be adequately served by a rapid transit system which would have its hubs in the downtown core. "Spokes" would feed the outlying communities and there would be transit

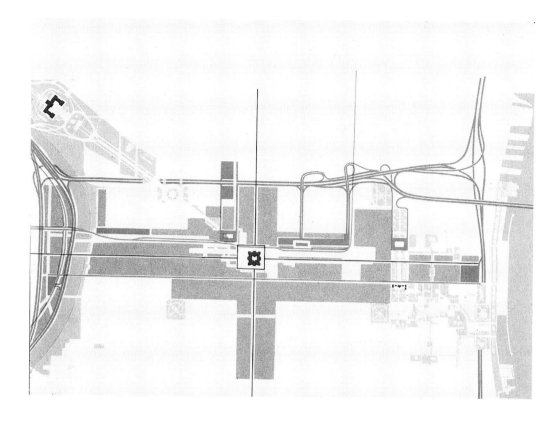

"spiderwebs" connecting the spokes. The "loop" would contain certain vital elements—transportation and convention centers, a civic auditorium, a complete cultural center, an international exhibit center, financial, shopping, and commercial centers, and an administrative or civic center. (quoted in Hebert 1959b)

FIGURE 32
Opposite: Forth Worth, Texas, 1956: View of downtown. Courtesy of Gruen Associates.

FIGURE 33
Revitalization plan for Philadelphia, Pennsylvania, 1973. Penguin USA (Bacon 1974, 271).

From the 1950s to the 1970s many downtown plans shared an interest in recapturing the importance and centrality of downtown by increasing the density of the core. In almost all these efforts, planners and designers were particularly concerned with the circulation of people and vehicles. As a way to improve downtown's accessibility, master plans of the 1960s promoted the construction of inner-loop freeways encircling the CBD and terminal parking facilities at the periphery of the core (Urban Advisors to the Federal Highway Administration 1968). The 1963 center city plan of Philadelphia is a good case in point (see figure 33). Philadelphia City Planning Commission Director Ed

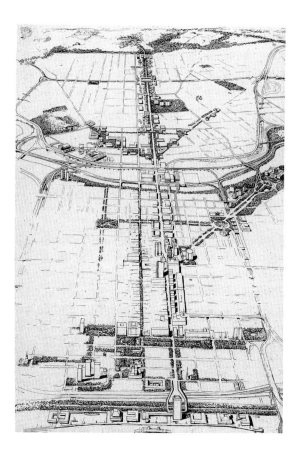

FIGURE 34
Aerial view of Market
Street design,
Philadelphia, 1973.
Penguin USA (Bacon
1974, 300).

Bacon drew inspiration from William Penn's original design for the city and utilized the historic landmarks of City Hall and Independence Hall as focal points for downtown reconstruction (see figure 34). Downtown was surrounded by an expressway loop, but at the core, primary emphasis was given to the accommodation of pedestrian traffic. Three levels of pedestrian walkways—below ground, at grade, and elevated—linked the city's five historic squares. In his well-known book *Design of Cities*, Bacon (1974) stressed the important role of "simultaneous movement systems" as generators of architectural form in the modern city.

The same interest in the orderly circulation and efficient organization of downtown was shared by a number of prominent plans of the period. Thus,

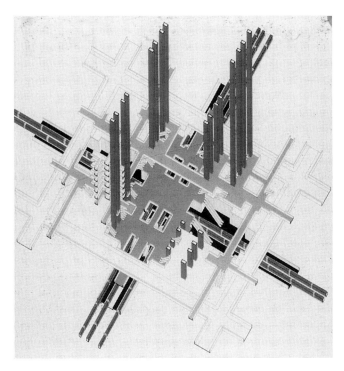

FIGURE 35
The access tree diagram
for midtown Manhattan.
Regional Plan Association,
Inc. (Regional Plan
Association 1969, 30).

The Second Regional Plan for New York issued in 1968, introduced the concept of the "access tree" as the guiding urban design principle for the reordering of Manhattan (see figure 35). The roots of the tree were the horizontal, underground subway lines; and the trunk was established by the vertical circulation of escalators and elevators which led to the branches, the public streets and private office corridors. In the words of the planners,

> The Access Tree is a principle for dealing with several functional problems of the CBD. In general it is a way to plan for efficient circulation, enhanced job choice and the great social interaction which is a requirement of an office center. Also, it shows the importance of taking the underground into account; it demonstrates the relationships among various modes of transportation within the center, proposing grade separations which favor pedestrian paths; . . . it demonstrates the linkages between the essentially horizontal public transportation systems and the vertical circulation in private buildings. (Regional Plan Association 1969, 31)

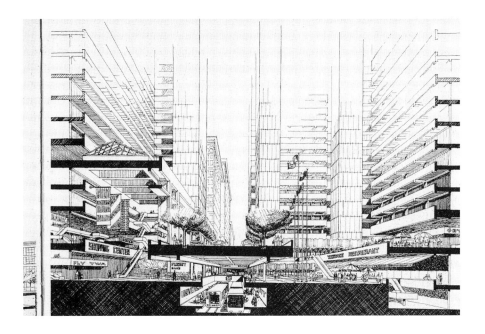

Inspired by Le Corbusier's ideal city, where movement modes were separated on the basis of relative speed, the access tree concept represented an effort to plan for the totality of downtown through an under- and above-ground circulation scheme (see figure 36). New nodes of clustered office-tower development were seen as hierarchically organizing urban form through an "alternating drama of high and low groups of buildings, of light and shadowed places, of closed and open space" (Huxtable 1968, 22).

The concept of downtown as a shopping center—a collection of functional parts in a unified whole, accessed by different means of transportation from the outside but only by foot on the inside—was also celebrated in the 1970 urban design plan for the Detroit CBD:

> The concept design provides a spatial distribution for all modes of access. Terminating the radial thoroughfares, modal transition points shift the speed and level and direction of travel entering the CBD. . . . Once within the CBD the sequence becomes a pedestrian affair. The design proposes a core of pedestrian spatial links connecting the modal transition points with the major activity centers in the CBD: the Con-

FIGURE 36
Opposite: Urban design
proposal for Manhattan,
1960. Regional Plan
Association, Inc. (Regional
Plan Association 1969, 49).

FIGURE 37
Downtown Detroit, 1995:
People mover system.
Photograph by Tridib
Banerjee.

vention District including hotels, entertainment, and Cobo Hall; the commercial
centers and specialty stores along Woodward Avenue; seats of city and county government fronting on Civic Center Plaza and the river; offices and finance comprising the highest form and population density in the heart of CBD; and two residential outcroppings tied to the pulse of the CBD but independent enough to assure
their own integrity. (Detroit City Plan Commission 1970, 6)

The essential public spaces for such a downtown were described as multilevel *terminals*, which would combine the various modes of arrival and departure into a building complex (see figure 37). These terminals were placed at
nodal points of the circulation network and had at their top a public square
surrounded by shops and restaurants.

Almost all modernist downtown plans incorporated public space in the form
of landscaped office plazas—at street level, below, or above—skywalks, and
pedestrian ways. But as in Le Corbusier's famous schemes for a utopian "city
of tomorrow," public open space was never a place for social activities; it served
merely to embellish the buildings, to accentuate their importance in the city

FIGURE 38
New York City, 1960s.
Courtesy of Redstone
Tiseo Architects
(Redstone 1976, 116).

fabric. Modernist downtown designs consisted of object-type buildings that are isolated from one another or form a series in a neutral space (Colquhoun 1985). Brochures, sketches, and renderings of different projects showed the modernists' predilection for the tower in the park—high-rises surrounded by limitless and abstract open space.

The tower was usually a megastructure. Occupying one or several blocks, a single building shell combined multiple uses: shopping, office, hotel, residential, and parking facilities, as well as walkways and plazas (see figures 38 and 39). The architecture was sleek and elegant, with modern materials (glass, aluminum, prefabricated concrete). Building facades lacked ornamentation, in accord with the doctrines of modernist design. The megastructure was often tied in with neighboring buildings through skywalks or underground concourses. Evident in these plans was an attempt to create a coherent, functional whole. But the desired coherence was in most cases artificial, since the architecture

FIGURE 39
Cleveland, Ohio, 1960s:
Park Centre. Courtesy of
Redstone Tiseo Architects
(Redstone 1976, 121).

of corporate buildings asserted their individuality and separateness from the whole. Being below or above grade, the link to the city did not usually allow any meaningful connection to the public environment. Megastructures invaded American downtowns in the 1950s and 1960s. Prudential Center in Boston, Renaissance Center in Detroit, Embarcadero Center in San Francisco, Charles Center in Baltimore, and Gateway Center in Pittsburgh all cut off existing streets to create superblocks of buildings and open spaces that were dramatically different in scale and architecture from downtown spaces of earlier eras. They were designed to exclude the social liabilities of modern downtown—the poor, the denizens of skid row, the homeless.

The architecture of such megastructures hoped to achieve the construction of a self-sufficient miniworld. Fortress-like facades were visually uninviting. Contact with the city outside was minimal. Transportation connections (parking, subway) were within the shell of the building. Retail activity was often

FIGURE 40
Fulton Mall, pedestrian
mall in Fresno, California,
1960s. Courtesy of Gruen
Associates ("Fresno and
the Mall," brochure
prepared by Victor Gruen
and Associates, 6).

enclosed inside the megastructure, placed around interior courts and walkways. This was in sharp contrast to the street-oriented retailing that characterized earlier downtowns (Beauregard 1986).

Another design solution to accommodate retailing in downtown was again influenced by suburban shopping center design. The creation of pedestrian (figure 40) and transit malls (figure 41) at the core of downtown required the closing of selected streets to traffic (in the case of transit malls, public transit was allowed to penetrate the mall) and landscaping them in suburban style with trees, benches, fountains, and other pedestrian amenities. During the 1960s and 1970s about two hundred American cities converted major downtown streets into pedestrian and transit malls in an effort to revitalize their downtowns (Robertson 1995). However, with the exception of a handful of transit malls (in Denver, Portland, Philadelphia, Minneapolis) most developments failed to spur retail activity; and their furnishings were later removed, and their right-of-way was given back to traffic.

The modernist model envisioned an urban environment broken down into different functional parts. The implicit assumption, however, was that all parts

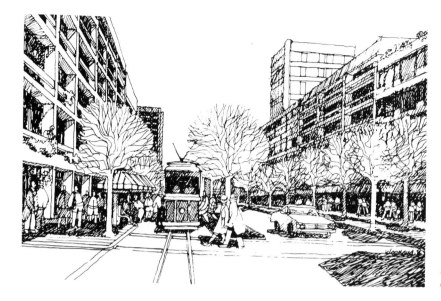

FIGURE 41
Revitalization of
downtown district,
transit mall in Seattle,
1974. Courtesy of Lee
Copeland, City of Seattle
(Barnett 1986, 156).

together constituted a coherent whole. During the post–World War II period, as American cities tried to confront the decline that had crept into their downtowns, a number of plans were drafted across the nation: Ed Bacon's scheme for Philadelphia, Charles Blessing's plan for Detroit, the Regional Plan Association's urban design plan for Manhattan, were all large-scale visions that aspired to plan for the totality of the downtown environment. As will become evident in the chapters to follow, this tendency would distinguish these plans from later "postmodern" developments, which tended to produce disjointed and discrete projects within the downtown (Colquhoun 1985; Boyer 1994). Similar to the other models examined in this chapter, the modernist model also required a prominent role for the public sector, which was perceived as the initiator of large-scale plans and as the regulator of private developments.

AFTER THE MODERNISTS: DESIGN BY PUBLIC POLICY

In the sixties, the modernist approach was challenged by social scientists and critics who were dismayed by the impact of downtown urban renewal projects on such established neighborhoods as Boston's West End or Los Angeles' Bunker Hill. In the name of removing physical blight, older urban districts were leveled without any concern for the social life and the sense of locality that existed in many of these communities. The critics questioned "physical determinism," the basic tenet of the modernist approach—the belief that designers know what is good for people and that environments designed according to these beliefs can actually improve people's sense of well-being. Critics considered such views anachronistic and megalomaniac (Banerjee and Southworth 1990). Some argued that designers deal only with nominal clients and are isolated from substantive clients, that is, the actual users of the environment.[9] The proponents of this argument believed therefore, that designers should know about the actual users of the environment—their needs, aspirations, desires, and the like. This view was consistent with the prevailing notions of advocacy, pluralism, and participatory planning and design.

It was at about this time, when the modernist designers were recoiling from this attack of social critics, that Kevin Lynch published his seminal work, *The Image of the City* (1960). Lynch did not believe in the deterministic, top-down approach to planning and design. He felt it was important for designers to know how people use and conceptualize an entity as complicated as the modern city before they propose any design schemes of their own. He indirectly rejected the modernist or even premodernist baroque design principles, which he saw as authoritarian and elitist.

In his explorations into the images of the American cities, Lynch focused on three downtown districts, those of Boston, Jersey City, and Los Angeles. He argued that the visual form of the American city is not always coherent or particularly legible. He proposed that city images—which can be defined in terms of such universal categories as districts, edges, landmarks, nodes, and paths—must be preserved, protected, enhanced, and more important, made legible. Lynch's methodology of interviewing people and asking them to draw maps opened up a new avenue for empirically grounding urban designers and making urban design a participatory process. This was Lynch's primary intent, as he himself admitted many years later (Lynch 1985).

Lynch's work generated considerable interest in downtown visual form. In the early 1960s, intraurban highway links were being completed, despite considerable opposition from the inner-city neighborhood groups. The new freeway loops around downtown opened up some dramatic vistas of the CBD. The visual form of American downtown as a totality and its components were never appreciated at this scale of movement before. In studies published in 1964 and 1969, Lynch and his colleagues examined not only the view from the road (Lynch, Appleyard, and Myer 1964) but also the imageability of such views from the public's perspective (Carr and Schissler 1969).

Soon, Lynch's methodology became a staple in the development of subsequent downtown urban design plans (see Southworth and Southworth 1973; Southworth 1989). Lynch himself was involved in developing the plan for the Government Center and the waterfront of downtown Boston, an area that included some of the cherished historic landmarks of the city. Based on Lynch's earlier analysis, the plans attempted to strengthen the visual and functional structure of the district; views of important landmarks were protected and, in some cases, opened up. Access to the waterfront was improved, visual linkages to various parts of the city were established, and a system of open spaces and pedestrian paths linking Beacon Hill to the waterfront was proposed (see Banerjee and Southworth 1990). Many other downtown urban design efforts in the sixties and seventies began with a Lynchian analysis, but as Lynch (1985) himself and Michael Southworth (1989) pointed out, not all of these efforts necessarily led to any coherent design schemes. In cities like San Francisco and Seattle, where visual form and scenic views matter most, the Lynchian approach was used to develop design guidelines and even legislation to protect and improve the appearance and design of the city.

Lynch's work led to a major shift in the design attitude, and this was reflected in the belief that by defining some larger public purpose and aims in the built environment, and by regulating private development within these guidelines, a good city form could be obtained. These ideas were vigorously pursued in New York City during Mayor John Lindsey's administration, and led to what were considered major urban design innovations. These included incentive zoning legislation,[10] special design districts, programs for saving landmark buildings and rebuilding theater districts, and shopping streets (see foreword by John Lindsey in Barnett 1974). Jonathan Barnett (1974) later referred to these innovations as urban design by public policy. The plan for lower Manhattan was a case in point. Faced with the task of creating design standards for new development on landfill areas along the waterfront, the design team began with the idea of preserving existing vistas of the waterfront along principal streets. The special zoning district created for lower Manhattan landfill development was ultimately based on three essential criteria: design continuity, visual corridors, and visual permeability. The design controls defined the "planes" that controlled the future building envelope.

This approach to downtown urban design—which was in accord with the idea that guidelines and regulations could produce a good city form, that one could "[design] cities without designing buildings," according to Barnett (1974, 29)—was also a tacit acknowledgment that the idea of urban design through capital improvements was defunct. This was still another rejection of the modernist approach.

The idea of incentive zoning—another contribution of New York urban design—became popular in many other cities, including Los Angeles and San Francisco. Indeed this was the beginning of a private-public deal making epoch, although incentive zoning would be ultimately abandoned in most cities. Urban design as public policy would be replaced by the present era of urban design by negotiation and privatization.

In the following chapters we will document how this vision of publicly initiated and guided design faded in favor of the increased role for and significance of the private sector in downtown restructuring.

3

CORPORATE PRODUCTION OF DOWNTOWN SPACE

The transition to a postindustrial economy has affected the circumstances of place making in these waning years of the twentieth century. Nowhere have the effects become more evident than in the urban form and imagery of American downtowns and the transformations in their public realm. In this chapter we seek to unravel the political and economic changes responsible for what has been coined the "urban renaissance" of American downtowns—the intensive investment of private capital and public resources from the seventies through the nineties to renew the image and function of downtown areas. We will discuss the municipal policies, the planning strategies and tools, and the negotiations and deal-making that now typically precede any project development in downtown today.

PRIVATISM AND THE PRIVATIZATION OF PUBLIC SERVICES

As we have seen in previous chapters, in the post–World War II years the downtown rebuilding process was an effort that involved public works and was initiated largely by the public sector. In the 1980s, however, downtown rebuilding became increasingly dependent on private investments. New political ideologies, fiscal constraints on municipal governments, and the dynamics of an increasingly corporatist economy dictated the public sector's dependence on private developers and corporations.

Privatism became the dominant cultural tradition affecting urban policy in the United States in the 1980s. The rise of the Reagan administration in 1981 brought together a new political ideology—New Conservatism—and subsequent attacks against "big government." The basic beliefs and assumptions of this ideology were the following:

- Freedom and individual liberty are endangered by a powerful government (McCraw 1984).

- The public sector is wasteful and inefficient because it lacks the profit incentive, whereas the private sector is inherently efficient, its efficiency being fostered by competition in the marketplace.

- Economic efficiency is a goal superior to social justice and equity (Savas 1982).

- Local initiative and voluntarism can substitute for extensive federal spending, social programs, and public-service provision.

The success of the tax-cut movements in the late 1970s (for example, Proposition 13 in California and Proposition 2½ in Massachusetts) contributed to a reappraisal of the ways in which public services are provided. The changes in the economic and political environment resulted in an increased tax awareness among American citizens in the late 1970s. In state after state, proposals advocating sharp decreases in state taxes and local expenditures emerged victorious from ballots. A fifty-state survey conducted by the *New York Times* and released in August 1979 found that thirty-seven states had cut taxes or imposed spending limits in 1979 (in Poole 1980). Having risen steadily for decades, state and local government taxes declined dramatically.

It is estimated that in California alone the passage of Proposition 13 (which served as a model to many citizen groups advocating lower taxes in other states) caused the state to lose $51 billion in revenues between 1978 and 1979 and between 1983 and 1984. The proposition stripped local governments in California of revenues amounting to 22 percent of their total budgeted expenditures (Schwadron and Richter 1984, 24). These huge losses were coupled with a sharp decline in federal aid for state and local budgets.

Starting in the 1970s the federal government drastically reduced its financial support and withdrew from its oversight role (Fainstein 1994). In 1974 Congress terminated the Urban Renewal and Model Cities Program, replacing it with the Community Development Block Grant, which switched the emphasis from large-scale redevelopment efforts to individual projects. In 1977 new legislation initiated the Urban Development Action Grant (UDAG) program

(UDAG), which made federal support for a project contingent upon the participation of private funds, with local governments acting as intermediaries. UDAG was specifically designed to help cities subsidize programs that could attract new private sector employment. The 1980s were defined by the Reagan administration's policies, which were characterized by massive cutbacks of urban programs. One of the administration's actions was the establishment of the President's Task Force on Private Initiatives, a task force that sought to overcome the shortcomings of government by promoting urban projects that were mostly private investments. The task force espoused the "shift from urban renewal bulldozer and antipoverty campaigns of the 1960s to limited, tightly negotiated urban development agreements between the public and private sectors in the early 1980s" (President's Task Force 1983, 5).

While the ideology of the Reagan administration shaped the directions of U.S. public policy in the 1980s, many actions of the administration were designed to favor private over public welfare. Implied in these actions were definitions of well-being and quality of life strongly related to market consumption (Wingo and Wolch 1982). Public services were curtailed and often sacrificed in favor of amenities and programs that helped protect and increase market efficiency. Publicly subsidized goods and services were seen as encouraging "rampant waste" and "thoughtless consumption," and as transferring an unfair burden to taxpayers.

Privatism was of course not a new phenomenon in American cities. According to Sam Bass Warner Jr. (1987, 202), "privatism is the quality which above all else characterizes America's urban inheritance." From very early on in the American urban history private business and institutions played an important role in municipal affairs, and private decisions have largely determined the pattern of urban development (Barnekov, Boyle, and Rich 1989). Throughout the nineteenth century and during the first decades of the twentieth century, private involvement in the delivery of local services was a distinctive feature of the American city. From the Chicago Chamber of Commerce, to the Allegheny Conference in Pittsburgh, to the Central City Association in Los Angeles, the influence of businessmen in civic affairs and downtown planning was decisive.

But starting from the Great Depression, government involvement in urban policy increased enormously. Federal urban programs, from the New Deal legislation of the 1930s to the Great Society legislation of the 1960s, made the federal government a new and active participant in urban affairs. As outlined in the previous chapter the role of the public sector in the reshaping of the downtown during the urban renewal era has been critical.

In the 1980s, however, privatism brought a new era in urban affairs, service delivery, and downtown planning. The ideology of privatism clashed sharply with the liberal values and ideals that introduced and institutionalized the welfare state. The ideology was a manifestation of different attitudes in public policy that reinterpreted and redefined the role of the state, individual liberty, efficiency and equity, growth and redistribution, the mix of public and private services, and the balance between public and private welfare.

Privatization—an umbrella term that covered a number of government initiatives designed to increase the private sector's role (Ascher 1987)—became the magic word of the 1980s. Privatization signified the introduction and extension of market principles into public service production and provision. Privatization also meant the withdrawal or disengagement of the public sector from specific responsibilities under the assumption that the private sector would take care of them. In certain cases privatization also meant selling public assets or contracting out public services (Barnekov, Boyle, and Rich 1989). According to Emanuel Savas (1982) privatization means many different things: voluntary or marketplace provision of goods supplied by the government, or what he calls "load shedding"; minimizing government involvement in service delivery by transferring the work to private vendors; encouraging competition; selling off publicly owned facilities to private bidders, and the like.[1]

THE RESPONSE OF MUNICIPAL GOVERNMENTS: PLANNING TOOLS

Local governments were forced to invent new strategies to cope with the new economic and political reality. These strategies involved one or more of several options: imposing user fees, contracting out the provision and sometimes the production of municipal services, becoming equity partners in private developments, and becoming increasingly entrepreneurial in an attempt to attract private funds and development. The common denominator of these strategies was the tendency to extend market principles into areas that were in the past considered to be outside the domain of the market.

The frantic search for non-tax revenue sources often led to the imposition of user charges for services once characterized as public goods. In California, local revenues derived from such charges grew by 40 percent between 1978 and 1980, the first two years after the passage of Proposition 13. By June 1979, exactly one year after the adoption of this proposition, cities and counties in the state had raised $125 million in new or increased user fees, about 19 percent of what they had lost in property-tax revenues (Poole 1980). Advocates of user fees emphasized the strong points of the market system: efficiency, reduction of "free-riders," responsiveness to demand (Fisk, Kiesling, and Muller 1978; Poole 1980; Savas 1982). Opponents pointed to the inability of market principles to address questions of need, the regressivity of user charges, the inequity against the poor, and the danger of disappearance of services not susceptible to pricing (Hanrahan 1977; Le Grand and Robinson 1984; Brooks 1984; Ascher 1987; Banerjee 1993a).

The effects of the tax-limitation movement, on the one hand, and the ideological motivation provided by the federal government, on the other, resulted in increased interest in contracting out public services in cities, counties, school districts, and special districts. Local governments came to view privatization as the panacea for their ailing economies and budget deficits. A 1981 survey by the California Tax Foundation identified eighty-seven distinct services being contracted out by cities and ninety-two by counties (Schwadron and Richter 1984). In many cities a whole range of services (parks and recreation, police, trash collection, transportation, public works, and so on) were handed over to the private sector, which carried the burden of provision and made profits from this new venture.

Tax-cut movements in combination with the curtailment of federal aid for cities in the 1980s increased the financial debts of local governments and intensified competition among cities for private investment. With the declining manufacturing base and the simultaneous expansion of the service sector, local governments actively sought to attract the new generation of industrial and commercial development to their jurisdictions by offering competitive packages of land and financing. Increasingly, municipalities became more actively involved in real estate and development (Fulton 1987; Frieden and Sagalyn 1989). "Mayors are now entrepreneurs. . . . They have become master orchestrators of public and private projects," asserted David Walker (in Barnekov, Boyle, and Rich 1989, 74).[2] Thus, local governments became increasingly corporatist in structure as they got involved in real estate deals, became an equity partner in private developments, and pursued joint-development projects with profit as the major motive (Savitch 1988; Frieden and Sagalyn 1989).

Mayors and city councils had often acted as civic boosters for their cities by promoting public works and real estate projects. But as Bernard Frieden and Lynne Sagalyn (1989, 285) explained, there was now a difference:

> Before World War II city development projects were limited to such clearly municipal functions as building streets, parks, schools, libraries, police stations, and firehouses. These were the public works that served a resident population, and city officials scattered them through the neighborhoods where people lived. The more recent agenda crosses the old barrier between public and private development by using public power and money to promote office buildings, hotels, convention centers, shopping malls, stadiums, and more. Now the projects are located away from places where most people live, concentrated instead in a downtown of corporate offices, business visitors, suburban commuters, and tourists.

The corporate center strategy   The new financial and political realities of the 1980s had profound effects on downtown planning. For many mayors and city councils, the cornerstone of development activity and economic growth had to be the downtown. The welfare of a city was commonly equated with the success and prosperity of its CBD. Cities, therefore, attempted to convert the core into a modern, efficient corporate center within a national and global network. According to Richard Hill (1983), the investment priorities of this "corporate center strategy" were "to transform the aging industrial city into the modern corporate image: a financial, administrative, and professional services center . . . [with] an emphasis upon recommercialization rather than reindustrialization, and an orientation toward luxury consumption that is appealing to young corporate managers, educated professionals, convention goers and the tourist trade" (105). The key elements of this approach included:

- The belief that what is good for business is good for the city.
- The dominance of private sector decisions in determining economic development outcomes (Brooks and Young 1993).

- The role of the public sector as a facilitator of private development and a promoter of growth and expansion, rather than as a regulator of development (Fainstein 1991).

- The effort to compete with other cities in attracting business and services and thus broadening the municipal tax base.

- The reshaping of the built environment and public realm of the downtown so as to better support corporate activities.

Downtown represented prime real estate for the location of national and international headquarters and support services such as accounting, advertising, investment banking, consulting, and legal firms. Retail specialty shopping and entertainment facilities had to be provided for the white-collar office worker. Hotels and convention centers could attract more businessmen and tourists. Luxury condos and refurbished brownstones could appeal to professionals who would choose to live near their work.

The corporate center strategy resulted in an unprecedented downtown building boom financed mainly by the international capital of the new global economy. Downtown office construction dwarfed the earlier booms of the 1920s and of the urban renewal era (Abbott 1993). In the thirty largest metropolitan areas, office construction in the first half of the 1980s grew at twice the rate of that in the 1970s, which in turn had outpaced that of the 1960s by 50 percent (Frieden and Sagalyn 1989, 265).

Frost Belt and Sun Belt cities alike pursued the corporate center approach as the best strategy for their interests. Politicians and planners in New York, Los Angeles, Chicago, Boston, Baltimore, Cleveland, Detroit, New Orleans, and Pittsburgh competed with varying degrees of success to attract office towers to their CBDs.

In Baltimore, Mayor William Donald Schaefer made downtown redevelopment the central component of his administration's strategy to restructure the city. Projects of the 1950s like the Charles Center and Inner Harbor were followed by the construction of a festival marketplace—the Rouse Company's Harborplace (see figure 42)—and the building of tourist facilities, urban entertainment parks, museums, restaurants, and upscale shops. According to Marc

Levine (1987, 109), "As Baltimore's industrial base continued to erode, downtown was envisioned as the heart of a 'new' Baltimore economy: a regional administrative and corporate services center, with entertainment and commercial facilities to attract tourists, conventioneers, and retail shoppers, and with quality housing to lure Metro Center professionals from suburbia."

In the 1980s downtown New Orleans experienced its greatest building boom since the city's commercial heyday in the 1850s. Office space more than doubled, from 7.7 million square feet in 1975 to over 16 million square feet in 1985. The tourist and convention trade and the construction of hotels kept pace with that growth (Brooks and Young 1993). An incentive-zoning program encouraged developers to provide open space amenities (plazas, gallerias, miniparks, arcades) in return for increased FARs. A study of UDAG projects in New Orleans found that the ratio of neighborhood to non-neighborhood projects was one to four, and 88 percent of the non-neighborhood projects occurred in the CBD (Janet Spraul in Brooks and Young 1993, 268).

In Pittsburgh, an ambitious CBD expansion program that came to be known as Renaissance II[3] brought a large expansion of offices, the development of a convention center, and the promotion of retail specialty shopping and entertainment in the downtown area (Law 1988).

In order to further boost New York City's global reputation, Mayor Edward Koch's administration wholeheartedly supported and stimulated private development in Manhattan and sought to expand growth in an already vigorous CBD.[4] In inflation-adjusted 1983 dollars, the value of Manhattan taxable real estate increased by $925.5 million from 1978 to 1986, while in the rest of the New York City it declined by more than $10 billion (Fainstein, Fainstein, and Schwarz 1988, 69). From 1985 to 1989 New York completed 39 million square feet of office space in Manhattan alone (Sudjic 1992, 240). As in other American downtowns, the building boom in New York included luxurious high-rise residential buildings, hotels, and festival marketplaces (such as Rouse's South Street Seaport) in addition to signature office towers (such as Minoru Yamasaki's World Trade Center). According to H. V. Savitch (1988, 47–48, 59),

> The cutting edge of the transformation is the construction of a whole new generation of skyscrapers. . . . The CBD boom, gentrification, and the replacement of working class households have worsened existing imbalances. The CBD is saturated with investment, the remainder of the urban core is overcrowded due to excessive demands placed upon it, and much of the first ring falls into deeper poverty and deterioration.
>
> . . . This is an impulsion towards corporatism, which stems from the city's perceived need to attract investment, increase the value of land, augment tax revenues, provide jobs, and advance toward a post-industrial order.

From the 1930s to 1950 only one office tower was built in the Boston downtown area. But between 1965 and 1987 sixty flashy office buildings gave this city a distinguishable skyline (Frieden and Sagalyn 1989). Its extremely successful Faneuil Hall Market, developed by the Rouse Company, established the standard for festival marketplaces (see figure 43).

Negotiation   The restructuring of the physical form of the American downtown in the 1980s involved a new type of relation between the public and the private sectors, between municipal governments and private developers. With the blessings of the federal government, cities started forming joint ventures

FIGURE 43
Boston, 1990: Faneuil Hall
Market. Photograph by
Anastasia Loukaitou-
Sideris.

and partnerships with real estate developers. Whereas in the past downtown planning was directed by the planners' wish for comprehensiveness—reflected in the master plans that cities adopted over the years—the impetus now was competitiveness, market rationality, and maximum returns on downtown real estate. As Susan Fainstein (1991, 25) has argued, "The new definition of planning as the process by which the government enables the private sector to invest profitably in urban space undermines an earlier, conservative perspective wherein government was viewed as antagonistic to business."

Both sides were well aware that they would gain from engaging in partnership with each other. Corporate interests realized that the restructuring of the downtown—necessary to compete in a postindustrial economy—would also create opportunities for enormous profit in land development. The relaxation of regulations, the provision of the necessary infrastructure, the permission to build over and beyond what was allowed by right, were some of the actions that the public sector could take to increase the profitability of a project. These entitlement powers gave planners some new leverage over the private sector (Fainstein 1994). Now they could ask for the provision of urban amenities, such as street improvements, open space, housing, and public facilities, in return for additional development rights.

Every partnership involves some trading and negotiation among partners to set the terms of the agreement. The new role of the public sector as a partner of private developers initiated bargaining and negotiation in downtown planning. Public officials traded their approval of variances or capital spending. Developers traded contributions to urban amenities.

Unlike earlier periods in which planners in their regulatory roles devised universal formulas for development in downtown, now each project is unique, tailored to the time, place, and specificities of development. The structuring and packaging of "deals" are complicated processes that are built around confidentiality and often take place behind closed doors to maximize flexibility and minimize disclosure of competitive bids (Barnekov, Boyle, and Rich 1989). The disposition and development agreement (commonly referred to as the DDA), the legal document that crystallizes the agreements between the two parties, is often hundreds of pages long and can contain dozens of amendments.

This new, "entrepreneurial" planning required a new type of agency to carry it through. For most U.S. cities urban redevelopment agencies (often called community redevelopment agencies) proved to be the mechanism for overseeing and promoting downtown building and restructuring.[5] As described by Timothy Barnekov, Robin Boyle, and Daniel Rich (1989, 76),

> These were set up by local government, received and administered public funds, and offered public incentives such as land banking and tax abatement schemes. . . . They were governed by executive boards. Their advantage was that their legal status as quasi-public, non-profit provided them with powers which were difficult or impossible for public agencies to exercise. . . . In effect the city through the development corporation could act as an investor and risk taker in partnership with private business.

It is estimated that over fifteen thousand economic development corporations were already in operation by 1980 (Barnekov, Boyle, and Rich 1989). Big downtown projects all over the country, like the South Street Seaport in New York, California Plaza in Los Angeles, Harborplace in Baltimore, and Moscone Center in San Francisco, are the products of the often not so public dealings of public development corporations with the private sector.

Carrots and sticks   As the competition among American downtowns intensified, planners and city officials had to develop a whole set of tools that acted as financial carrots for developers: land-assembly programs, land write-off or write-down, tax abatements, tax-increment financing,[6] facility lease-back arrangements, and zoning incentives. Robyne Turner (1992) distinguishes between two types of strategies that are followed by the public sector to facilitate private development: "supply side" strategies offer economic development incentives to reduce business costs, and "demand side" strategies use public resources to invest in local economic development and in the creation of attractive sites for developers.

In 1987 researchers from the Urban Land Institute (ULI) asked planners in more than sixty-five cities to describe their newest land use controls (implemented through zoning regulation) in downtown. They found that downtowns of first- and second-tier cities have developed a formidable inventory of planning carrots to induce development (Lassar 1989). In the 1980s many cities initiated a comprehensive rewrite of their downtown zoning ordinances. Since then zoning variances have been rewarded to eager developers in return for plazas, public atria, galleries, and the like, as well as for retail frontages, subway entrances, and transportation improvements. These special provisions have allowed office buildings to tower well above the existing height limits. Trump Tower in New York, for example, was given so many bonuses that eventually it reached a 21.6 FAR, almost twice as high as what was originally perceived to be the maximum for the area. Planners in Los Angeles suggested to the developers of First Interstate World Center—the tallest structure in the city—that they build an eighty-five-story tower instead of the fifty-story structure originally anticipated for the site.

New York was the first city to initiate incentive zoning in order to encourage developers to provide urban plazas within their project site. Each square foot of plaza area was credited with ten square feet of office space. Between 1961 and 1973 every developer who put up an office building in New York took advantage of the plaza bonus. It has been calculated (Kayden 1978) that for every dollar spent by developers for the creation of plazas they made a return of forty-three dollars on the extra office space they were able to build. When plazas "flooded" the Manhattan landscape, New York planners started giving bonuses for indoor atria, subway entrances, and arcades. In a sample of fifteen projects in New York that used incentive zoning, the value of the public amenities totaled $5 million, while the market value of the bonus floor area was estimated by the comptroller as $108 million (in Frieden 1990, 426).

The early New York precedent of incentive zoning was copied widely by other cities throughout the country in the late 1970s and 1980s. In New Orleans, for example, a rigorous incentive zoning program made allowances for certain downtown buildings to have FARs of up to eighteen to one, in exchange for miniparks, arcades, and plazas. In addition, as we will later discuss, Los Angeles and San Francisco have experimented with incentive zoning.

In general, incentive zoning was enthusiastically received by the development community all over the country. Most developers responded to this opportunity to obtain increased FARs for valuable commercial space by providing some public amenities. As we will show in the presentation of our case studies, developers also grasped the fact that the enrichment of their projects with public space could be profitable if the space was closely connected to commercial facilities and private services.

Municipal governments have also used other carrots to stimulate private development downtown. They have often set up assessment and tax districts, where a portion of property taxes levied on structures within the district is returned to it for various improvements. To help developers who want to increase their building's floor space, planners have often allowed them to purchase "air rights" or transfer them from one building to another. Sometimes planners have even ignored negative environmental impacts, justifying such actions in terms of the greater good served by developer contributions to public amenities (Fainstein, Fainstein, and Schwartz 1988).

Thus, in the 1980s cities used their zoning ordinances not as fixed documents but rather as the starting point for negotiation with the private sector. Wanting to boost their downtown image as a corporate center and ensure amenity contributions from developers, municipal governments made a lot of concessions to them. Only a handful of cities (Boston, San Francisco) have decided to use sticks to prevent excessive commercial development in downtown. These have taken the form of impact fees, where developers are required to pay a negotiated or set sum to the city's budget; exactions, where builders of commercial projects have to supply some public facility or amenity as a condition for building downtown; and linkage fees, where developers have to build or finance low-income housing, day-care centers, or even social services like job training (Alterman 1988; Keating 1986; Dreier and Ehrlich 1991).

Many researchers have analyzed the public-private partnerships of various cities (Hartman 1984; Levine 1987; Savitch 1988; Frieden and Sagalyn 1989; Sudjic 1992; Fainstein 1994). Overwhelmingly, they have found that business interests have dominated downtown development priorities. In an economic and political climate of market liberalism, it is real estate developers and their corporate clients who shape the form and function of the central city. Nowhere is this more evident than in the emerging urban design of the new downtown.

PRIVATIZATION OF DOWNTOWN: THE LOS ANGELES EXPERIENCE

Downtown rebuilding efforts have changed not only the cities' skylines but also their public realms. A distinctive feature of the new downtown is the variety of open spaces created through private enterprise: plazas, paseos, gallerias, roof gardens, and arcades. The proliferation of these open spaces in American downtowns is a phenomenon worth studying if we want to comprehend the making of the new downtown and the impact of politics, policies, and processes on urban form. In fact, we would argue that public open spaces have become the leading metaphor for understanding the structure and design of the contemporary North American downtown.

Public open spaces appear to be amenities for downtown office workers, corporate clients, tourists, and conventioneers. These spaces, though privately owned, are by agreement available for public use and are presumed to be in the public domain. In most cities, they are the only new public spaces that have been added to downtown areas in recent years. In response to some of the incentives described previously (tax abatements, special zoning arrangements, bonuses) and other perceived benefits, developers increasingly have complemented their projects with open spaces. Today the supply of such spaces by the private sector represents a fundamental change in the creation and consumption of public space in downtown.

The privatization of public space, the transfer of responsibility for the production, management, and control of downtown public space to the private sector, is a relatively recent form of private involvement in open-space provision.[7] Traditionally, public open spaces were publicly acquired, created, owned, controlled, and managed. They were accessible to the public and available for individual or communal activities (Scruton 1984). Even though in the past the private sector played a role in shaping the public realm (for example, early city and regional plans sponsored by business organizations and philanthropic grants of private lands for public parks), the public sector was expected to offer the leadership and was considered responsible for the planning, design, and management of open spaces. In recent decades, however, urban plazas built with private money, usually in downtown areas, have become the modern American version of public space.

Public space privatization in American downtowns can be attributed to three interrelated factors (Loukaitou-Sideris 1991):

- The desire of the public sector to attract private investment downtown and, at the same time, relieve its economic burdens by utilizing private resources for the provision of urban amenities.
- The responsiveness of the private sector to development incentives and its willingness to participate in public-private partnerships and incorporate public spaces within private development projects.
- The existence of a market demand from certain sectors of the population for the facilities and services that the privately built open spaces offer. The "urban pathology" of traditional public spaces—that is, the perception, and often the reality, that public squares and parks are the locus of urban problems—and the desire of office workers, tourists, and conventioneers to be separated from threatening groups, the "undesirables" as William H. Whyte (1988) calls them, opened a market for spaces that are produced, maintained, and controlled by the private sector.

To illustrate some of our points we will now turn to a case study and examine the privatization of public space in downtown Los Angeles. A visitor to downtown Los Angeles will not fail to notice that a considerable number of new developments have dedicated parts of their sites as landscaped plazas available for public use.[8] The part of downtown with the densest new construction is the CBD (composed by the Bunker Hill and Financial Core redevelopment

FIGURE 44
Downtown Los Angeles
districts. Drawing by
Liette Gilbert.

areas), approximately at the geographic center of the sprawling metropolis (see figure 44). In the last three decades a major building boom, financed to a great extent by private capital, has transformed the CBD into a prime financial and corporate node of the Pacific Rim economy (Soja, Morales, and Wolff 1983). The downtown rebuilding, beginning with the Bunker Hill urban renewal project in the 1960s, has systematically segregated the contemporary CBD from the historic downtown to the east.

This accelerating growth and development has gone hand-in-hand with in-migration that has brought waves of homeless people and tenants with very low income, as well as undocumented workers, mainly from the Third World. Thus, downtown Los Angeles is a mosaic of people with different cultural, racial, occupational, and economic backgrounds. The sharp division between wealth and poverty in Los Angeles is clearly reflected in the urban form. As we will elaborate in chapter 5, the city has two downtowns, one next to the other: the rich, flashy, corporate, modern downtown of the First World and the poor, derelict, abandoned downtown of yesterday, which is beginning to look like the Third World.

Starting in the 1960s the focus of public expenditure in Los Angeles shifted toward major urban renewal programs aimed at the revitalization of the CBD. The Los Angeles Community Redevelopment Agency (CRA) was created to be the primary public organization responsible for all redevelopment projects within the downtown district. The relationship between the CRA and private developers is critical in terms of the provision and allocation of public open space. As part of its efforts to restructure downtown, the CRA initially pursued an incentive zoning program. This strategy allowed the agency to encourage private developers to provide various public amenities within the project site in exchange for enhanced development rights beyond the constraints of zoning ordinances. Specifics of such public benefit improvements, negotiated between the developers and the agency staff, were incorporated in development agreements. As a result of this process the supply of downtown open space under private jurisdiction and control has significantly increased in recent years. The same cannot be said for traditional public spaces. Development or remodeling of such spaces has remained on planners' drawing boards for years.

In order to assess the effects of privatization on the physical layout and social uses of space, we have selected as examples three downtown Los Angeles plazas—Security Pacific Plaza, Noguchi Plaza, and Citicorp Plaza—all of which were created through a public-private negotiation process. Each plaza occupies a prominent location within a different redevelopment area of downtown. Security Pacific Plaza is located in the Bunker Hill area (the premier corporate district of downtown), Citicorp Plaza is within the Financial Core (the commercial-retail heart of downtown), and Noguchi Plaza is at the center of Little Tokyo (the booming and prosperous Japanese community of Los Ange-

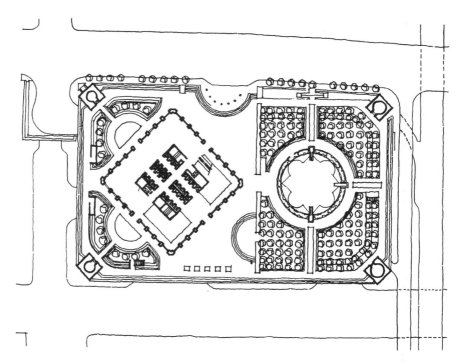

FIGURE 45
Security Pacific Plaza: Site
plan. Courtesy of Security
Pacific Plaza.

les). Each plaza is attached to a different primary use. Citicorp Plaza is an urban mall with retail uses. Security Pacific Plaza is a typical corporate plaza. Noguchi Plaza is associated with cultural uses (being part of a complex that includes the Japanese American Cultural and Community Center and the Japanese Theater).

Each plaza conveys a different physical image: Security Pacific Plaza resembles a formal garden in repose situated awkwardly in the midst of urban activities. As a garden it seeks isolation from its surroundings. Its spatial configuration, reminiscent of classical landscape design, emphasizes axial symmetry, harmonious proportions, pleasing relationships between the different parts. The careful arrangement of plant materials, the uniformity of trees and planters, the axial organization of the water channels, signify orderliness and harmony—attributes in sharp contrast to the disordered and chaotic environment of the surrounding city (see figures 45–47).

FIGURE 46
Security Pacific Plaza,
1996: View of the
garden. Photograph
by Liette Gilbert.

FIGURE 47
Security Pacific Plaza,
1996: Sculpture court.
Photograph by Liette
Gilbert.

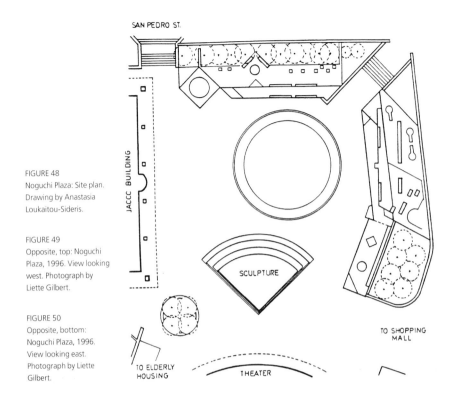

SAN PEDRO ST.

JACCC BUILDING

SCULPTURE

TO SHOPPING MALL

TO ELDERLY HOUSING

THEATER

FIGURE 48
Noguchi Plaza: Site plan.
Drawing by Anastasia
Loukaitou-Sideris.

FIGURE 49
Opposite, top: Noguchi
Plaza, 1996. View looking
west. Photograph by
Liette Gilbert.

FIGURE 50
Opposite, bottom:
Noguchi Plaza, 1996.
View looking east.
Photograph by Liette
Gilbert.

Noguchi Plaza can be compared to a ceremonial court, ready to serve as the stage for scheduled events, festivals, and celebrations (see figures 48–50). It is, however, a semiprivate court, turning away from the world to reveal its contents only to "initiated" visitors. The plaza is occasionally used for organized events and performances, but the space is not designed as a setting for spontaneous human activity. The plaza seems to encourage solitude and meditation. It is conceived as a work of art; the setting is designed as an outdoor museum court.

Citicorp Plaza was characterized by its designer, Jon Jerde, as a grotto, an artificial hole in the ground that "swirls" people away from the activity of the street (see figures 51 and 52). The plaza also resembles a sanitized bazaar. It aspires to create a lively, festive, diverse commercial environment, but the diversity seems at times preplanned and artificial. Citicorp Plaza screens out most of the attributes that make a bazaar successful: a variety of people and merchan-

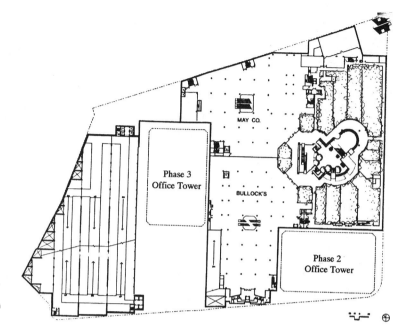

FIGURE 51
Citicorp Plaza: Seventh
Street–level site plan
(1983). Does not reflect
current improvements.

FIGURE 52
Opposite: Citicorp Plaza,
1991: Sunken court.
Photograph by Anastasia
Loukaitou-Sideris.

dise, intense, spontaneous activity, and elements of spectacle and surprise. Design here is clearly intended to appeal to upscale consumers.

Using these three plazas as examples, we can examine the effects of privatization at two different levels: its effects on the provision and production of space and on design and physical representation.

Provision and production of space   All three plazas are supposed to be open and accessible to the public. As prescribed by the DDAs, the responsibility for the provision of public space is supposedly shared by both the public and the private sectors. Our study has shown that this is not exactly the case.

On the surface it would seem that the CRA would retain the upper hand in the negotiation process because of its power and clout. After all, the agency is quite autonomous financially; it has the right to design approval, and it has the power to give density variations and enhanced development privileges. However, a closer look at the agency's political and administrative structure and insights gained from interviews with key actors suggest that the balance of

power often tilted toward the private sector: developers usually set the terms in the negotiation process. As one CRA planner confided, "When you deal with the big developers they have a lot of power. There are political ramifications. They have the power, they have the money and they will use it. There is always a certain amount of pressure. When there are battles they can go over your head and that is their option too."

The CRA is politically dependent upon City Council. All agreements have to be approved by the agency's board (appointed by the mayor) and by City Council. In the past, developers have applied political pressure to achieve their intentions. As another CRA planner explained,

> Our job is to make development happen, not to chase the developers away. Developers are investing millions of dollars on a project. They can say "if you make us build this there is no way we can continue," or "public open space may look nice, but it has inherent security problems." We invest considerable amount of time during the pre-agreement and selection process. We do not want to see afterwards everything falling apart. It is reasonable to think that we should get to agree.

The CRA is a redevelopment agency. Its purpose is to promote development, not hinder it. Developers, if pressed too hard, can always threaten to take their money and leave. Developers know how to take advantage of the fact that economic growth, the generation of revenues and the enlargement of its tax base, is a major goal of the CRA. As a representative of the Prudential Development Company (the owner of Citicorp Plaza) stated, "The CRA gets additional property taxes assessed for those densities above what a developer can do by right. So it has an incentive to cooperate with us."

During the negotiation process, the CRA often relies on its ability to offer developers density variations. Developers are often willing to trade something for the right to build additional floor space. But the design and planning of public open space are seldom important issues during the negotiation and development process. Public space provision has become a low priority objective for city officials. According to the planners interviewed, the cost of assembling land and using it for noneconomic purposes is prohibitive. Public open space is considered an unproductive allocation of land and is devalued as an amenity. The public sector is content to trade off negative externalities and transfer the responsibility for the provision and maintenance of public open space to the private sector. Development frameworks and guidelines are loose and flexibly written so as not to discourage or constrain private initiatives. But this lack of an overall urban design framework for downtown and the planners' inability to impose strong design and development guidelines are losses for the city, which misses the opportunity to strengthen its urban form and pedestrian activity.

Design and physical representation   A great deal of creative talent is devoted to making urban plazas attractive and distinctive. These three plazas project distinct physical images. At the same time, however, they display some common qualities and characteristics. Introversion is an attribute common to all three spaces. Their exteriors give few clues to the space within. Design features are utilized to achieve an inward orientation of these spaces, which are supposedly open to the public: high enclosing walls, blank facades, isolation from the street, deemphasis of street-level accesses, major entrances through parking structures, and the like. These design features control access to and use of space and facilitate effective deployment of security measures. These defensive design postures insulate the space from the outside environment, thereby fragmenting and disconnecting the space from the surrounding city fabric.

Design objectives for all three plazas reflect a desire for escapism and relief from the city. Architects and developers interviewed referred to their spaces as "oases" deliberately designed to look and feel different from the rest of the urban context. The intention of design is to create a sharp contrast between the gray exterior space and the bright interior courts and atria. Yet, as we talked to the architects of these plazas, it became clear to us that they all aspired to resurrect an idealized, even nostalgic image of the public realm. Indeed, many plaza designers referred to the classical plazas, squares, and open spaces of medieval and baroque European cities as their inspiration. The poetics of design is clearly different from the politics of the production of these spaces, as will be discussed in chapter 7.

Another common characteristic of all three plazas is the rigidity of their design, which demands that users adapt their behavior to the requirements of the setting and encourages visitors to be passive spectators. Nothing is left to chance, nothing can be moved, rearranged, or easily changed. In all three spaces, design emphasizes orderliness rather than spontaneity. None of these spaces provides an appropriate setting for children to run freely, couples to lie on the grass, or big groups to congregate. Formal receptions with appropriate decorum and attire, however, may be possible.

In order to serve the purposes of developers, the designers often strive to create settings for an exclusive class of users. Chic architecture and stylish, highly ornamental, and elegant materials are intended to attract and impress the affluent and at the same time promote the feeling of affluence. The design of corporate plazas, like Security Pacific Plaza, usually borrows heavily from the modernist doctrines—clear-cut layout, hardscapes,[9] fixed benches, colors drawn from a limited palette of grays, browns, and pale greens. Abstract ornamentation, for example, a sculptural or water element, is often a limited attempt to break away from the standardization and universality of the modernist design scheme. Shopping plazas like Citicorp Plaza are often dressed in a postmodern costume. The stylishness, superficiality, and impression of affluence that postmodernism sometimes seeks blends well with the purposes of commercial enterprises. Shopping plaza postmodernism uses a pastiche of colors and design elements borrowed from various styles. Design treats space as a commodity to be consumed.

In both office and shopping plazas the visual language of design is utilized to promote cues consistent with the goals of private enterprise. The design characteristics commonly present in the plazas—introversion, fragmentation, escapism, orderliness, and rigidity—are consistent with the objectives of control, protection, social filtering, image packaging, and manipulation of user behavior.

Downtown open spaces like the ones discussed here can be found today in almost every downtown in the United States. They are part of cities' redevelopment efforts, which more often than not are based on a corporate center strategy. Genuine public spaces, whether parks, squares, playgrounds, or recreational facilities, have been consistently devalued as amenities and redefined as planning problems to be eliminated or privatized (Davis 1985).

Corporate plazas are loved by developers and redevelopment agencies alike. They are perceived as enhancing the corporate milieu, as enhancing downtown's glitter and its image as "world center." As we will discuss in a later chapter, a great deal of design talent and effort, as well as money, goes into the development and packaging of these spaces, which as set pieces often represent attractive environments for the users. It should also be said that plazas offer comfort and a secure "refuge" to some legitimate groups of downtown users: advanced service professionals, white-collar office workers, women workers for whom security in public places is a major concern, and increasingly smokers, who are banished these days from most interior work spaces, especially in California cities. However, on the basis of the findings of this study, we wish to raise a number of issues and concerns regarding the privatization of the downtown public spaces.

As other researchers have found for other cities, the acclaimed public-private partnership in Los Angeles between the city's Community Redevelopment Agency and the private developers has effectively meant corporate domination of public policy and a form of dependency of the public on the private sector. It was clear from our interviews with developers and planners that the two sectors are not, contrary to previous claims (Poole 1980; Bennett and Johnson 1981; Savas 1982), equal collaborators in the development process. In Los Angeles the role of the public sector in the determination of open space provision and functions is minimal. Our case studies show that the private sector is usually in a better position to determine the outcome and to set the terms of the negotiation and deal-making process. This finding is quite consistent with the theory of the economic dependency of cities in the era of postindustrial capitalism (Kantor 1988) and other similar studies focusing specifically on downtown (Frieden and Sagalyn 1989). The bargaining relationship between cities and the large corporations that have come to dominate urban economies has tilted in favor of the latter. Cities are forced to "sell" their downtown space mostly to large corporations in order to effectively compete with one another.

Thus, the private developers have become the city builders, and private interests determine what gets built where and when. Bonuses to developers can be seen as negative externalities, the costs of which (for example, increased traffic congestion) are borne by the public. One could also question the wisdom of giving such bonuses and density variances for an amenity that most probably would have been provided by the private sector even without the incentive. All the developers we interviewed indicated that they perceive plazas as directly beneficial to their building, as enhancing its image and desirability to tenants.

It is only very rarely that any strategic planning has been done by the public sector regarding what sorts of public space priorities should be set, how much public space is needed in downtown, where it should be located, and which models of public space can best serve the needs of various user groups. As a result the need for plurality and diversity in the provision of public open space is not served well by the privatization pattern. In Los Angeles, for example, the divide between west and east, new and old, and rich and poor in downtown has been widened by the allocation of all new open space in the form of corporate plazas on the west side of the new downtown. We will discuss this further in chapter 5.

4

PART TWO

THE

POLITICS

OF

DEVELOPMENT

■

Dependence on private investments and initiatives for downtown rebuilding has changed urban politics and the very nature of the public realm (Savitch 1988). Today, private investment is generally seen as performing functions in the public interest (Hartman 1984). The public sector has become a facilitator; it responds to, reacts to, and sometimes regulates private initiatives. There is, however, often give-and-take in these public-private transactions. Developers often require enhanced development rights, zoning variances, land write-down, financial guarantees, or improvements in order to initiate investment. Planners request in return certain urban amenities, usually public open space, street improvements, public art, and in some cities, day-care centers and housing. In this context the form of the contemporary downtown is a product of negotiation, bargaining, and deal-making between city governments and private developers. This process has affected downtown's public realm, since it is now the market that is expected to supply downtown open space and other public amenities.

In recent years the downtown public realm has been the focus of considerable academic research. William H. Whyte's pioneering work on plazas (Whyte 1973, 1980, 1988) is representative of a body of literature that examines the design and use of downtown plazas and the reasons for their success or failure. Back in the early 1970s, Whyte and some of his students formed the Street Life Project to study how people use open spaces in the center of the city. Their study focused on many New York plazas, which were the recent products of the city's incentive zoning program. Using time-lapse photography Whyte and his students sought to understand why some plazas were popular while others remained empty. They found that many plazas lacked basic amenities: seating, food concessions, shade, water elements, landscaping (Whyte 1980). Their size, shape, purpose, location, and design were mostly the outcome of economic decisions not necessarily made for the public good (Whyte 1973). Whyte (1988) showed how simple design features—sun, water, seating, food, activities, and the like—can lead to the successful use of plazas. Whyte's findings and recommendations resulted in drastic changes of the incentive zoning provisions in the New York City code.[1] His book *The Social Life of Small Urban Spaces*, and the film with the same name, continue to influence the new generation of downtown planners and urban designers.

Others have sought to expand Whyte's work by producing comprehensive design guidelines for public open spaces (Cooper Marcus and Francis 1990). Some studies have focused on plaza users and their needs (Mozingo 1989; Franck and Paxson 1989; Sommer and Becker 1969). Still other researchers have analyzed the social dimensions of contemporary downtown open spaces (Chidister 1988; Brill 1989), their contribution to contemporary public culture (Francis 1988), and their availability for user control (Francis 1989).

The work of Whyte and others has considerably enhanced our knowledge of the role and function of urban plazas. Yet there have been few attempts so far to document the design and development process in the creation of downtown open space. The nature of the process has not been systematically examined. The story of the policy objectives, design guidelines, development agreements, deal-making, and negotiations that underlie these open spaces has yet to be told. Furthermore, how this process is affected by a particular city's culture of planning and development has also not been documented.

In this chapter we discuss the process of creating downtown open spaces in Los Angeles and San Francisco—two cities that have used distinctively different policy approaches in forming public-private partnerships. Both cities are facing the challenges and problems of growth, and both represent multicultural environments, mosaics of distinct social worlds with different values and needs. Both cities have been in the forefront of negotiating a range of essential development improvements that are seen as serving a public purpose. By studying these cities we hope to understand similar trends in other American CBDs.

In examining the process of development in these two cities we had several questions in mind: How do negotiations and deal-making shape the final outcome? How is the process different in these two cities? What do these open spaces mean for developers and corporate owners? Are they really necessary from the corporate perspective? How are they expected to be used, managed, and maintained? Can anyone be excluded from these spaces? Indeed, how valid is the presumption that these spaces are in the public domain? To address all these questions we studied eight plazas—four in Los Angeles and four in San Francisco—that were representative examples of recent downtown open space development in the two cities. The sites selected in Los Angeles were Citicorp Plaza, California Plaza, Bunker Hill Steps, and Figueroa at Wilshire Plaza. The case studies selected in San Francisco were Crocker Center, Grabhorn Park, Rincon Center, and One Hundred First Plaza.

DEVELOPMENT OF DOWNTOWN OPEN SPACE: A TALE OF TWO CITIES

In the last thirty years the downtowns of Los Angeles and San Francisco have experienced major building activity.[2] Downtown San Francisco added about 36 million square feet of new office space between 1965 and 1983 (San Francisco Department of City Planning 1983). Office inventory in downtown Los Angeles has more than doubled, growing from 12.5 million square feet in 1977 to almost 26 million square feet at the end of 1990; at least another 7 million square feet are expected to be added by the end of this decade (Community Redevelopment Agency 1991). Both Los Angeles and San Francisco have quite enthusiastically pursued joint ventures and partnerships with the private sector, but with distinctively different planning styles and policies.

In San Francisco regulatory, comprehensive planning is the norm. The planning department is now the public agency that oversees and controls most developments downtown. In the fifties and sixties, the redevelopment agency was the all-powerful force in shaping downtown's development, particularly in the area south of Market Street, which was considered the "great divide" that separated the business district from lower-income neighborhoods and transitional land uses (Hartman 1984). The massive Yerba Buena project, featuring George Moscone Convention Center, is a major legacy of that era. In recent years the San Francisco Redevelopment Agency (SFRA) has come to play a much diminished role in downtown development.[3]

Planning in San Francisco is mission oriented. The comprehensive plan of the mid-eighties grew out of organized citizen demand for a citywide master plan. Dennis Keating and Norman Krumholz (1991) have characterized the 1985 downtown plan (San Francisco Department of City Planning 1985), which came out of this process, as a growth-management device. The plan addresses commercial development, housing, historic preservation, open space, urban form, and transportation and sets a rigid and consistent class of rules, which establish the framework of planning in San Francisco.

A major section of the plan discusses the city's objectives for downtown open space. It should be noted that prior to the adoption of the plan, San Francisco experimented for some years with an incentive zoning strategy to ensure public open space in its downtown district. Each square foot of plaza area was credited with six, eight, or ten square feet of additional building space (depending on the zoning district) up to 15 percent of the basic allowable gross floor area. The planning code specified the dimensions, characteristics of access, and proportions of the plaza space to be occupied by landscaped features. Nevertheless, it was found that "The code failed to provide any qualitative guidance for the design of open space. As a result, a number of plazas downtown are only marginally useful because they are either inaccessible, are seated in the shadow of buildings, and/or lack seating or other amenities that make people feel welcome and comfortable" (San Francisco Department of City Planning 1985, 50).

To correct all this, the downtown plan adopted a much more aggressive stance. Developers of high-rise buildings must provide usable indoor and outdoor open space that is accessible to the public and must pay into the city's park fund two dollars for each square foot of office space. Although the plan gives priority to plazas and parks, it also allows for the provision of eleven types of public open space (see table 1). The plan specifies their minimum size, location, access, seating arrangements, landscaping and design, commercial services, food, sunlight, wind, and public availability (hours of operation). Some additional review functions were added as a result of citizen initiatives. One such popular initiative that has particular bearing on the location and design of open space is Proposition K, passed in 1984. Commonly known as the "no new shadows" rule, it requires that the designers of proposed new buildings demonstrate *ex ante* that the buildings will not cast any additional shadows on existing downtown open spaces. Shadow and wind simulation studies are now part of the environmental review process in San Francisco.

It is no surprise that developers and architects consider such close scrutiny somewhat overbearing. Developers also complain about the increased costs of development due to what they consider unnecessary delays in the process. The

Table 1. Types of Downtown Open Space in San Francisco

Types	Description	Size	Location
Urban garden	Intimate, shielded, landscaped area	1,200–10,000 sq. ft.	Ground level adjacent to side-walk, through-block way, or building lobby
Urban park	Large open space with natural elements	Minimum 10,000 sq. ft.	
Plaza	Primarily hard-surface area	Minimum 7,000 sq. ft.	Southerly side of building, not near other plaza
View/sun terrace	Wind-sheltered area on upper level	Minimum 800 sq. ft.	2d floor or above in place with spectacular views
Greenhouse	Partially or fully glassed-in enclosure	Minimum 1,000 sq. ft.	In places too shady or windy to be used as open space
Snippet	Small, sunny seating space	Various sizes	On new or existing building sites
Atrium	Glass-covered space in building interior	Minimum 1,500 sq. ft.	Interior of building or block
Indoor park	Interior open space; glass wall along street	Minimum 1,000 sq. ft.	Building interior adjacent to sidewalk or public open space
Galleria	Through-block passage lined with retail	Minimum height 30 ft.	In any approved galleria
Arcade	Covered passageway defined by building setback and columns	Minimum width 10 ft., minimum height 14 ft.	As identified in pedestrian network plan
Pedestrian walkway	Seating area on a sidewalk of a street or mall or in an exclusive pedestrian walkway	Various sizes	As identified in pedestrian network plan

SOURCE: Excerpted from San Francisco Department of City Planning 1985, table 1.

plan's annual cap of 450,000 square feet of new office space had in the past forced developers to compete rigorously for the privilege to build in San Francisco— a process that is commonly referred to as "the beauty contest."[4] According to one developer, it now costs $1 million to enter the contest. Furthermore, architects typically complain that a lot of creativity is taken away from them because the planners decide all the details.

In contrast to the deterministic style of planning in San Francisco, planning in Los Angeles displays drastically different qualities. The city's planning department has very little to do with planning in downtown. They seem to have yielded to the redevelopment decisions of the Community Redevelopment Agency (CRA). In 1972 a preliminary general development plan was privately prepared under the auspices of the Committee for Central City Planning, Inc. (CCCPI 1972), an organization representing the downtown business interests. But this plan has had no real effect on the direction of downtown development so far. Now, after more than twenty years of redevelopment work, a strategic plan for downtown has been developed (see chapter 10). Even this effort has turned out to be an oddly fragmented process shared by the city planning department and the Strategic Planning Task Force.

In Los Angeles, overall policy and design frameworks are absent, and development agreements are struck on a more ad hoc and opportunistic basis than in San Francisco. As explained in the previous chapter, the Los Angeles CRA is the primary public organization responsible for all projects downtown. Since the purpose of the CRA is to promote development through tax-increment financing, its time-discount rate is rather high. Immediate project implementation is more urgent than long-term visions. In San Francisco incentive zoning utilized specific formulas, but in Los Angeles the agency and the developers negotiated bonuses on a project-to-project basis.

Two official documents establish the outline for redevelopment in downtown Los Angeles: *The Redevelopment Plan for the Bunker Hill Urban Renewal Project* and *Design for Development: Bunker Hill, Los Angeles, California* (Community Redevelopment Agency 1959, 1968). *The Redevelopment Plan* shows land uses, circulation patterns, and general location of buildings in downtown. *Design for Development* sets some broad objectives for development. Neither document shows any particular vision as to the role and function of public open space in the contemporary downtown environment. The only reference in either document regarding open space is strategic in nature:

> A project-wide organization of open spaces and buildings will assure a balanced composition, individual identity and profitable investment in an exciting urban environment. Integrated organization of all open spaces which recognizes the significance of the topography consists of plazas, either at street level or above, roof decks, recreation and leisure areas, building setbacks, etc., linked by the pedestrian circulation system.[5] The principal objective is the creation of an interrelated arrangement welding the parcels into a unified urban complex centered around plazas. Buildings should combine to give definition and enclosure to these open spaces, and maximum integration between development on each side of the project boundary. (Community Redevelopment Agency 1968 4, 7)

These two documents are very general, schematic, and, in part, ambiguous. Still the language of the text reveals the way public open space is perceived by the planners. The words "individual identity and profitable investment" capture well the basic goals of contemporary downtown planning and urban design.

Unlike San Francisco, Los Angeles has no specific formulas, guidelines, or universal requirements. A disposition and development agreement (DDA) is drawn up for each project and covers the outcome of negotiations between parties prior to the initiation of a project. Since the agency has the right of design review, it has obviated the need to set specific open space requirements and design constraints. The planning climate in Los Angeles is more conducive to negotiation and deal-making, a fact that is appreciated by the development community. Table 2 gives a comparative summary of the differences in planning styles and policies in San Francisco and Los Angeles.

San Francisco and Los Angeles have also developed different planning styles and policy approaches. But do these differences matter? Do they actually have any effect on the downtown public realm and urban form? In order to answer this question we will now turn to our case studies. Documenting the design and development process of eight downtown spaces gives us an understanding of the politics of modern downtown building.

Table 2. Phases and Characteristics of Planning Process, Los Angeles and San Francisco

	Los Angeles	San Francisco
Planning agency	Community Redevelopment Agency	City Planning Department
Phases	a. Bunker Hill urban renewal project (beginning in 1959)	a. Incentive zoning CBD zoning plan (1968–1983)
	b. Tax-increment financing with incentive zoning (from late 1960s)	b. Downtown plan process (1981–1985)
	c. Strategic plan (1990 onward)	c. Downtown plan (1985 onward)
Characteristics	a. Compliant	a. Assertive
	b. Entrepreneurial	b. Consistent
	c. Ad-hoc and incremental	c. Synoptic
	d. Opportunistic	d. Mission-oriented
	e. Open-ended	e. Established rules
	f. Politically fragmented	f. Politically unified
	g. Weak citizen involvement	g. Strong citizen involvement

Crocker Center: an alley transformed   Crocker Center in downtown San Francisco is a successful mixed-use development that features office and retail space housed in new buildings and refurbished historic structures (see figure 53). The three-level Crocker Galleria with its sixty-two shops and restaurants is the centerpiece of the whole project (see figure 54). The galleria occupies a public right of way—the old Lick Alley—which used to be a midblock passage between Post and Sutter streets. Since the alley itself was never formally vacated the galleria technically remains a public easement. Planners were reluctant to vacate the alley mainly because of an earlier controversy over vacating a street access at the Transamerica building site. Their reluctance was clear in early negotiations with the planning department. Recalls David Larson, an architect with SOM, the design firm which undertook the project, "There was an

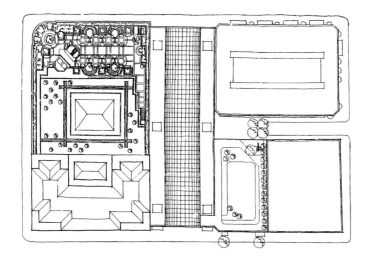

FIGURE 53
Crocker Center: Site plan
(roof level). San Francisco
Department of City
Planning.

FIGURE 54
Crocker Galleria, 1991:
Interior view. Photograph
by Anastasia Loukaitou-
Sideris.

alley . . . at the same position where the Galleria stands. The city said it was a public space. It had to be maintained as a public space. So that led to the idea that there would be an open circulation space between the two buildings."[6]

The planning for Crocker Center began during the incentive zoning era of downtown planning. Preliminary ideas for the project were first presented in January 1970 to the San Francisco Department of City Planning by Edmund Chandler of Crocker National Bank. The bank was interested in developing the entire block bounded by Montgomery, Post, Lick, and Sutter as the site for an office tower in about five years. Another office building was to be added later on the middle parcel, the building at Post and Montgomery was to be torn down for a plaza, and a building of major historical significance at 111 Sutter was to be replaced by a low building. In other words, total clearance and rebuilding on the site were envisaged at that time, and the bank also wanted a major zoning change.

After the bank had presented its preliminary thoughts, the city's planners immediately went to work. By early August, Richard Hedman, the principal urban designer for the city had prepared an urban design analysis with three alternative schemes for developing the site. This analysis made several recommendations: saving the existing facade of the original bank building and the main banking hall, keeping the corners of the street block intact, creating a system of interconnected pedestrian spaces, including the historic Hallidie and Aetna buildings in the visual domains of the new pedestrian space, and providing a roof garden for public use (see figure 55). These guidelines would ultimately influence the final design of the Crocker Center.

The planning of Crocker Center was to take almost another ten years before all the issues were to be fully resolved. In mid-1975 such issues as the impact of BART, vehicular access and parking, pedestrian circulation, historical landmark issues, transfer of development rights, and other general environmental, political, and permit process issues continued to occupy the agenda of Crocker Center planners in their discussions with the planning department staff. By 1978, the bank had acquired additional properties on the block, prompting the popular columnist Herb Caen to note in a June 8 *San Francisco Chronicle* column, "Entre News: Would you believe 72-story twin towers in the block bounded by Montgomery, Post, Kearny and Sutter? You don't have to, but

now that Crocker Bank has acquired most of the property in that block, the tower's plan has reached the model stage."

Yet, the bank planners accompanied by their SOM architects and the planning department staff were far from reaching an agreement. At the end of the summer of 1978, they were still negotiating over the location of two towers, a bonus for pedestrian access, and the like. Finally in October of 1978, Crocker Bank announced in a press release its plan for developing a portion of the block adjoining its historic headquarters building. The bank proposed to preserve the existing banking hall built in 1908, as well as its twenty-two-story office building at 111 Sutter Street. The proposal also called for expanded retail space and an office building. The idea of a three-story retail galleria was introduced for the first time. No details of the total square footage or building heights were given in the press release, although the planning department staff was aware that the proposed scheme—which was predicated on a 700-foot tower— would require major zoning changes.

The day after the Crocker plans were announced, Rai Okamoto, the then planning director, wrote to Robertson Short, the senior vice president of Crocker National Bank, that "certain proposals which we have seen would require major changes in the Planning Code before they would be allowable." In particular he referred to "changes which would be required in the zoning ordinance pertaining to height." He also pointed out, "this project is significant enough in scope and close enough to Market Street to require that it be subject to discretionary review procedures and, of course, environmental impact review of the City Planning Commission."[7] He did mention, however, that overall some elements were consistent with the intentions of the existing master plan, particularly street-level activities and preservation of the lower portion of the historic bank building.

The public opposition to high-rise construction was gaining strength in San Francisco at this time. Rai Okamoto recalled that Mayor Diane Feinstein was also opposed to the bank's attempt to exceed the allowable height limit. Finally, in March of 1979, the bank conceded to public opposition and agreed to scale down the proposed tower to the current height limitation of five hundred feet. According to a *San Francisco Chronicle* story, the bank's board of directors was concerned about passage of an anti-high-rise initiative, which was gaining strength. This initiative was opposed by the downtown and business interests. According to this story, "Facing growing public opposition to high-rise construction, Crocker Bank officials said yesterday they will scale down their planned 700-foot tower at Post and Kearny streets. . . . Thomas B. Wilcox, chairman of the bank's board of directors, said the company would reduce the height of its planned skyscrapers to conform to the present height limitation of 500 feet at that site" (Robinson 1979, 1, 22).

Finally, and despite some contentious public hearings, in late June of 1979 the City Planning Commission approved the Crocker Center project as amended (see figure 56). A month later, the City Planning Commission adopted a resolution enumerating various conditions and requirements to be met by the project, and certified its environmental impact report (EIR). It took another two years to finalize the configuration of the roof garden.

Planning by negotiation seems to have worked for both the project developers and the city planners. The planning department's help was critical for the bank to build over the vacated public alley and to overcome public opposition to high-rise construction in downtown. In return the bank had to scale down

FIGURE 56
Crocker Center, 1991:
View from Market Street.
Photograph by Anastasia
Loukaitou-Sideris.

its initial concept and amend its design. Downtown San Francisco gained a new urban mall. But the mall's public space is in no way geared to all San Franciscans. Despite the early sensitivity to the public-easement question, the galleria is no different than any other corporate open space. Access and public presence are carefully controlled and monitored by vigilant security guards. The galleria is closed at night.

Grabhorn Park: an off-site open space   Grabhorn Park is an innovative response to the requirement for privately created public open space for new office developments in downtown San Francisco, which was formalized as part of the 1985 downtown plan. This small park, provided by the developers of the property located at the corner of Sacramento and Montgomery, is off-site, on a separate lot a couple hundred feet away from the office tower (see figure 57). The negotiations for this open space, however, began long before the 1985 downtown plan was approved.

According to Martin Brown of the Empire Group, the original developer of the project, the development process started in 1978 with the assembly of ten

FIGURE 57
Grabhorn Park, 1991.
Photograph by Anastasia
Loukaitou-Sideris.

(later to become eleven) parcels, amounting to a little over 26,000 square feet. Although there was no downtown plan at the time the initial ideas were considered, the tradition of providing public space was very much in place, mainly because of the deals made earlier during the incentive zoning era. The Empire Group developers knew, therefore, that while it was not explicitly defined, they had an obligation to provide public open space. Their first idea was to provide a galleria, which was incorporated in the initial design. This was finalized into a plan and subsequently reviewed and approved by the planning department. In the proposal existing buildings, amounting to a little over 34,000 square feet, on four of the eleven parcels were preserved, but their air rights were added to the overall computation of the floor area ratio (FAR). A basic FAR of 14:1 allowed the Empire Group to propose a new twenty-four-story building with ground-floor retail shops, and a pedestrian arcade connecting Sacramento and Commercial Streets. In June of 1984 the City Planning Commission granted the final conditional use authorization.

Soon after the initial plan was approved, the Empire Group began to have second thoughts about the galleria, for several reasons. First, since the site itself was rather small, there was not enough room for an effective galleria. Second, the cost of providing a galleria appeared quite steep. Third, it would have been in shade all day, a condition that is not acceptable in San Francisco. Fourth, and finally, some of the Chinatown neighborhood groups, who were involved in the early negotiations because of the project's proximity to that neighborhood, were concerned that the local residents might not feel welcome at the galleria because of its corporate environment.

At this point, the developers made a strategic choice. They realized that it would be advantageous for them to buy an adjacent property and create an off-site open space. Since it was off-site, it did not have to be a formal environment as in other corporate plazas and, therefore, would not be intimidating to the neighborhood residents. Also the developers would not have to worry about providing security. Okitami Komada, executive vice president of Mitsui Fudosan Corporation, the owner of 505 Montgomery, was not so sure. He expressed his misgivings about the off-site park, arguing that it did not contribute much to the prestige of the corporate building or the welfare of his tenants.

Nevertheless, during the planning stage the developers felt that meeting the open space requirement off-site would not be any more expensive than creating the galleria. The developers also saw that by meeting the public space requirement on an off-site location, they could also increase the leasable floor space of the building by additional 15,000 square feet. As it turned out, according to Martin Brown, the total cost of creating Grabhorn Park was between $1.5 and $2 million, including site acquisition, demolition, and construction costs. This figure also included landscaping and street improvements along that entire block of Commercial Street.[8]

The developers, a general partnership by now known as 505 Montgomery Associates, along with 642 Commercial Partners, and the owners of the 642 Commercial Street site (the proposed park site) submitted the off-site idea to the San Francisco Department of City Planning. They proposed to provide approximately 2,000 square feet of "publicly accessible open space in the form of a ground level landscaped park" on Commercial Street as an alternative to the "enclosed open space within the retail arcade of approximately 1,860 square feet."[9] The city planners responded to the idea favorably, and in early 1988, after almost a year of negotiations about the specifics of park design and the associated street improvement, the project modification was approved by the City Planning Commission. The 505 Montgomery Street project was completed in the spring of the following year, receiving a temporary permit of occupancy in May of 1989, more than a full decade after the Empire Group began assembling the land. The planning department was clearly pleased with the park and streetscape improvements (light fixtures, benches, trees) on Commercial Street.

The collaboration and negotiations seemed to have worked, especially from the city planners' point of view. The project met the open space objectives of the downtown plan. Grabhorn Park can be seen as a successful step toward the creation of pedestrian and worker amenities in the corporate downtown of San Francisco. Yet some doubts linger. For example, one could question the appropriateness of the park's location in light of our findings that show that this park is not used much, even during lunch hours (see chapter 6). One could question the wisdom of not pursuing some linkage with food vendors. And one could also question more generally the effectiveness of the proposed pedestrian network system and whether it is served by appropriate generators or destinations of pedestrian traffic.

Rincon Center: a mixed-use development   Rincon Center is one of the most glamorous mixed-use development projects in San Francisco in recent years (see figure 58). It is a combination of new and old structures occupied by residential, office, and retail space. The development of Rincon Center was also quite complex, given all the conditions and requirements of the various agencies that became involved, and the complex financial arrangements that the project entailed.

Rincon Center represents a different regime of San Francisco's downtown development and urban design. It is an example of a different form of entitlement process and agency patronage, namely, that of the SFRA. Thus the Rincon Center project shares the institutional characteristics of the Los Angeles cases we will later discuss, since development at any site in downtown Los

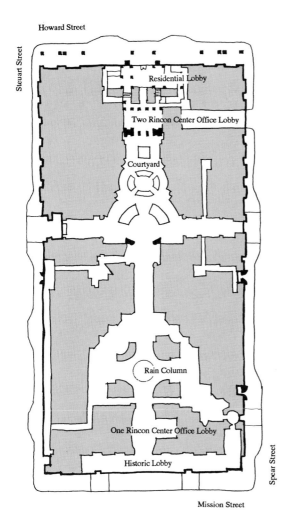

Howard Street

Steuart Street

Residential Lobby

Two Rincon Center Office Lobby

Courtyard

Rain Column

One Rincon Center Office Lobby

Historic Lobby

Spear Street

Mission Street

FIGURE 58
Rincon Center: Site plan.
"Rincon Center,"
brochure prepared
by Rincon Center, A
Development of Perini
Land and Development
Company.

Angeles is controlled by the city's CRA. But this similarity is only superficial, since San Francisco's City Planning Commission had an opportunity to comment on the design concept and, later, to be involved in the entitlement of the Rincon Center project—much more than what would be the norm for the Los Angeles Planning Department.

According to Frank Cannizzaro, who was at the time the SFRA's project director for the Rincon Center development, planning and development of the waterfront had always been a very significant issue in local politics.[10] Although there was a general interest in the redevelopment of the area, it was very difficult to reach a consensus about what should be done. There was conflict among interest groups, who had their own objectives: office development, housing, preservation of maritime and commercial uses, improvement of transportation infrastructure, and the like. In 1976 a planning effort was undertaken under the leadership of the SFRA. By 1978 this process was formalized to include the staff of the San Francisco Department of City Planning and the Port of San Francisco, and a very large citizen advisory committee. This process ultimately produced a consensus that was the basis for a plan for an area that extended from Market Street to the China Basin area. Approved by the San Francisco Redevelopment Agency in October 1980 and called the Rincon Point–South Beach Redevelopment Plan, the plan tried to accommodate all of these objectives. The underlying goal was to create more housing within a mixed-use waterfront environment. As was expected, the gradient of proposed density of development increased toward Market Street, and the specific properties to be included within the plan became a matter of "political give and take," according to Cannizzaro.[11]

The block containing the Rincon Annex to the U.S. Postal Service was included within the plan boundaries. The Rincon Annex, designed by Gilbert S. Underwood and built in 1939, is according to one report (San Francisco Department of City Planning 1979), considered one of the fine examples of large public buildings designed in the Streamline Moderne style of San Francisco architecture (see figure 59). The Maritime Museum, also built in 1939, is another example of that style. These were all members of a class of WPA-sponsored buildings built throughout the nation in the 1930s. The architectural style reflected the then modernist design principles influenced by machine age technology. But the real treasure of the Rincon Annex was its art, especially the famous murals by Anton Refregier covering four hundred feet of wall space.

Around 1977 the Postal Service realized that the Rincon Annex was not large enough for its operation. At the same time, because downtown San Francisco was experiencing a real estate boom, they also became interested in increasing the value of their property holdings. But the real challenge, according to Cannizzaro, was how to transform the planning concepts into reality and to obtain

FIGURE 59
Rincon Center, 1992:
Old post office building.
Photograph by Anastasia
Loukaitou-Sideris.

approval by the Postal Service. Negotiations with the Postal Service continued for about a year and a half to determine the most sensible type of development in terms of the intent of the plan, good urban design, and sound economics. On the basis of this study the Postal Service sent out a request for proposals (RFP) to interested developers. The RFP, based on an agreement the Postal Service had with the SFRA, stipulated that the proposal must include retail and housing and that the Postal Service would retain ownership with the provision of a sixty-five-year ground lease.

The Postal Service received four bids and decided that the proposal from Perini Land and Development Company was the best from an economic point of view. Even after the bid was accepted, negotiations went on for some time. According to Jay Mancini, who was hired by Perini Land and Development Company as a general project manager at that time, some of these had to do with the ground-lease agreement, the rights of the landlord and the tenant, insurance, future refinancing and reappraisal, requirements for property main-tenance, and the like.[12] The developers also had to negotiate with the SFRA over the owner participation agreement (OPA), which stipulated how much of the housing was to be low and moderate income and dealt with the hiring of minority business in the construction and with the requirement for public arts, open space, and so on.

From the development point of view, the RFP presented several constraints. Because commercial (office) space could not rise above six stories and the housing had to be placed above the office floors, office space could not have the best view, which is most attractive for the professional and corporate tenants of contemporary downtown office buildings. According to Mancini, this situation did not make much economic sense because the higher floors, if rented as office space, would command higher rents.

Reflecting on the entitlement process, Mancini felt that overall the SFRA was reasonably flexible in their demands. With respect to the plaza requirement, the agency had specified a minimum amount but left the specific design details for the developers to decide. Toward the end of the negotiations, the agency started bringing in more and more downtown plan requirements, or what Mancini referred to as the "creeping downtown plan,"[13] which affected the shape of the top of the towers, shadows, the amount of open space, and the like. In the end, while the Rincon Center developers were able to escape the "beauty contest" that started immediately after the downtown plan was published, they still had to respond to some requirements; for example, they had to undertake a rigorous shadow analysis in order to demonstrate that the Rincon Center residential towers would not cast significant new shadows on the proposed park along the Embarcadero.

The least problematic, interestingly, was the open space requirement. According to Mancini, the developers would have provided significant open space even if there had not been such a requirement. Because they were not able to build an office tower, they had to create a very lively and interesting space, and retail uses had to help them pay for this open space (see figure 60). According to its developers the real philosophy of this project was based around the concept of open space, which was perceived to reinforce retail activity.

Rincon Center today is a "basilica" of trade and commerce (see figure 61 and also chapter 7). There is a touch of medieval urbanism here, since people can live, shop, and work within one city block. But the diversity of the social context that usually characterizes medieval open spaces is missing. Ultimately the owners determine the policies for the use of the open space, with an eye

FIGURE 60
Rincon Center, 1992:
Outdoor space between
office and residential
towers. Photograph by
Anastasia Loukaitou-
Sideris.

FIGURE 61
Rincon Center, 1992: The
atrium. Photograph by
Anastasia Loukaitou-
Sideris.

to keeping their tenants, retailers, and clients happy. Noisy people, homeless, denizens of skid row of any sort, are escorted off the premises.

One Hundred First: open space above a garage   One Hundred First is a high-rise office tower next to the Transbay Terminal in downtown San Francisco (see figures 62 and 63). To comply with the city's open space requirement, the developer has converted the roof of a three-story garage into a sun terrace, an

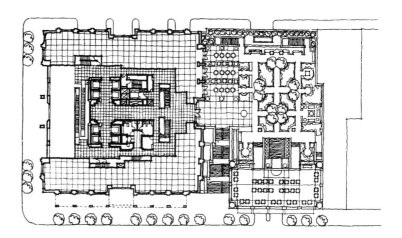

FIGURE 62
One Hundred First Plaza:
Site plan. Courtesy of
Jeffrey Heller, FAIA,
Heller, Manus Architects.

FIGURE 63
One Hundred First, 1991:
Approaching view.
Photograph by Tridib
Banerjee.

FIGURE 64
Opposite: One Hundred
First Plaza, 1992: The sun
terrace. Photograph by
Anastasia Loukaitou-
Sideris.

area with substantial landscaping that can seat approximately six hundred people at full capacity (see figure 64).

Complying with the open space requirement probably was the easiest part of the process of getting the project approved. As a test case for the downtown plan, the design of the building was subject to rather close scrutiny and various demands from the Planning Department. This scrutiny led to controversy and disagreement over the architectural design of the building, and ultimately another architect, Jeffrey Heller (a native of San Francisco and a partner of Heller and Leake) was brought in to design the building to the satisfaction of the Planning Department. The process was a contentious and lengthy one that left the original architect, Richard Keating, and the developer, Michael Barker, rather embittered with the whole experience.

The developers first met with the planning department staff in March of 1983 to discuss potential land acquisition, the future direction of office development in downtown San Francisco, and the feasibility of the site in that context. Apparently at that time they were completely in the dark about the forthcoming downtown plan, which was in the final stages and only five months from publication. Land assembly involving three parcels was completed in April with the developers' understanding that the FAR allowed was 14:1 with a height limit of 550 feet. In May the developers had a "full scale meeting" with Dean Macris, the director of city planning, and his staff, and in June an initial design presentation was made to the city planning staff.[14] The initial reaction to the conical form of the building with set backs was favorable, although the planners expressed "great concern" over future shadows on the open space in front of the Transbay Terminal building. In response to these concerns, extensive shadow studies were completed in August. Meanwhile the downtown plan was published (also in August) with specific guidelines for bulk control that applied to four components of a structure: the base, lower tower, upper tower, and upper tower extension. In October a second scheme was presented to the city planning staff reflecting the "three-tiered step-back version."[15]

In November, the Office of Environmental Review, which oversees the preparation and approval of EIRs, required full compliance with the downtown plan. This meant many new requirements in addition to bulk control. By March of 1984, shadow issues still had not been resolved. A new design scheme (the third) was produced to reduce the bulk and improve the shadow impact. But as the first planning code revisions to incorporate the guidelines of the downtown plan were published, new requirements—a child-care facility, housing contribution, park fee, and so on—were imposed on the project, although not all of them had direct bearing on the design of the building. The planners requested new shadow studies, new wind studies, a reduced and more slender building form, and compliance with a new 10:1 FAR as stipulated in the downtown plan. More design reviews followed in late April to consider the amended design (still the third scheme). By the middle of June a revised planning code document was published, which, according to the developers, "seriously impacted the upper tower design of the building and loading dock requirements which (if literally followed) would 'gut' the majority of the ground floor lobby area and reduce upper floors to a very inefficient size and design layout."[16]

In early August, the developers were informed by the Planning Department that the shadow impact was no longer an issue, but the building's bulky appearance remained a concern. This was a direct result of the Planning Department's desire for an elegant building, but the height restriction of 550 feet and the developers' needs for sufficient floor space were major obstacles. Finally, in September the developer of the project retained Heller and Leake to finalize the design of the building. Although the construction began in 1985, by the middle of 1988 occupancy permits were still being held up by, among other things, restoration and completion of the top of the building to the satisfaction of the Planning Department. While Heller's design mediation helped to resolve the aesthetic concerns, the product remained less than satisfactory to many observers. The extensive redesign efforts considerably strained the initial budget and, thus, directly affected the quality of building materials and details. Today, Richard Keating, the original architect, refuses to associate himself with the final design of the building. To some local connoisseurs of design, One Hundred First will always be "the building that looks like a fire plug" according to one senior staff member at the San Francisco Department of City Planning.

Architect Richard Keating was skeptical about the open space requirements and argued about the cumulative effects of individual open spaces at a larger scale:

> The planners insisted on having public open space as an amenity. It sounds like a good idea. But do you need public open space on a site like that, where you have public open space right across the street? This is a simplistic and silly idea, that all buildings should have plazas. Then you have leaky public open spaces all throughout. The only choice that the developers had was to put the public open space so much high and you needed stairs to reach it.[17]

Architect Jeffrey Heller, on the other hand, spoke positively about the effect of the downtown plan on creating better open space:

> All you have to do is to look at the buildings that were approved in the 1970s versus those in the 1980s. The open spaces are much better. Open space reduces the block density and in doing so it brings us back to a wider organization of urban form, which is very important. . . . There needs to be open space between towers . . . in an urban core like this, if you don't have spaces between towers, it's windy, it's bad, it's a mistake![18]

In this project, as in others, the open space—despite requirements for sun, seating, food, landscaping, public access, and the like—was the least problematic requirement of the design. According to developer Michael Barker, the cost of providing the space was around $1.5 million, less than 1 percent of the $175 million price tag for the project as a whole. He talked about the need for provision of amenities in office buildings and stressed that he would have included open space even without any formal requirements.[19]

Today the sun terrace is a bright and comfortable space that is almost exclusively used by the tenants of the adjacent One Hundred First tower during lunch break. Despite the rather imposing grand stairs there is little hint that there is a place intended for the public (see figure 65). To a stranger the stairs may simply indicate another entrance to a corporate looking building. In that sense the sun terrace contributes little to the public realm of downtown San Francisco.

Citicorp Plaza: an upscale mall and offices   Citicorp Plaza, which opened officially in 1986, occupies two consolidated blocks in downtown Los Angeles and pro-

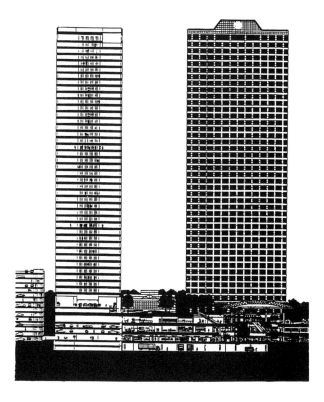

vides 1.9 million square feet of luxury office space and an urban mall (see figure 66). Once visitors pass the information and security booth at the entrance, they are isolated from the city while being in the middle of it. Mall users are drawn—by means of elevators and escalators—to the lower levels with shopping and to the very bottom level, which is an open-air food court (see figure 67). The upper level of Citicorp Plaza, the "roof" as the developer calls it, offers a parklike setting of 2.5 acres interspersed with pieces of public art (see figure 68). This is "the best hidden space in downtown," as one user put it. No sign along the street reveals the existence of this open space, which is intended to serve for the lunch breaks of the office tenants.

The seeds for the development of Citicorp Plaza were planted in the late 1970s, when Oxford Properties, Inc., a Canadian development firm, purchased from AMMCO Realty a block of downtown land with the intention of build-

FIGURE 68
Citicorp Plaza, 1996:
Upper level view.
Photograph by Liette
Gilbert.

FIGURE 67
Citicorp Plaza, 1996:
Escalators connecting
different levels.
Photograph by Liette
Gilbert.

ing a major office development. The site was limited to an FAR of 6 : 1, and the developer turned to the CRA for a variance. This was the beginning of a series of negotiations between the developer and the agency. At that time (early 1980s) the CRA was very much concerned that two major department stores (Bullock's and May Company) were planning to leave the abandoned and decaying east side of downtown. The agency wanted to find space to accommodate them on the west side of the CBD, thus preventing their exodus from the downtown area.

The two parties came to the negotiation table with specific items on their agenda. Developers wanted a large density variation in order to build three high-rise office towers, as well as the evacuation of a street that intersected their site. The CRA pressed for a mixed-use development that would include office and retail space, a parking structure, a hotel (which was never built), and some amount of open space. In 1981, the environmental impact report (which found that the proposed project would result in some unavoidable, significant environmental effects) was approved by the CRA (the agency ruled that the effects could be overridden by the anticipated benefits). The agency and the developer signed an OPA. For the amount of $5 million the developer got a density variation of 1.2 million square feet of additional commercial space (FAR 9.5 : 1). In addition to the three office buildings the developer agreed to build 350,000 square feet of retail space and accommodate the two department stores. The CRA agreed to vacate the street and also contributed $11.5 million for the construction of a parking garage (Citicorp Plaza 1981).

The OPA between the public and private sectors defined three development phases. Phase 1, which included a forty-two-story office tower, a retail plaza, a parking structure, and open space, was officially completed in 1986. In the same year Oxford Properties transferred its interest to the Prudential Company. One year later (1987) a new private partnership, the South Figueroa Plaza Associates, was formed between Prudential (25 percent) and MMA Plaza Associates (75 percent), a subsidiary of the Japanese Mitsubishi Estate Company, and this partnership was responsible for the negotiation of the next two phases with the CRA.

From our interviews with CRA planners and the private developers, it became clear that the latter had more power during the negotiation process. Both parties conceded that the sum of $5 million was an extremely favorable rate for the purchase of such a big variance in an expensive downtown area. Regarding the issues of publicness and accessibility one CRA planner stated, "It was the CRA's intention that there is some place where the public can always go to. But this did not happen. There are no official public easements now. The place was not exactly intended as a public park, but we wanted it open and available."[20]

The developers' objectives regarding the plaza space were outlined by a manager of the Prudential Company:

We wanted to provide a clear transition between the office buildings and the retail mall. When you have a corporate client you do not want to force him to mix with the typical mall shopper. Open space serves as a nice transition. We also wanted to have a nice central area that is not going to feel like you are in the middle of downtown. We did not want carts and street vendors. We do not have enough space and they do not make a lot of money. . . . We wanted a very safe park. We have tons of security, a small army taking care of things. . . . The users we want to attract are our tenants, their employees and other downtown employees.[21]

Architect Jon Jerde was brought in to reconcile with his design the different demands promoted by the corporate tenants, on the one hand, and the retail tenants, on the other. Jerde wanted to link the plaza space to the commercial street environment. The developer would not, however, give up for retail the prime real estate value and the exposure of the corner. Jerde also wanted more retail and more open space. According to him, the project does not have the appropriate "critical mass" to attract enough people. Jerde's original vision of the physical form of the plaza was quite different from what was eventually realized:

I did not want it to be tailored in that way. I wanted it to be a park, very softscape with gravel rocks. I always described it as a grotto, with water at the bottom, as you wander down through its rings in a totally landscaped environment—getting very little view across—with little things that I described as 'perfume bottles,' little architectonic bubbles that would break up the open space but would not have a lot of physical presence. Now my gravel has turned to granite and my water has vanished. These are things that always happen to projects. It is a continuous battle to reach a resolution. You give one to get another.[22]

Citicorp Plaza gives a clear example of how market imperatives can define the purpose and functions of place making in downtown. Negotiation between the public and private sectors during the redevelopment process was guided by economic principles and objectives. On the one hand, the agency's considerations were formulated by its desire to embellish downtown's potential as a regional retail center. On the other hand, the developer was preoccupied with issues of marketability and profitability. The CRA considered open space as a required amenity, but did not prepare specific guidelines for its form and usage.

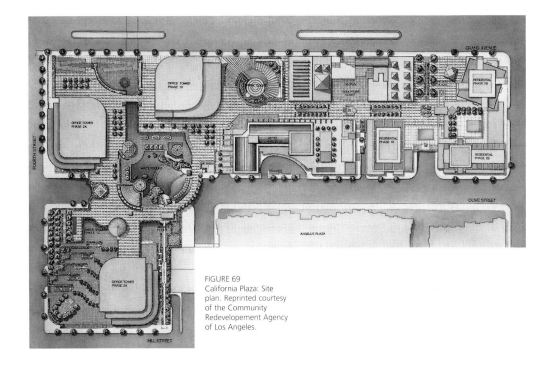

FIGURE 69
California Plaza: Site
plan. Reprinted courtesy
of the Community
Redevelopement Agency
of Los Angeles.

The developer treated open space as a commodity item that could help sell his
project to perspective tenants and clients and enhance its financial success.

California Plaza: emphasis on arts and culture   California Plaza is a master-planned
project, a city within a city, that covers five unified city blocks and features
three office towers, three residential high-rise buildings, the Museum of Contemporary Art (MOCA), a luxury hotel, and parking facilities, all of which
are linked through a series of open spaces, courts, and landscaped plazas (see
figure 69).

California Plaza is located in the 136-acre Bunker Hill redevelopment district of Downtown Los Angeles. As already explained in chapter 1, Bunker Hill
in its heyday at the turn of the century was a fashionable residential neighborhood with elegant Victorian mansions and pristine backyards. Today Bunker
Hill stands as the premier corporate mixed-use node of downtown, with lus-
trous office towers, modern high-rise apartment buildings, commercial-retail

complexes, luxury hotels, and corporate plazas. Responsible for this dramatic transformation of the cityscape is the CRA, which in 1959 designated the by then declining neighborhood as a redevelopment area. In 1960, utilizing federal funds, the CRA began acquiring property, relocating residents and business, demolishing buildings, and clearing the land. This activity was accompanied by massive regrading of the area, in order to enhance its redevelopment potential. Overcoming local opposition, the CRA proceeded to realize its vision and transform Bunker Hill into the prominent symbol of a revitalized downtown: "an attractive day and nighttime activity center with grade-separated pedestrian system, landscaped parks and plazas, fine arts, entertainment facilities, and controlled urban form" (Community Redevelopment Agency 1973, 8).

The current site of California Plaza was the last undeveloped piece of land in Bunker Hill. These five unified blocks were seen by the CRA as a unique opportunity to give Bunker Hill an active "heart," an environment that could combine commercial and cultural activities, and act as a regional magnet for tourists, residents, and office workers. In its scheme for the site, the redevelopment agency departed from its previous policy. Instead of offering the parcels to different developers, the CRA decided to offer them as a single entity.

In October 1979, the CRA issued an official request for proposals (RFP), which yielded responses from five developer-architect teams. The RFP specified the programmatic requirements of the project, the amount and type of land uses, but did not specify an urban design framework. The selection jury included CRA staff, three CRA board members, and real estate consultants. Of the five competition entries, two finalists emerged as the leading contenders. One was the Bunker Hill Associates—formed by Cadillac Fairview, a giant international development corporation—which had Arthur Erickson as its principal architect and was supported by two local architectural firms: Kamnitzer, Cotton, and Vreeland, and Gruen Associates. The other finalist was Maguire Thomas Partners (MTP), a Los Angeles development firm with a team of well-known architects put together by the late Harvey Perloff, the then dean of Architecture and Urban Planning at UCLA. This design team was managed by architect Barton Myers and included architects Cesar Pelli, Charles Moore, Frank Gehry, Ricardo Legoretta, Robert Kennard, and the firm of Hardy Holzman Pfeifer and also landscape architect Lawrence Halprin.

The design solutions offered by the two teams were very different in concept. Myers's approach, which was much more consistent with the city grid and followed the original block layout, arranged the different buildings on seven different blocks. This scheme sought to define public space as an extension of the sidewalk, creating at the same time a definite street wall. Halprin and Moore designed a linear promenade along Grand Avenue to rejuvenate what was previously a dead-end street and, at the same time, to link California Plaza to the Music Center. Projections from the buildings, which Moore called "noses," created interruptions and playfully orchestrated a link between public space and the building facades. At certain points the open space intruded into the interior of the block through arcades, arches, cornices, and grand portals.

The concept behind the Erickson scheme was quite different. According to Tim Vreeland, who was a member of the design team during the initial stages of the project, Erickson saw the opportunity to design a superblock as a unified whole as a "highly desirable architectural gesture." [23] Following a modernist, Corbusian idea of space, he created a large uninterrupted open space expanding from Grand Avenue and unifying the whole development. Freestanding towers were strategically planted in the open space.

Ultimately, however, what decided the competition's outcome were financial rather than design considerations. According to a former deputy director at the CRA, Rob Maguire, a relatively young developer, had not established the kind of track record that Cadillac Fairview had, and did not seem to have the capability to bring in the financial resources that the project required. Thus, in July 1980, the CRA's board voted to award the entry of Bunker Hill Associates. In the negotiation between developers and the agency staff, the CRA offered the developers the right to build on the property utilizing an FAR of 10:1 in exchange for certain public benefits. Each phase of the project was associated with a benefit to the city to be funded by the developer and, ultimately, by rent assessments. During Phase I MOCA was to be built. During Phase II the developer was to provide a large outdoor performance space for festivals and concerts. Finally, Phase III would be accompanied by the restoration of a historic Bunker Hill funicular, the Angel's Flight.

After a series of meetings that focused mostly on the nature of financial incentives and requirements, the agency and the developers signed a DDA in September 1981. Regarding open space the DDA stated,

There is to be an exciting variety of open spaces located throughout the site, total-ing approximately 5.5 acres. Central to these spaces is to be the Central Performance Plaza [now Watercourt] serving as the major open space focus for the development. This large, multilevel space on the podium and plaza level is to be a pedestrian gath-ering and entertainment center for a variety of developer-programmed and spon-taneous outdoor activities and events. . . . It is to contain approximately 1.5 of the total of approximately 5.5 acres and will span Olive Street.

Other open spaces are to include a landscaped plaza between the two office tow-ers at Grand Avenue featuring a retail food or drink pavilion, the entrances to the performance plaza and proposed future transit station located on lower levels. . . . A variety of courts and gardens are to provide a setting along Grand Avenue for mu-seum activities, retail shops and the hotel. This open space along Grand Avenue is to have the effect of a large, but carefully delineated space defined by the residen-tial buildings to the east, offices to the south, hotel to the north, and Grand Ave-nue to the west. This open space would also contain the museum and have smaller scaled elements and level changes incorporated within, providing pedestrian scale and activity. Pedestrian use and activity of this space must be clearly visible and accessible from Grand Avenue. Parcel Y-1 will include terraced recreational and garden areas and spaces for retail shopping. . . . Throughout the open spaces shall be water features . . . elements such as pools, cascades, streams and fountains care-fully planned to add sparkle, pleasant sound and visual delight. (California Plaza 1981, Attachment No. 3, p. 3)

The developer was obligated to provide evidence of financial commitment by July 1982 and to begin construction by the end of September. Because of financial hardships the developers missed the deadline and negotiated a year's extension with CRA. At the end of the year, however, Cadillac Fairview was in even worse shape. So in 1983 Metropolitan Structures, a joint venture of Metropolitan Life Insurance (one of the original five competitors) was brought in by Cadillac Fairview as the general managing partner.

It was at this time that major changes affected the physical layout of the project, and neither the CRA nor Erickson was able to prevent them. The character of the performance space changed to include water features (see fig-ures 70 and 71), the hotel site moved southward, and the residential towers and hotel were commissioned to different architects. A former CRA official is quite critical of how the project has evolved: "I think it is unfortunate that Erickson's original concept was not realized more closely. I think there is no architectural

FIGURE 70
California Plaza, 1996:
The Watercourt.
Photograph by Liette
Gilbert.

FIGURE 71
California Plaza, 1996:
Entrance from Grand
Avenue. Photograph by
Liette Gilbert.

coherence at all with the hotel and the housing. It is a lost opportunity and quite an irony because Erickson's scheme was the one providing the opportunity for integrated development. Now it is fragmented pieces."[24]

But the current CRA project management for Bunker Hill claims that there shouldn't be any complaints about the quality of the project or the level of the CRA's commitment to downtown Los Angeles. This commitment, as the CRA planners admit, has so far been primarily geared towards fostering the growth and development of the new downtown and transforming it into a place efficient for business and attractive to tourists and middle- and upper-class residents. These goals are clearly reflected in the urban form and imagery of California Plaza.

Bunker Hills Steps: a public passage   Inserted between two office towers, the Bunker Hill Steps are a grand stairway (see figure 72). The Steps link new development on top of the hill with the city below. Like many other places and plazas produced by the private sector in downtown Los Angeles, the Bunker Hills Steps are only a small part of a megadevelopment project, which features two high-rise buildings (the seventy-three-story First Interstate World Center and the fifty-two-story Gas Company Tower) with office, retail, and parking facilities, as well as two major open spaces: the Steps and the West Lawn of the Los Angeles Central Library.

The deal that enabled the development company, Maguire Thomas Partners (MTP), to put together a $2 billion development package has been characterized as the "single biggest commercial real-estate transaction in the history of Los Angeles" (Greengard 1988). It included the building of the two skyscrapers, the renovation and expansion of the Central Library, the development of the library's West Lawn into green space, and the linkage of upper and lower Bunker Hill through the Steps.

The origins of the project go back to 1979, when the debate over the fate of the Central Library was progressing into a spirited fight. Preservationists, the American Institute of Architects, and the Los Angeles Conservancy, along with citizens groups, were fighting to restore the Moorish-style library building designed by Bertram Goodhue in 1926. City officials, however, were flirting with another idea: relocation of the library collections to another site, demolition of the landmark building, and eventual replacement by a pair of office towers.

FIGURE 72
Bunker Hill Steps, 1996.
Photograph by Liette
Gilbert.

As both sides were hanging on to their cause, it became evident that any attempt to develop the site would result in a long litigation process, which would halt any action, including the restoration of the old building, for years.

It was at that point that MTP and Robert Anderson of ARCO jointly funded a $300,000 study to explore financial and design options to save the library. As a means to restore and enlarge the old building, the study proposed the transfer of development rights from the library parcel to an adjacent lot, the building of a high-rise, and the ultimate use of money generated by the building (revenues and taxes) to restore the library. The city quickly expressed its interest. According to a CRA planning director, MTP's proposal was ingenious because it showed the city a way to privately finance the restoration and expansion of the Central Library. The 1979 study became the core of the redevelopment plan, eventually worked out seven years later after a long series of negotiations between MTP and the CRA, the Los Angeles Planning Commission, the Central Library Commission, and City Council.

But by late 1984, the cost of refurbishing the library had jumped to a staggering $110 million because of inflation, the continuing deterioration of the structure, and more ambitious plans for expansion. There was no way that the initially proposed fifty-story office tower could generate enough revenue to cover this cost. So the height of the building had to be increased. There was an obstacle: downtown's FAR restrictions would not allow a building of the height that both developers and planners wanted.[25] It was then that the CRA came up with the concept of a "designated building site." This designation, which was approved by City Council, allowed the pooling together of three different parcels (the library parcel and the parcels that would eventually contain the First Interstate World Center and the Gas Company Tower) into one project site.

Meanwhile, the proposed tower kept growing higher and higher in order to give developers' more leasable floor space, provide the city with more revenues, and meet the increasing cost of renovation. At one point the CRA even suggested the building of an eighty-five-story building. The problem was solved finally when the planners came up with the idea of a second tower. "It was an opportunity to make the deal that much more lucrative," stated Maguire (Greengard 1988).

It was at this point that the idea arose for steps creating a pedestrian link between upper Bunker Hill and the financial core. The Bunker Hill Steps were a developer-initiated project. The agency agreed that part of the costs for the construction of the steps ($12 million in total) would partially fulfill the developers' obligation to provide 1 percent for public art (see chapter 8). The scope of development section in the CRA/MTP agreement summarizes the basic ideas espoused in the design of the Steps:

> Immediately west of the Library Tower [later renamed First Interstate World Center], adjacent to the Wells Fargo Bank property, a series of terraced stairs designed by Lawrence Halprin will be built. These stairs will serve as attractive outdoor open space, as well as provide pedestrian linkage between the intersection of Hope St. and New Hope Place with the north sidewalk at Fifth St. The Steps will include a minimum of one terrace of sufficient dimension to accommodate outdoor dining, sales kiosks, and other activities. . . . All publicly accessible spaces, including sidewalks, lobbies, and the Bunker Hill Steps, shall be attractively landscaped or finished with high-quality materials. Water features will be provided at appropriate locations within or alongside the Bunker Hill Steps.

The CRA had no actual input in the drafting of these design guidelines and the criteria for the "Library Tower" and the Steps, which were put together after the design process was over! According to a MTP representative, "If you read the public document there are specific design criteria, but these were written following MTP's preliminary design proposal. It was not that you have the criteria and the design follows. It was not that the deal made the building, but exactly the opposite."[26]

Because of their function as a public passage, the Bunker Hill Steps are more welcoming to the public than other privately owned open spaces. But, in terms of control, this project is not very different from other open spaces built under the auspices of the private sector. The Steps were dedicated to the city, but MTP is still responsible for their maintenance and security. The space is secured by cameras and a fine-tuned system of roving guards. The developer has the ability to intervene in cases when a behavioral problem arises.

The development of the Steps is a quite typical example of how it is mainly corporate activity that prescribes and alters the urban form of downtown areas. The Steps were not the product of a preexisting city framework or master plan. They were proposed by the private sector and came about as a small part of a larger deal designed to serve private purposes as well as to generate revenues for the city.

Figueroa at Wilshire: leftover space for plaza   Figueroa at Wilshire Tower, which opened in May 1991, is a fifty-two-story office tower in the heart of downtown Los Angeles. The first three levels of the tower contain a grand lobby entered through terraced foyers (see figure 73). The tower is rotated forty-five degrees from the city grid, but this is not readily apparent at the street level because of the architectonic articulation of the facade with a series of openings. The part of the lot not covered by the building (the residual space) is designed as an L-shaped plaza.

The developer of the project was Mitsui Real Estate Development, the largest real estate company in Japan. In the early 1970s, Mitsui, prompted by increasingly strict controls on new development at home and what were perceived as widening opportunities in the United States, decided to venture into the U.S. market. Mitsui Fudosan (U.S.A.), Inc., was formed in 1972. After a

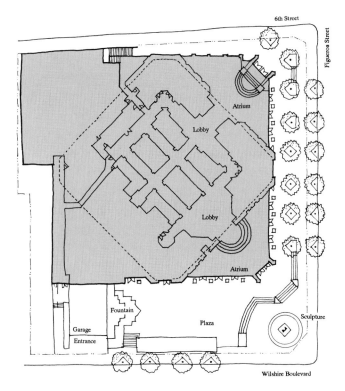

series of projects in Seattle, Honolulu, New York, and San Francisco, Mitsui
Fudosan (U.S.A.) purchased in the early 1980s a prime piece of real estate in
the heart of downtown Los Angeles.

With plans to create a flagship building, Mitsui developers were not content
with the allowable FAR of 6:1. In the early 1980s developers whose property
fell within the CBD plan could increase their FAR to a maximum of 13:1 by
following one of two options: variation or transfer of development rights. Most
developers requested a variation from the CRA. In exchange for the additional
square footage of commercial space, developers had to provide some form of
public amenities. This was in essence an incentive zoning system, the specifics
of which were negotiated between the developer and the agency. Alternatively,
developers could opt for a transfer of development rights (TDR) from adjacent
underdeveloped sites. This transfer was usually a private transaction that in-

volved the exchange of funds between private parties. Once a deal was final-ized, the planning commission had to give its approval, and the CRA was not involved in the process. Mitsui Fudosan (U.S.A.) opted for the latter procedure and in 1983 received approval from the planning commission to increase its FAR to 13:1 by transferring the development rights from five different sites, all of which were in the vicinity of their property.

The TDR document approved by the Planning Commission contained some minimum requirements regarding open space, street improvements, landscap-ing, and art work. On the issue of open space the document stated

> That not less that 15% of the site, not including walkways, shall be open and un-obstructed to the sky and shall be used for park-like purposes (except recreational facilities) for public access, which may include, but is not limited to landscaping, art works, benches and outdoor cafes.
>
> That all open areas not used for buildings, driveways, parking areas, recreational facilities or walks shall be attractively landscaped in accordance with landscape devel-opment plans prepared by a licensed landscape architect or licensed architect. (Los Angeles Department of City Planning 1983, 2)

The owners of the project were more than happy to comply with the open space requirement. As an executive of Mitsui stated, "Public space is very im-portant to enhance our building. We see it very positively. I think that the existence of open space increases the marketability of our project. Our tenants like our atrium [lobby] space and the plaza element. We would have created it even without the requirement. There is nothing that we are doing on this project which is not voluntarily in excess of any requirements."[27]

A CRA planner, however, stated the following regarding the plaza space: "This project was very different than other projects that fell within CRA's ju-risdiction. There were no public easements required or real trading involved. The Agency had not required a public plaza at this site. Basically, the develop-ment proceeded on its own power. This location was not identified as one that needed additional public open space. If it had been built by a retail developer retail could help activate the street."[28]

From the initial stages of the project Mitsui Fudosan reasoned that "Ameri-can architects know what Americans like better than Japanese architects."[29]

Accordingly, they chose a local architectural firm, A. C. Martin Associates, which has been active in designing various downtown buildings for over half a century. In 1986, after some initial frustration in their attempt to market and prelease their building, Mitsui also hired a American firm, Hines Interests Limited Partnership, to oversee the design development, construction, marketing, and leasing of the building, as well as to manage the completed project.

Hines decided to enter into an OPA with the CRA. This was described as a burden by the company, but it clearly had advantages for the developers. As they stated,

> We agreed to enter into an OPA which brings with it a large number of requirements, in order to gain the CRA's endorsement of the project and ratification of the previously existing, but dated Environmental Impact Report, which would have otherwise required a whole drawn-out public process of its own, and possibly a new EIR altogether. In doing so, we subjected ourselves to many requirements, such as the prevailing wage policy and the huge amount of hassle you go through just to show you are in compliance with each policy.

In 1987 Hines negotiated with the CRA the vacation of an alley at the west part of the property. The existence of the OPA allowed the company to convince the city to vacate the alley and deed it to the CRA, and to negotiate directly with the CRA for the acquisition of the alley without a public bid process.

The actual design guidelines for this project were relatively minimal, quite flexible, and generally patterned according to the plans presented to the CRA by developers. As in the case of the Bunker Hill Steps, the design guidelines for the open space were also drafted and incorporated into the OPA after the review of the drawings by the CRA. This relaxed development climate and the CRA's project-to-project approach were actually praised by the building owners. Their sentiments are shared by the development community in Los Angeles. The CRA's aggressive pro-growth approach coincides with private development interests.

As does every open space under private control in downtown Los Angeles, the Figueroa at Wilshire Plaza features a series of plaques that remind users that this is "private property, permission to pass revocable at any time."[30] Security

FIGURE 74
Figueroa at Wilshire,
1996: View of the plaza.
Photograph by Liette
Gilbert.

FIGURE 75
Figueroa at Wilshire
Plaza, 1996: Entrance.
Photograph by Liette
Gilbert.

guards are present inside and outside the building. "The plaza is available for public use but not for undesirables," stated the building owners. "We don't design for homeless people to come in," stated architect David Martin, who speculated that "there is something about the corporate edifice and the very expensive building facades that intimidates the homeless."[31] As are so many other open spaces built by the private sector, this is clearly a corporate milieu, the realm of the white-collar office worker (see figures 74 and 75). Fire and water do not mix in the minds of private developers, regardless of what the sculpture at the corner of Wilshire and Figueroa mischievously implies (see chapter 7 for a description of the sculpture).

EVALUATION OF THE PROCESS: CONSENSUS RATHER THAN CONTENTION

In this era, private market forces have been consistently favored as the only source capable of stimulating urban investment. As has been argued, downtown has been "taken over by another kind of market culture, one made by real estate speculators, institutional investors, and big-time international customers" (Zukin 1991, 198). In such an economic and political climate, the private production of downtown's public realm has been seen as an inevitable phenomenon. In the last two decades almost all major U.S. cities have, following often different planning approaches, relied on the private sector for the supply of their downtown public space. But have the differences in planning and policy affected the final outcome—the form, function and uses of downtown? We will be devoting several of the following chapters to this question, drawing from our eight case studies. We will start here by comparing and evaluating similarities and differences in the production processes in San Francisco and Los Angeles.

As we have discussed, the private provision of public open space became a legislated requirement in San Francisco after the implementation of the 1985 downtown plan. In Los Angeles it is a less formal, quasi-mandatory, negotiated item that has often been traded for special development privileges. Because of its downtown plan, the city of San Francisco is in a stronger position to guide and direct the development process than the city of Los Angeles, where planning is opportunistic and more responsive to the intents of the private sector. What is interesting, however, is that in both cities, provision of public open space through the private sector has never been a stumbling block in negotiations between developers and planners. In none of the eight spaces that we studied did we hear any complaints about the public space requirement. Developers were more than glad to build, maintain, and operate such spaces.

Open spaces, many of which are programmed to include food and retail services, are now standard features of the architectural design. Office and commercial developers perceive open space as an element that is necessary for the enhancement of corporate image, an element that can bring more prestige and invite attention to the buildings. Developers believe that open space increases the profitability of office buildings and helps them attract and retain tenants. In today's competitive office market this is not a small consideration. Open spaces are, in effect, necessary for developers to keep up with the Joneses, to remain competitive in attracting tenants. Images of landscaped plazas dominate the marketing brochures and films that advertise and promote development projects.

Plazas cost little to build and maintain. Typically, costs do not exceed 1 to 2 percent of the overall costs of development. Programming and maintenance costs are typically recovered through rental income. It is not surprising that developers and their corporate clients do not object to providing public open space. In fact it is they who in most cases propose the development of such spaces.

In general, providing plaza space has not been a matter of contention between public and private sectors. The lack of debate over the plazas' design and function can be attributed to the fact that city planners and developers have reached a consensus on what is presumed to constitute the downtown public realm: inward-oriented, landscaped open spaces that have adequate seating, food, and areas of sun and shade and are built with elegant materials for the use of the white-collar office worker. As already mentioned earlier in this chapter, the strategy for downtown development in San Francisco, Los Angeles, and many other American cities is to make downtown efficient for business firms and attractive to visitors and middle- and upper-class residents. The transformation of the aging core into the modern corporate center is truly remarkable. In this context public open spaces are not exactly democratic or public, intention and expectation to the contrary notwithstanding. As will be discussed in a later chapter, this new public realm is designed and furnished to appeal to specific user groups.

The overall goal of downtown transformation and regeneration shared by most American cities has led to many similarities in their urban form, a topic that will be further explored in chapter 7. Like other researchers (for example, Fainstein 1994), we were struck by the extent to which similar economic structures have led to similar physical outcomes, despite quite different political and institutional traditions. The independent deal-making associated with each project has reinforced a fragmentation of the urban form in downtown (Fainstein 1994). Thus, even in San Francisco, despite the existence of a comprehensive master plan and design guidelines for downtown and despite the integrated planning style, the downtown public realm appears to be fragmented and disconnected from the rest of the urban fabric. More emphasis is placed on the aesthetic appearance of the building than on its surrounding urban space. Guidelines promote the idea of public space as a set piece that complements the building but does not "tie in" with the rest of the city. Emphasis is given to the architectural style of the building, the form of the plaza, the colors and texture, the seating and landscaping, but not to urbanistic objectives such as coherence, continuity, linking of districts, and pedestrian connections.

The new downtown public realm is designed to be autonomous from its surrounding context. It is the typical "market landscape," where each product attempts to out perform its immediate competition. In that sense urban plazas and other corporate open spaces are a reflection of a market-driven urbanism —planned, designed, and packaged to satisfy a predetermined clientele. The corporate downtowns in Los Angeles, San Francisco, and other American cities are at odds with the old downtown—the Main Streets and public squares of yesteryear. What is left of the earlier downtown is derelict, ignored, or forgotten, as indeed are many of its denizens. This duality of the modern day American downtown is the focus of our next chapter.

5

It was a Sunday afternoon in the fall of 1987. We had just walked out of the Biltmore Hotel in downtown Los Angeles at the end of a national conference of planning educators. As we crossed the street to enter the parking garage below Pershing Square, we saw a young Latino father with two very young children—maybe two and four years old—caught in somewhat of a pickle on the escalator leading to the parking level below. The father, precariously balanced on the escalator with one child in his arms and a tricycle in his free hand, had already descended halfway down when he discovered—alerted by a child's scream—that his older boy was stuck at the top of the escalator with his bicycle caught between the railings. While the boy kept crying the father was frozen, panicked, and helpless, most likely wishing that he had another set of arms and legs and could instantly transform himself into Superman and climb up the moving steps to help out the boy.

As we dislodged the bike and helped the boy get down the escalator, while his thankful father waited helplessly at the bottom, questions reverberated in our mind: Why were they here? Didn't the father know that Pershing Square was patently dangerous? Certainly it was no place for kids to play or ride their bikes. After all, it was common knowledge that Pershing Square had been taken over by the homeless, the indigent, and the drug dealers and addicts (see figure 76 for a behavior map of Pershing Square drawn by USC planning students in 1988). Office workers avoided it at all cost. The Biltmore, a fine and elegant hotel fronting the square, found it to be a nuisance and a liability and had constructed a new entrance on the opposite side of the block. The Jewelry Mart and the corporate offices facing the square shared the same feelings no doubt. Physically the square had become increasingly derelict and run down (see figure 77). The fountains and the pools had no water in them and had become receptacles for trash and litter. The benches were broken, the rest-

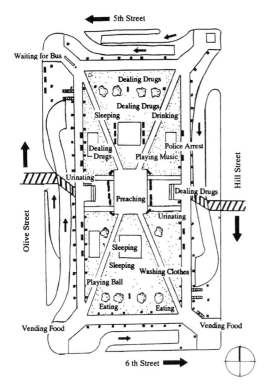

FIGURE 76
Pershing Square: Mapped
activities. USC Urban
Design Studio conducted
by Tridib Banerjee.

FIGURE 77
Pershing Square, 1986:
Aerial view prior to its
facelift. Photograph by
Anastasia Loukaitou-
Sideris.

rooms closed (see figure 78)—to discourage the homeless and the drug dealers—and the once green lawn had long ago succumbed to ever expanding patches of dirt. Pershing Square was biding its time to be renovated, waiting for its old and worn face to be lifted, for the bags and the wrinkles to be removed.

We will come to the face-lift of Pershing Square presently, for it represents an important symbolic act in the urban design saga of downtown Los Angeles. Returning to our story of the young father and children, the question remains, why were they there? The obvious answer, it seems, is that there are few public parks where residents of downtown and its immediate neighborhood can take

FIGURE 78
Pershing Square, 1986:
Condition before facelift.
Photograph by Anastasia
Loukaitou-Sideris.

the children for a Sunday outing. This father and his children were certainly residents of the downtown area, and we suspect that they were immigrants and new to the area. They did not seem particularly poor. Both the father and the children were well clothed, the children had their own bikes, and the father could afford the five-dollar fee for parking in the garage. We don't know if this family and others like it were regular weekend users of Pershing Square, a part of the weekend social life that thrived undaunted by the indigents and pushers, or whether this was a mere aberration. We tend to think that it was the latter, and that it is quite possible that this father, realizing his mistake, was in the process of making a quick exit.

THE DUALISM OF PRIVATE AND PUBLIC SPACES

According to the recently published *Los Angeles Downtown Strategic Plan* (1993), some 26,000 people live inside the "freeway ring" today. In the Bunker Hill and South Park areas, isolated pockets of upper- and middle-income residents (mainly households without children) account for about the third of the population, but the remaining are poor. Most live in single room occupancy units (commonly known as SROs) and shelters for the homeless. Some 3,200 children, mainly of Latino descent, live in run-down establishments of the downtown frame. They reside mainly in the Eastside Industrial District or Central City East in overcrowded housing surrounded by parking lots, warehouses, and industrial sites.[1] They play in the streets, abandoned industrial sites, and empty parking lots in the midst of trash and litter. This is the ultimate paradox. Although modern American downtowns have created a significant amount of corporate open space through mandates or negotiations, there is little open space that serves the poor residents.[2]

This is not the only paradox that manifests itself in the two faces of downtown urban form. This dualism has several dimensions, all of which are imbedded in the social ecology of downtown. One important dimension is the sharp contrast between the private and the public realms. A second is the contrast between the new and prosperous "Gold Coast" (Davis 1987) financial and office district and the old and languishing Main Street of an earlier era. A third dimension is the separation of the white-collar and the blue-collar workforces and the contrast between their respective work environments. A fourth has to do with the spatial expression of the increasing income gap between the rich and the poor, its telltale signs being the contrasting built forms. The final dimension of the dualism is the First World versus Third World dichotomy, which is strengthened as the growing immigrant labor force working in the downtown sweatshops contributes to the street life and the upper- and middle-income, professional, white-collar, and mainly white office workers remain cloistered in sanitized office towers, clubs, cocktail lounges, and restaurants.

These parallel dimensions are in part outcomes of market processes reflected in the landscape of the market economy. Others result from the changing dynamics of a global economic order. Given this reality that defines the political economy of urban form, it is not clear that the urban design efforts we have reviewed so far could have stemmed the tide of the inexorable market processes. In fact many of the well-meaning efforts of urban design may have further exacerbated the dualistic structure of the downtown urban form. We will examine these issues later in this chapter.

Paul Goldberger, the architectural and urban critic for the *New York Times*, questioned the limit of urban design in an article entitled "Why Design Can't

Transform Cities?"; speaking of New York, he seemed particularly concerned about the widening gap between the opulent private space and the deteriorating public domain. "New York has always been a city in which richness and poverty shared turf, but never so dramatically as now. The city's great monuments, from Grand Central Terminal to Grant's Tomb, house homeless people; so do the terraces of Central Park and entryways of churches. It is so common to see vagrants on the sidewalk that few people pause any longer to notice them; they have become part of the landscape, like street lamps and park benches" (Goldberger 1989, H1). What concerned Goldberger most was a growing loss of humanity in American cities—not that they have become more "harsh and dirty," but that they have "become so indifferent to the very idea of the public realm." He comments further: "Today in Los Angeles and Miami, in Boston and Chicago, as well as New York, we build great, shiny skyscrapers, but they are private, not public. We build enclosed arcades and shopping malls, but they, too, are private. Corporate office towers but not housing, private arcades but not parks: these choices stand as the symbols of our age."

As we have seen in the previous chapters, development efforts to create spaces that are presumptively public have been part and parcel of the new urban design downtown, but the publicness of these spaces remain indeterminate and contested (Ellickson 1996). It is best to think of the use of these spaces not as a right but as a privilege, one that is limited to white-collar office workers, as dictated by the social ecology and design of downtown space. The fear of crime and so-called incivilities associated with the public domain has increased security and surveillance measures in these corporate spaces. In an essay entitled "Fortress L.A.," Mike Davis (1990) graphically describes these design features in his critical interpretation of the emerging architecture of Los Angeles. William H. Whyte (1988) has also criticized the kind of "fortress architecture" that isolates major downtown projects from the surrounding streets.

Aside from the qualitative differences between the private and public spaces, there is also a major inequity in the way these spaces serve the general public. There is a gross mismatch between the location of corporate open spaces and the demand for public open space. The map of downtown Los Angeles in figure 79 identifies streets with major pedestrian traffic and areas that the CRA has designated as major pedestrian districts. The map shows clearly that

DOWNTOWN LOS ANGELES
Pedestrian Activity

Pedestrian Zone (Designated)

Moderate Intensity
High Intensity

the older, historic core of downtown is the least served by open spaces and other pedestrian amenities, while the new downtown of recent years seems overstocked with such benefits. A similar map of San Francisco shows a more equitable distribution of open spaces (see figure 80), although close scrutiny reveals that most of the open spaces south of Market Street did not exist until recently (Hartman 1984). Furthermore, most of them are corporate open

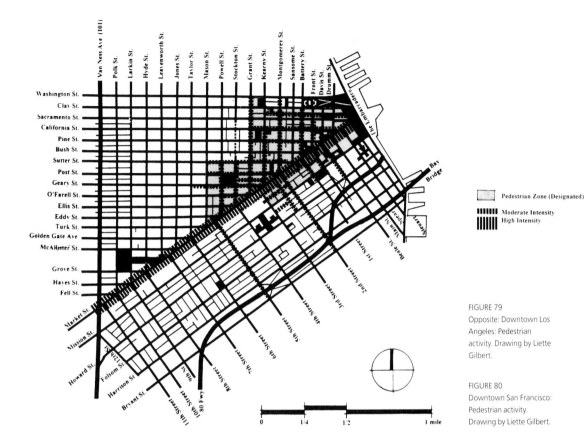

Washington St.
Clay St.
Sacramento St.
California St.
Pine St.
Bush St.
Sutter St.
Post St.
Geary St.
O'Farell St.
Ellis St.
Eddy St.
Turk St.
Golden Gate Ave
McAllister St.

Grove St.
Hayes St.
Fell St.

Van Ness Ave (101)
Polk St.
Larkin St.
Hyde St.
Leavenworth St.
Jones St.
Taylor St.
Mason St.
Powell St.
Stockton St.
Grant St.
Kearny St.
Montgomery St.
Sansome St.
Battery St.
Front St.
Davis St.
Drumm St.

The Embarcadero

Bay Bridge

Market St.
Mission St.
Howard St.
Folsom St.
Harrison St.
Bryant St.
11th Street
10th Fwy
9th St.
8th Street
7th Street
6th Street
5th Street
4th Street
3rd Street
2nd Street
1st Street
Beale St.
Main St.
Spear St.

☐ Pedestrian Zone (Designated)
▥ Moderate Intensity
▦ High Intensity

0   1/4   1/2   1 mile

FIGURE 79
Opposite: Downtown Los
Angeles: Pedestrian
activity. Drawing by Liette
Gilbert.

FIGURE 80
Downtown San Francisco:
Pedestrian activity.
Drawing by Liette Gilbert.

spaces—Rincon Center, Hill Plaza, One Hundred First Plaza, and the like—where the denizens of skid row are not welcome, notwithstanding the intent of city planners to create truly public spaces. Even in San Francisco's massive Yerba Buena project, which features some new public spaces south of Market Street, including George Moscone Convention Center, uses of these spaces are carefully monitored.

In Los Angeles, even the preeminent public space, historic Pershing Square, has recently been "reclaimed." The new urban design symbolizes a territorial claim—a claim that the space now belongs to the new downtown of corporate owners and their white-collar office workers. In the next section, we will consider the history of the recent urban design efforts to reclaim this public space.

REINVENTING PERSHING SQUARE: GENTRIFICATION OF A PUBLIC SPACE

Located on the "symbolic economic boundary line between those who live and those who work in downtown Los Angeles" (Pershing Square 1989, 1.2), Pershing Square was created in 1870 out of a federal land grant. With its informal collection of trees and shrubs and its picket fences to keep the cattle and horses out, it served as a public commons for many years. At the turn of the century it was redesigned in a more formal layout, with fountains and sculptures, and given its present name. Newly constructed commercial and cultural buildings, including the Biltmore Hotel and the Philharmonic Auditorium, since demolished, surrounded the square. The period between the two world wars represented the glorious years of Pershing Square, when it truly was the heart of an upbeat downtown. Its decline began after World War II, when the original downtown lost its preeminence with the centrifugal forces of freeway development, suburban expansion, and growth of competing centers. This metropolitan decentralization in turn led to downtown urban renewal projects as part of an attempt to hold the center. But thirty years of redevelopment efforts that produced a new financial and business district on the west side managed to further exacerbate the steady decline of Pershing Square.

Pershing Square was a forgotten public space until the mid-1980s, when the leading edge of downtown redevelopment finally engulfed this historic square. The Biltmore Hotel had gone through a major renovation including the addition of a new tower. Barely a block west, the First Interstate tower was complete, and the library complex was being renovated and expanded. On the northeast corner of Pershing Square, the elegant Gas Company Tower designed by Richard Keating with a massive mural by Frank Stella was finished at about the same time. A few years earlier, on the block southwest of the square, the historic Oviat building was renovated by Wayne Ratkovich, an influential downtown developer specializing in historic buildings. The Red Line subway construction was about to begin, and Pershing Square was designated as a station site with a portal from the square itself. Major public and private investments were being poured into the area. There was reason for the property owners facing Pershing Square to be uneasy about the derelict and languishing public space.

The 1984 Olympics created an opportunity for recapturing the square, although plans to revive the square began much earlier (Kaplan 1983; Soble

FIGURE 81
Pershing Square
Competition, 1986:
Winning design by SITE.
Courtesy of SITE
Environmental Design.

1984). In the summer of that year the square was transformed into a temporary "French countryside" for an alfresco black-tie opening party thrown by the downtown patrons of the square (Reichl 1984; Gindick 1984). Although the Olympic festivities were short-lived, the effort to recapture Pershing Square from the drug dealers and indigents began in earnest soon thereafter.

The Central City Association, an organization representing downtown business interests, created the Pershing Square Management Association to initiate the revitalization efforts for the square. In conjunction with the mayor's Office, the Community Redevelopment Agency (CRA), the Department of Parks and Recreation, and the Cultural Affairs Commission, the group organized an international design competition for the square. In the middle of 1986 the juries reviewed some 242 entries from seventeen countries. The jury was held in Pershing Square itself, where all the entries were on display. The winning scheme was prepared by a New York firm, SITE Projects, Inc. Their scheme for Pershing Square was a "metaphorical carpet" that attempted to capture various aspects of the "Los Angeles experience" (see figure 81). But as it turned out the SITE design, with a projected cost of over $20 million, proved to be too expensive. Furthermore, according to Leon Whiteson, an architectural and urban critic for the *Los Angeles Times*, the design failed to address the fundamental social question: Whose park is it? Seemingly unaware of the rhetorical nature of his question—given the obvious intent of the downtown business interests to recapture the square—Leon Whiteson (1994) asked, quite seriously, "Does it belong, as it has historically, to the largely Anglo Bunker Hill–Grand Avenue commercial establishment? Can it connect with the Latino population of Broadway? And what about the rights of those urban casualties who find some measure of refuge from the dangers of Skid Row in its open lawns?"

In 1991, Maguire Thomas Partners, perhaps the most influential actor in downtown redevelopment, led the effort to develop an affordable plan for Pershing Square. The firm had just finished the complicated Central Library project and had established a good working relationship with the CRA. In approaching the new plan, the firm tacitly acknowledged the existence of two very different downtowns, described in terms not of old and new, or rich and poor, but of Anglo and Latino. Nelson Rising, then a Maguire Thomas senior partner, commented, "We recognize that making a connection between the two main constituencies that border the park is crucial to its success." Using a stronger term, Whiteson spoke of the need for the new plan to breach the "urban apartheid" that split up the central city in segregated enclaves (quoted in Whiteson 1994).

In a seemingly conciliatory gesture, Maguire Thomas hired well-known Mexican architect Ricardo Legoretta and Philadelphia-based landscape architect Laurie Olin to develop the new scheme. The design itself, however, appeared to be less than conciliatory, opting to divide the square into two parts: a northern section with an amphitheater and a grassy area with benches ostensibly for the Anglo crowd, and a southern section for other users, focusing on a shallow pond connected to a screen wall with a dramatic waterfall, and an egregious 120-foot purple campanile that apparently marks the division between the two parts (see figures 82 and 83). The design is apparently inspired by the traditional Mexican plaza—the *zócalo*—with its bright colors that are the signature of the architect's postmodern "Latinismo" style.

The Latin theme in the design of the square is gratuitous and puzzling. The indigent users of the square shared poverty, substance use, and despair, not a

FIGURE 82
Pershing Square after
the facelift, 1996: New
fountain. Photograph
by Liette Gilbert.

FIGURE 83
Pershing Square after the
facelift, 1996: Campanile.
Photograph by Liette
Gilbert.

Latino heritage. Indeed indigents represented all ethnic groups: Anglos, Latinos, African Americans, Native Americans, and so on. As far as the Latino users of Broadway and Main Street were concerned, it was not clear that the rhetoric of design necessarily translated into any special appeal for the residents and shoppers of the "other" downtown. Whiteson had the same misgivings and felt that the design "mannerisms may be too artful and abstract to attract the populist Broadway crowds" (Whiteson 1994).

The apparent Anglo-Latino polarity of downtown Los Angeles continued to be a convenient opening line, even when Whiteson managed to ask more fundamental questions about the dualistic nature of the downtown urban form: "Will it dissolve the stubborn social membrane that isolates Latinos from Anglos, Broadway from Bunker Hill? And will it help heal the widening metropolitan rift between have's and have-not's made blatant in the contrast between spruce downtown office workers and their homeless and desperate fellow citizens?" (Whiteson 1994).

The irony of reinventing Pershing Square is that while the park has been rebuilt according to Legoretta's postmodern "Latinismo" design, and the denizens have been shooed away under careful surveillance of the Los Angeles police, the plaza, although colorful—in fact, somewhat phantasmagoric—is basically a brooding and empty space (see figure 84). There are occasional noon concerts organized by agencies responsible for the reinvented square, but they lack the spontaneity, verve, and bustle of the multiethnic crowd of the Broadway corridor.

Such irony notwithstanding, Pershing Square is an example of how urban design can be used as a tool for "reclaiming public space" (Ellickson 1996). There is a growing concern today, authors like Ellickson argue, that the incivilities of public spaces—panhandling, vagrancy, people sleeping in parks or on sidewalks, and other "street nuisances"—are on the rise and are a major source of annoyance for the general public. He also suggests that such incivilities are particularly common in the public spaces of American downtowns, and argues that America's downtowns will not remain viable unless street users are seen as having responsibilities as well as rights (Ellickson 1996). While the legal scholars debate the constitutional rights of the homeless and the destitute, some communities have already developed measures and ordinances to discourage

FIGURE 84
Pershing Square after the facelift, 1996: Emptiness. Photograph by Liette Gilbert.

such incivilities. Ellickson himself proposes zoning as a mechanism for insuring civility in public spaces.

As we have discussed elsewhere, downtown corporate plazas, including Pershing Square, have already used not so subtle design mechanisms, in combination with strong surveillance measures and the right of exclusion, to obviate such incivilities in these spaces. Critics like Mike Davis (1990) and Steven Flusty (1994) have referred to them as "fortress architecture" and "architecture of paranoia." Politically, design mechanisms are more expedient than having to legislate civility in public spaces. That it seems to have worked only accentuates the inequities between the two downtowns.

There are other examples. Scollay Square in Boston was similarly redeveloped in the sixties through an urban renewal project and converted to a sanitized urban space—the Government Center. Similar approaches are being tried today in other downtowns. Most notable is the grand urban design scheme currently underway for reinventing New York's historic Times Square.

Big change is afoot, under the leadership of the Disney Company, to convert Times Square from a center for street crime and adult theaters and bookstores to the center of the entertainment industry (Netzer 1978).

THE THIRD WORLD METAPHOR

The rhetoric of Pershing Square revitalization planning suggested that the reinvented square would serve the important function of uniting the two downtowns—the Anglo and the Latino. This reference to the Anglo and Latino downtowns is in a way a tacit acknowledgment of the increasing "Third World-ization" of not just Los Angeles but also other major cities, especially

FIGURE 85
Opposite, left: Los
Angeles, 1996: Broadway
Street. Photograph by
Liette Gilbert.

FIGURE 86
Opposite, right: Los
Angeles, 1996: Mural on
Broadway Street
reflecting Latino heritage.
Photograph by Liette
Gilbert.

FIGURE 87
Los Angeles, 1996: Mural
on Spring Street
celebrating the Latino
origins of the city.
Photograph by Liette
Gilbert.

New York and Miami. In Los Angeles, the downtown is centrally located within an inner-city area that a *Daily News* article has described as the "nuevo Los Angeles"—the Los Angeles of the immigrant population (see figure 85). This area includes parts of Hollywood and the neighborhoods of South Central and East Los Angeles and contains over a million people, the majority of whom were born outside the United States. The concept of a Latino downtown is really an oblique reference to a downtown of immigrants, where although Spanish may be the dominant language, one may also hear a cacophony of Chinese, Korean, Tagalog, and other dialects. Author David Rieff (1991), who has called Los Angeles the "capital of the Third World," would certainly agree (see figures 86 and 87). Speaking of California as a whole, he argued that the state is now "at least as much part of the Third World as the First, and growing more so every day. A simple drive downtown would have confirmed this fact . . . " (Rieff 1991, 118).

Nuevo Los Angeles' dual downtown of the Anglo core and the multiethnic immigrant periphery may indeed be seen as both a microcosm and an outcome of the emerging global economic order. Various analysts have suggested as much (see Mollenkopf and Castells 1991; Sassen 1991; Portes, Castells, and Benton 1989). What the corporate planners and developers see as a dual downtown consisting of an Anglo and a multi-ethnic part can also be described as having a First World core surrounded by a Third World periphery.

What is intriguing about this core-periphery metaphor is that it echoes the model of global economic order suggested by the Latin American "dependency" school (see Frank 1967, for example) many years ago and supported by other scholars (Amin 1974; Wallerstein 1984). In this model, the Western industrialized countries were seen as comprising the prosperous core of a global economy, served by a periphery of primary-resource-producing, poor Third World countries, who are the market for manufactured goods produced in the core countries. In effect, this was a model of neocolonialism, and it was quite influential as an alternative explanation for Third World underdevelopment and poverty.

In this image of a global economic order, underdevelopment was seen as causally linked to development. The Third World was always seen as dependent on the First World. This theoretical framework also led to an explanation of the dualistic economy—that is, the existence of an informal, traditional economy functioning parallel to a formal, modern economy—and, ultimately, of the dualistic urban form that is typical of many Third World cities (see Castells 1977b). Brazilian geographer Milton Santos (1975, 197) further elaborated this relationship between formal and informal economies in national and regional urban space as a type of "spatial dialectics."

Santos's model of the dialectics of shared space provides, as an interesting by-product of this Third World metaphor, a theoretical framework for looking at the dualism and competition between public and private space. The movement to recapture public space—as manifested in revitalization efforts from Pershing Square to Times Square, and as defended by their protagonists like Robert Ellickson (1996) and Fred Siegel (1991), who argue that the very survival of

American downtowns is in jeopardy if such initiatives are not taken—can be seen as an argument in this dialectic. Downtown urban design has so far reflected little understanding or acknowledgment of this essential dialectic of shared space. The rhetoric of Pershing Square revitalization managed to bring forth a tacit admission of this reality, but not much else.

Yet a form of dualism—separation or division by income and occupation—has always existed in American cities. In the story "South of the Slot," Jack London talked about the division of San Francisco by the Market Street slot for cable cars. "Old San Francisco . . . was divided by the Slot. . . . North of the Slot were the theatres, hotels, and shopping districts, the banks, and the staid, respectable business houses. South of the Slot were the factories, slums, laundries, machine shops, boiler works, and the abodes of the working class" (quoted in Hartman 1984, 54).

As Chester Hartman (1984) points out, there are similar "South of Market" districts in many American cities, and these districts historically have provided the important economic function of sheltering and maintaining a reserve army of skilled and unskilled workers in an industrial economy. In his analysis of the politics of the Yerba Buena project and the neighborhood opposition to it, he emphasizes the historical social function of this district.

In order for urban design to mediate in this spatial dialectic of a polarized downtown, the designers must understand the political economy of the emerging global economic order that has produced the more recent dualism of American cities. The new dualism we consider here must be examined in the context of what H. V. Savitch (1988) describes as "post-industrial cities." Referring to New York, he discusses two very conspicuous social orders. On the one hand, there are the prosperous, well-educated, professional individuals, either single or living in small households, who enjoy a privatized world of personal services, security, education, and leisure. On the other hand, there is the order of poverty and despair consisting of people who are poor and live in public housing, ride public transit, and depend on public services and welfare. Often they are homeless, and they sleep in streets and on park benches. Savitch argues that the postindustrial economy has passed them by. As the demand for postindustrial skills increases, they fall further behind. We might add to Savitch's observation that these are mainly the people who are increasingly seen as the root of incivility in public places and as a growing threat to the public order. The prosperous social order of Savitch's New York meanwhile retreats to its private city, what Trevor Boddy (1992) refers to as the "analogous city." This metaphorical retreat is what former Labor Secretary Robert Reich calls "secession of the successful" (Reich 1991, 16).

Dualism is the theme of a collection of articles edited by Fainstein, Gordon, and Harloe (1992). Focusing again on New York, they talk about two separate economies with quite distinct loci of neighborhoods and social systems. Like Savitch, they too refer to the lifestyle of, on the one hand, a "new service class" that has "reconquered" parts of the inner city by gentrification and, on the other hand, the people who live outside or at the margin of the labor market, yet in close proximity to the former group. The growing ranks of the latter group are not localized to traditional skid row or "South of the Slot" districts of old downtowns; they have now infiltrated the exclusive parts of downtown. This new dualism smacks of the typical Third World city, where slums and squatters coexist with luxury hotels, shopping districts, high-rise condominiums, and offices. It is not surprising, therefore, that the Third World theme permeates the portrayals of New York and Los Angeles in popular literature and media. Consider, for example, Tom Wolfe's (1987) *Bonfire of the Vanities*; a CBS *Sixty Minutes* segment entitled "Calcutta on the Hudson"; a set of articles and editorials published in the *New York Times* under the title "New Calcutta" (see *New York Times* 1987, 20, A25; 1988, E10; 1989, A18; 1990, E20); Kristin Koptiuch's (1991) "Third-Worlding at Home"; and of course, David Rieff's (1991) *Los Angeles: Capital of the Third World*.

The dualistic model of New York and other Western cities is not without its critiques. Essays edited by John Mollenkopf and Manuel Castells (1991) on New York City contain an extended critique of the "dual city" metaphor. They have argued that "the complexity of New York's social structure cannot be reduced to a dichotomy between the two extremes of the scale of income distribution." They base their account on a six-fold division of the occupational structure of New York City, distinguishing between an upper stratum of executives, managers, and professionals, on the one hand, and clerical workers, service workers, and those who remain at the margin of or outside the formal labor force, on the other. They suggest that while the interactions between these six groups are many, the dominant role is played by "the upper professionals of the corporate sector who form an organizational nucleus for the wider social stratum of managers and professionals." They further argue that the "remaining social strata occupy increasingly diverse positions." Thus, "cultural, economic and political polarization in New York takes the form of a contrast between a comparatively cohesive core of professionals and a disorganized periphery fragmented by race, ethnicity, gender, occupational and industrial location, and the spaces they occupy" (Mollenkopf and Castells 1991, 254).

These are important observations that point out that the notion of dualism does not necessarily capture the complex dynamics of social and economic changes in a city like New York. There are many dimensions of inequality and polarization that involve ethnicity, gender, occupation, and income. In addition, as Jonathan Raban (1974) would argue, a metropolis like New York is intrinsically "soft," intractable, and ephemeral, and it eludes easy categorization. The city is full of many parallel realities, overlapping experiences, incessant mutations. Studies of actual Third World cities—which are the source of the dualism metaphor—have also shown that such categorizations are untenable. Even the nexus between the urban formal and informal economies is quite complex, and the relationship can be seen more as a continuum than a dichotomy (Banerjee 1993b; Santos 1975).

These caveats notwithstanding, one cannot overlook the very different economic and social systems and built forms that coexist in contradistinction to each other in downtown environments. Although we must be cautious about using the First World–Third World metaphor, there is little doubt that many of the features of the "lower circuit" of Third World social systems are manifest today in the two faces of American downtowns: homelessness, marginality, and most significantly, a growing informal economy.[3]

HOMELESSNESS AND THE INFORMAL ECONOMY

Much has been written about the extent and causes of homelessness in the United States (Rossi 1989; Dear and Wolch 1987; Jencks 1994). Although estimates of actual homeless are often debated (Ellickson 1990), almost all major cities report some homeless population, with cities like Los Angeles, San Francisco, and New York reporting the largest numbers (Dear and Wolch 1987). Although precise estimates are not available, it is safe to assume that the bulk of the homeless population is found in the skid row district or in the margin of the downtown area.[4] The median age of the downtown homeless is thirty-five to thirty-eight years, close to one-half of them are homeless for six months or more, and interestingly one-half to three-fourths of them have a high school or college education. They are predominantly male (three-fourths or more) and minority ethnic groups (about one-half black and one-quarter Latino). About one-third are homeless because of substance abuse, but one-third to one-half are homeless because of lack of money or job (Wolch/Dear Consultants 1992). And of course they are drawn to the downtown location because, first, there are service providers and, second, it is easier to survive in the niches and crevices of abandoned buildings and untended back alleys, streets, and public places.

While most of the homeless are not squatters, and U.S. cities will never tolerate the type of extensive squatter settlements commonly seen in Third World cities, a growing number of squatters can be seen these days in vacant lots, under freeway bridges, and even in underutilized parking lots. Because they are still small in number relative to the vast expanses of urban wasteland that characterize much of downtown, these residents of "cardboard condominiums"—as they are jokingly called—are ignored by the authorities unless there is political pressure to do something about this "problem." When in the late eighties the business owners in the vicinity of Los Angeles' skid row district complained about the homeless on their front step affecting business, Mayor Bradley's administration in Los Angeles created a holding area—not unlike the internment camps of the World War II era—and rounded up the downtown homeless and brought them to the camp. Subsequently a more formal but smaller "tent city" of geodesic domes was established in an abandoned parking lot with downtown corporate funding and under the leadership of Ted Hayes, an activist for the downtown homeless.

Today the homeless problem is tacitly accepted as structural and enduring. The recent *Los Angeles Downtown Strategic Plan* includes recommendations that concede this point (Community Redevelopment Agency 1993).[5]

Beyond the homeless problems, American downtowns are also experiencing marginality, a term commonly used to refer to the condition of the population of the lower circuit in Latin American cities.[6] In the United States, we see at least two types of marginality. One type is defined by the homeless and those who are in the margin of the labor market, as discussed by Susan Fainstein, Ian Gordon, and Michael Harloe (1992). The latter have fallen out of the labor market because of obsolete skills, or have not acquired necessary skills to be absorbed by the labor market of the formal-sector economy. They are the "proto-proletariats" (see McGee 1982) of the postindustrial society. The second type of marginality is an attribute of the immigrant culture of the illegal aliens. They assemble at the street corners in the periphery of downtown, patiently waiting for a chance to be hired as day laborers. Because they are mostly undocumented, they are willing to work for wages far below the minimum.

Finally, we must consider the rise of the informal economy and its pervasiveness in the older, poorer face of the downtown. Alejandro Portes, Manuel Castells, and Laura Benton have argued that the "informal economy, in all the ambiguity of its connotations, has come to constitute a major structural feature of society, both in industrialized and less developed countries" (1989, 1). In her study of the informal economy of New York City, Saskia Sassen-Koob (1983) makes several observations. First, the informal economy has grown rapidly in recent years. Second, the informal economy permeates a whole range of industrial sectors, including apparel manufacturing, construction, vending, toy manufacturing, and the like. Third, other sectors such as packaging, photo engraving, jewelry making, and the like are also, to a lesser extent, affected by this economy. Fourth, informal economy activities tend to locate in densely populated areas with a large immigrant populations. Fifth, emergent sweat shop–type activities are very much a part of this sector. Finally, there are indications that such activities are dispersing to various parts of the metropolitan area.

In the case of Miami, Alex Stepick (1982) reports a heterogeneous informal economy, shaped by ethnicity and immigration. He argues that there are two distinct informal sectors, one of which is closely linked to the mainstream economy, while the other is isolated from the formal economy. The former is developed by Cuban immigrants, while the latter is mainly a result of the more recent Haitian immigration. Although systematic studies are sparse, it is common knowledge that in the case of Los Angeles, the garment industry is heavily integrated with the informal economy. At the metropolitan scale, much of the informal economy is in the service sector, which includes personal services, domestic help, gardening, home repair, and the like. Downtown serves as the

FIGURE 88
Los Angeles, 1996:
Vendor in Pueblo Plaza on
El Grito Day. Photograph
by Liette Gilbert.

consumer market for the people who earn their living in the informal economy (see figure 88). Broadway and many side streets and alleys have become the physical setting for this informal economy.

Authors like Castells (1977b), Mollenkopf and Castells (1991), Fainstein, Gordon, and Harloe (1992), King (1996), Savitch (1988), and Sassen (1991) have argued that the current metamorphosis of Western cities and their CBDs is the inexorable outcome of a changing global economic order. Global capital, transnational and multinational corporate interests, and investment decisions have shaped not only the highly volatile labor markets but also the urban form. In an international, competitive marketplace both capital and labor have become quite mobile, despite formal barriers. Thus, it is this global transnational and multinational capital—first Japanese, Canadian, British and German, now Taiwanese and Hong Kong—that is transforming the new downtown skyline. At the same time massive numbers of immigrants—many illegal—from the poor rural areas of Third World countries are now pouring into the downtown, thus shaping its landscape of marginality.

CHALLENGES FOR URBAN DESIGN

Integration or, more appropriate, mediation of these disparate but parallel transformations in the built form is the single most critical challenge for downtown urban design. The integration of the two downtowns and the assimilation of the periphery into the core will remain formidable tasks. In the absence of an alternative vision, the dystopian scenario of *Blade Runner* will remain the operational model of assimilation and integration.

The recently completed strategic plan for downtown Los Angeles, inspired by the ideals of "new urbanism" (see Katz 1994; Calthorpe 1993), projects a vision of integration through physical design and planning (Downtown Strategic Plan Advisory Committee 1993). According to this vision, two pairs of north-south *avenidas* and two pairs of east-west *avenidas* will strategically link all parts of the total area. Four civic squares will be located at the intersections of these avenidas. In addition, there will be neighborhood parks in residential areas within one-quarter mile walking distance of future residents of downtown. Will the strategic plan make a difference, or will this be Pershing Square on a larger scale? We will return to this point in our concluding chapter.

6

The new downtown corporate spaces reflect some of the broader changes that have occurred in public life. The loss of public life is a familiar critique of contemporary urbanism, especially when it is compared to preindustrial, precapitalist forms of urban development. More recently some have argued that public life has undergone a transformation rather than a decline (see Brill 1989). In this chapter we will review some of the common debates and discourses on this subject. In addition, we will investigate the forces that led to changes in the public realm and analyze their impact on contemporary downtowns and their uses.

A consideration of public life should begin with a definition of terms. "Publicness" and "privateness" are concepts by which our Western liberal society "organizes such areas of social life as involve ascriptions of access, agency and interest" (Benn and Gaus 1983, 25). Public life involves relatively open and universal social contexts, in contrast to private life, which is intimate, familiar, shielded, controlled by the individual, and shared only with family and friends.[1]

Public life traditionally combined a number of characteristics: it was directed toward some common benefit; it was open and accessible to everyone for observation or participation; it was shared by a diverse group of people and thus required tolerance of different interests and behaviors (Brill 1989); and, finally, it was characterized by common tradition, coherence, and continuity, which transcended an individual's life span (Arendt 1959).

Public life performed several functions and served many goals: it was a forum for political action and representation, the political realm par excellence (Arendt 1959); a common ground for social interaction, intermingling, and communication; and a stage for social learning, personal development, and information exchange. Public life often helped shape public concepts of gover-

175

nance, religion, and social structure. Public activities included entertainment and ceremonials, socializing and playing, commerce and marketing, political meetings and demonstrations, distribution and collection of news, water collection, and sometimes even punishment and executions (Lofland 1973).

Many of these public activities took place at the city center, which was a shared, common ground, the focus of social, political, and religious activities. As we discussed in chapter 2, public spaces were symbolically placed at the heart of the city center. The Spanish plaza, the French place d'armes, the New England common, were all built to facilitate civic functions, sharpen civic awareness, and remind people of their civic privileges and duties (Jackson 1984b).

Public life has changed in a variety of ways. In previous centuries engagement in public life was a daily necessity for all citizens (Brill 1990), but today it is a matter of choice. Many formerly public activities have disappeared or retreated inside the private realm of the household. The polarization of urban society, which sociologist Richard Sennett traces back to the development of nineteenth-century capitalism, has found a physical expression. Today, many find the public realm inhospitable, unpredictable, and intimidating. Those who can afford to have tried to shield and protect themselves from its vagaries (Sennett 1977).

Public behavior and decorum have also been transformed. As we will later discuss, there are certain expected and often enforced rules of behavior in contemporary public places. As Sennett explains (quoted in Hitt et al. 1990, 52),

> For Americans today, the public realm is a silent realm, which is not the way it once was. In the 18th century both men and women were very verbal in public. The public places—coffeehouses, assembly rooms, court halls—were sociable places. Silence began during the Industrial Revolution when women were driven from the public realm. Their presence in public was suddenly considered unseemly, unladylike, particularly for middle-class women. They were confined at home. In the 1980's, when women began to return to public space, it was only in terms of consumption—going to stores, shopping.

Many sociologists stress the increasing social apathy toward public life by pointing at low voter turnouts and low participation rates in political and communal activities. They argue that public life has become spatially disjointed, dispersed, and discontinuous, and they refer to studies of social networks that reveal the limited numbers of those actively involved in public causes (Sennett 1977; Gottdiener 1985).

Social scientists have long lamented the social alienation, depersonalization, and emptiness of public life in the complex environment of the American city. As early as 1938, sociologist Wirth wrote, "Cities generally, and American cities in particular, comprise a motley of people and cultures of highly differentiated modes of life between which there often is only the faintest communication, the greatest indifference, the broadest tolerance, occasionally bitter strife, but always the sharpest contrast" (Wirth 1938, 20).

The loss of the political character of the public realm is emphasized in the acclaimed work of Hannah Arendt, *The Human Condition* (1959). More recent sociological works are also concerned with the decline of community in American cities. Richard Sennett (1977) bemoans the "fall of public man" in contemporary urban societies. He argues that public life is in a state of decay and emphasizes a loss of civility resulting from urban residents' obsession with private life. David Riesman's (1961) characterization of society as a "lonely crowd" and his discussion of a form of social organization where "inner direction" is the dominant trait for individuals underscore this trend. Lyn Lofland (1973) argues that finding themselves in a "world of strangers," modern urbanites seek to minimize encounters with the unknown when in public. They do so by privatizing space, creating home territories, urban villages, and exclusive clubs, all of which form a comfortable cocoon. These strategies are similar to what Erving Goffman (1969, 38–42) describes as "involvement shields"—a variety of barriers and negative sanctions that individuals construct when in public. In a similar vein, Stanley Milgram (1970) argues that the modern urbanite draws boundaries in certain social transactions, develops filtering devices to block all but the most superficial forms of social involvement, and allocates less time to social activities. All these mechanisms not only protect but also estrange the individual from the public environment. Christopher Alexander (1967, 61) argues that the modern urbanite suffers from an "autonomy-withdrawal syndrome." He claims that urbanization has allowed individuals to withdraw from the more demanding public realm into their private worlds. In preindustrial societies, intimate contacts were characterized by face-to-face association and cooperation. However, modern urban societies have found no way of sustaining intimate contacts. While the contacts may have increased in number, their quality has diminished and become trivial. Gerald Suttles (1972, 21) also sees public life as being segmented into a series of "defended neighborhoods" and describes as a prevalent residential pattern the "communities of limited liability" (9), where loyalty, participation, and a sense of community are lacking. French philosopher Henri Lefebvre (1971) attributes the loss of the public realm to the capitalist nature of Western society, its basis in private ownership, individualism, and the pursuit of private purposes. In recent years, urbanists and social critics, namely, Edward Soja (1989), Mike Davis (1990), and Michael Sorkin (1992), have argued that this loss of public life threatens the basic humanity of cities.

CAUSES FOR THE DECLINE OF PUBLIC SPACE

A central argument of the works in the preceding section is that public life has all but disappeared in cities.[2] The traditional definition of public life as a concrete and homogeneous construct (Arendt 1959) and the role of public space as the facilitator of social interaction and shared communal feelings have been obscured by sociopolitical, cultural, and fiscal forces. In the following sections, we will discuss the various forces that have influenced these transformations.

Changes in social ecology and the increased complexity of the city   The complexity of the social environment is considered by many to be a decisive factor in the decline of public life. The increased density and heterogeneity of the modern city cause an overload of stimuli in the form of frequent and different encounters and experiences as well as ambient information (Milgram 1970). The complexity of the social environment has contributed to the fragmentation of the public realm. More so than other contemporary societies, the American urban context is composed of a rich variety of races and cultures and represents an amalgam of social groups with different values and symbol systems. The cultural landscape of the American city is composed of more or less well-defined social areas. The layout of urban artifacts follows the norms that are considered appropriate by the groups that control these areas (Duncan 1978). Thus the new downtown and its public realm are full of signs and symbols (buildings, spaces, public art) that perpetuate and underscore the power and importance of the corporate edifice, and exclude unrelated uses.

Since the social ecology of the American city is a composite of constantly shifting groups, each often striving for territorial identity, the picture of the public realm as a unitary and homogeneous construct is untenable. Sociability in American society today is defined more by the club culture than by mere communality. As the population has become more and more diverse and heterogeneous, social classes and ethnic groups have become increasingly isolated from each other and have withdrawn into their respective enclaves. These centrifugal tendencies have resulted in alienation from public experience. It can be argued that the notion that one unique public realm can incorporate and collectively express all societal values is a fiction. The American urban context is rather a collection of different realms that sometimes overlap but are most often rigidly separated or purposely segregated. These realms are group specific and are defined by cognitive and perceptual schemata shared within each group.

In the last decades the gap between the prosperous and the poor has widened, making the city an immeasurably worse environment for the latter. High levels of affluence and prosperity contrast sharply with the growing levels of deprivation among the urban poor. Increased mobility has enabled the middle and upper classes to seek new options, move away from social problems to communities of their choice, and create clubs and exclusive territories. Increased affluence has helped the substitution of private spaces for public ones.

Suburban fragmentation   Suburbanization has segmented urban form and expanded growth beyond the "minimum space-time requirement for the maintenance of patterns of human communication" (Castells 1977a, 5). Zoning has helped the segregation of uses in the city. It has banned mixed land use and separated residential space from work, social, and public activities. This differentiation in function has reduced the potential for social interaction. It has stripped public space of a basic component, the overlay of activities in one single territory, which could contribute to diversity (Jacobs 1961).

The suburban landscape favors the private and the parochial realms over the public (Lofland 1989). Planned unit developments are zealously protected and private spaces. Their streets, parks, pools, and meeting halls are for the exclusive use of their residents. Suburbanites commute with their private cars from home to work, often without having to set foot on public grounds. While the suburban landscape has been considered as the apotheosis of privatism and seclusion, similar processes of privatization, segregation, and exclusion have happened in recent decades in the corporate edifices of CBDs, a phenomenon that some have called the "suburbanization of downtown" (Boddy 1992, 150).

Fear of crime   The fragmentation of the public realm has been accompanied by fear, suspicion, tension, and conflict among social groups (Walzer 1986; Berman 1986). The modern urbanite is far more concerned with personal and property safety than with public life. Individuals fear and wish to avoid people different from themselves. It has been argued that " 'being inside' becomes a powerful symbol for being protected, buttressed, coddled, while 'being outside' evokes exposure, isolation, and vulnerability" (Boddy 1992, 140). This fear results in the spatial segregation of activities in terms of class, ethnicity, race, age, and occupation, the gating of residential communities, and the designation of certain locales as appropriate for certain persons and uses (corporate downtown, skid row area, communities for the elderly, ethnic ghetto, and so on). Many public environments are highly segregated according to this pattern and are designed to appeal to specific target groups.

Advances in technology   Technological innovations have tremendously shaped urban life and urban form. Modern technology permits and encourages the transfer of previously public and collective actions to private compartments (Harris 1987). Advances in communication and transportation technology, as well as household "mechanization," affected sociospatial organization. In previous eras, public spaces represented settings for information exchange and communicative interaction, whereas now this role is carried out by the telephone, the radio, the television, the fax machine, and the Internet. Physical presence is not necessary for communication anymore, since effective and convenient electronic substitutes for person-to-person contact are now being offered. In addition, new entertainment options and leisure activities (cable television, videos, and computer and electronic games) are increasingly home oriented and private.

Technological advances have made many social activities independent of context or location. The automobile brings closer distant parts of the city, other cities, and the countryside. This increased personal mobility has de-emphasized dependence on specific local public spaces. One does not have to rely on the neighborhood playground for recreation, and the large central park has lost its importance as the therapeutic antidote for urban life. As Melvin Webber (1964) has argued, it seems that modern life no longer depends on and does not exist within a framework of contiguous space. In these "non-place urban realms" proximity and propinquity are no longer prerequisites of community. But these "non-place urban realms" often result in strangely passionless landscapes, which deny deep experiences and close attachments (Relph 1976).

Changes in the family and in employment structure   Family structure and family life, as well as the nature of work, have undergone deep transformations. The combined influence of these changes has affected traditional lifestyles. The conventional nuclear family has suffered from high divorce rates, childlessness, and mobility of family members. By 1980 only 7 percent of households in the United States were traditional single-income nuclear families, while 30 percent were dual-career couples with no children. Many traditional public space activities had the family as their focus. With the shrinking of the nuclear family, these activities have faded or disappeared.

The employment schedule, the time required to get to and from work, and the increasing geographical separation of employment and residence have put extra strains on place ties. Officially, working hours have been reduced to forty per week, and vacation time has become institutionalized. Yet, as Henri Lefebvre (1971, 104) has argued, the amount of "compulsive time" (time spent not for work or leisure but for transport, official formalities, and obligations) has increased at a much greater rate than leisure time. Thus "obligatory activities" have increased at the cost of "discretionary activities" (Chapin 1974, 37–38). The constraints of time budgeting have also affected the use of public space.

THE RESURGENCE OF THE PUBLIC REALM?

The idea that there has been a gradual decline in public life has certainly been contested. The social alienation hypothesis promoted by Louis Wirth (1938),

Georg Simmel (1950), Stanley Milgram (1970), and others has been criticized by studies that have found a vibrant social life within subsegments of the public—small social (often ethnic) groups within larger urban contexts (Gans 1962; Suttles 1968). Some have argued that urban life does not necessarily produce estrangement from close associates or familiar groups. It is rather the unknown and socially dissimilar elements, which one encounters quite often in public spaces, that are perceived as threatening (Fisher 1981).

Others have argued that there are some misconceptions and a certain degree of false nostalgia regarding public life of the past, which in reality was never as diverse, dense, classless, or democratic as is now imagined (Brill 1989; Krieger 1995). While Frederick Law Olmsted and other park advocates called for social justice and democracy in the public parks of the late nineteenth century, the public landscape was—even then—quite contested, with the elites clashing with the masses over the rules of behavior in public (Mozingo 1995). The neighborhood playgrounds of the 1920s and 1930s reflected the segregation of inner-city neighborhoods. These public spaces did not necessarily encourage the democratic intermingling of and socialization between classes.

Some have even talked about a resurgence of the public realm, pointing to the new forms of public association and communication that now take place in settings completely different than the traditional public places. Many new types of public interaction are hosted not in physical spaces but in the "virtual space" of the interactive media (Brill 1989, 1990; Chidister 1989; Hitt et al. 1990). The vast popularity of the Internet attests to a flourishing public communication, albeit quite different from person-to-person contacts. Enthusiasts of high technology have even claimed that "the Internet revolution is likely to replace the binary world of public and private space with space open to pluralism and diversity" (Krieger 1995, 77).

Finally, some have pointed to the popularity of new urban malls, festival marketplaces, shopping plazas and arcades, skyway systems, and pedestrian streets as a sign of a reconstituted public realm. As already discussed, these spaces are privately produced, are often part of megadevelopment projects, and are closely linked to retail and services. They have been principal elements of the renaissance of many American downtowns in the 1980s and 1990s. Developers and city planners have often claimed that these spaces represent the new public realm of contemporary downtowns. In order to examine the validity of this claim we examined the social profile of our eight case studies. We surveyed the users, managers, and owners of these downtown sites, and—following William H. Whyte's lead (1980, 1988)—made systematic observations of the types of activities that take place in some representative spaces in San Francisco and Los Angeles.[3] What follows is an account of our findings.

USERS: EXCLUDING THE "UNHOLY" AND "UNWASHED"

A common attribute of the new generation of downtown public spaces that we studied is the homogeneity of their social context. These spaces are frequented by users who are for the most part white collar, upscale, and clean-cut. These settings contrast sharply with the surrounding public streets, which are much more racially and socially integrated. Design cues and management practices send the signal that this is a limited access territory—the realm of the white-collar office worker or the upscale consumer. As integral parts of the new corporate downtown, these spaces are designed and programmed to appeal to a very specific clientele, and they have been quite effective in achieving their goals. The majority of all our survey respondents were white-collar workers, ranging from business executives, managers, and lawyers to professionals and computer technicians. The great majority of these users came from the immediate vicinity, covering a distance of less than two city blocks (see figures 89 and 90).

Without exception, all the places we studied had more male users than female users. Users were characteristically well educated (the majority reported at least some years of college), most were white, and the vast majority fell in a limited age range from twenty to fifty (see figures 91 and 92). Both children and the elderly were almost absent among users with the rare exception of a few families (tourists or shoppers) wandering around the premises on weekends.

Users in all spaces were characteristically well dressed. Absent were the homeless, street vendors, or denizens of any sort. The exclusion of the "unholy" and "unwashed," as Lyn Lofland (1989) describes them, results from a combination of factors. For one, private management is quick to assert its authority, often converting the space into a limited-access territory. Control is the operating principle. "Hard" control eliminates certain "undesirable ele-

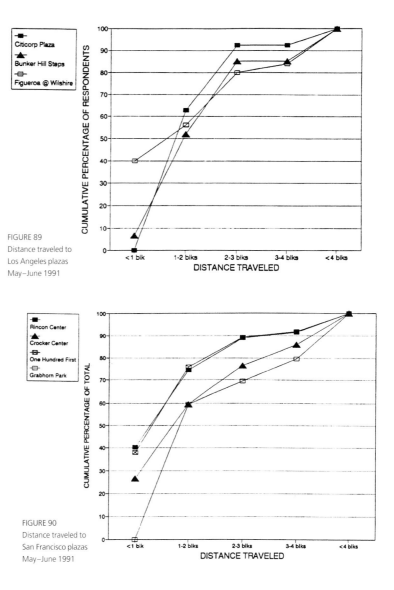

FIGURE 89
Distance traveled to
Los Angeles plazas
May–June 1991

FIGURE 90
Distance traveled to
San Francisco plazas
May–June 1991

ments" by using vigilant private security officers, surveillance cameras, and regulations that either prohibit certain activities from happening or allow them only by issuing permits, programming, scheduling, or leasing. "Soft" control focuses on symbolic restrictions: for example, the lack of facilities that could appeal to certain people or encourage functions deemed undesirable (public

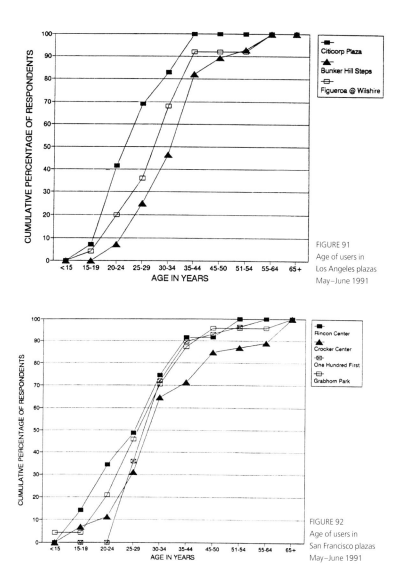

FIGURE 91
Age of users in
Los Angeles plazas
May–June 1991

FIGURE 92
Age of users in
San Francisco plazas
May–June 1991

restrooms, food vendors, sand boxes) and design features that seek to achieve a subtle closure and screening of the undesired elements. The corporate edifice, thus, becomes intimidating to certain segments of the public. In all spaces we studied (with the exception of Grabhorn Park, which is not directly linked to a corporate tower and is quite modest in its design), the "opulence" of design materials, the rigidity of design and programming, and the perfection of architectural form send clear signals as to the spaces' territorial identity. Control strategies are successful in eliminating undesirable elements from the grounds. Homeless and other denizens who wander in the surrounding downtown streets of Los Angeles and San Francisco were absent in these spaces.

These rigid control practices sometimes extend to traditional public spaces. As discussed in chapter 5, Pershing Square, the historic public park of downtown Los Angeles, has been retrofitted by a private development firm, Maguire Thomas Partners (MTP). The security of the square involves what Dan Gifford, vice president of MTP, calls "a four-pronged approach, that make it uncomfortable for the wrong element to be there." Each of the prongs is a different set of uniformed personnel: park rangers, LAPD officers, transit police from the nearby station, and a private security force contracted by the developer (quoted in Newman 1995, 49). In Saint Julian Commons, a skid row park, at the edge of downtown Los Angeles, the sprinklers are turned on every night to prevent the homeless from sleeping on its grounds. Fenced community gardens in some inner-city neighborhoods admit "members only."

It became clear from our interviews with developers, managers, and security officers of many downtown open spaces that the undesirable population includes not only criminal elements and dangerous individuals but also street vendors, musicians and other public performers, noisy teenagers, children, and in general everyone who does not conform to the management's standards of appropriateness or whose presence might damage the image of a clean, proper, and safe environment. Sometimes even appearance or clothing is the sole basis for excluding potential users.

In general, owners and managers of the new public realm give three good reasons for exercising rigid spatial control: maintenance, liability, and marketability. Since maintenance costs burden the owners, they have an incentive to ban people and activities that are perceived as potential threats to the space. Owners are in general liable for all facilities and spaces that fall within their property lines. The liability crisis of the last decade, which was accompanied by skyrocketing insurance costs, makes owners and managers very sensitive to any perceived risk. Finally, these spaces are a marketable commodity for the private sector and are designed to suit the needs of the office tenants. Since these tenants (as the surveys have shown) prefer safe, protected, and orderly settings, owners seek to eliminate any distraction that can spoil the image of a perfect environment.

USES: RIGIDITY, CONTROL, AND ORDER

There is a certain protocol for use of and decorum in downtown plazas. Spontaneous activities are rare. A group picnicking on the lawn, a tired office worker sleeping on a bench, and an individual climbing up on a sculpture's pedestal are the few nontraditional activities we encountered. The absence of diverse user activities is partly a reflection of the plazas' social context and the range of behavior settings. After all it is hard to imagine how office workers could lie on the grass while keeping their business attire intact. More important, management practices discourage or ban noisy activities, loud portable radios, drinking of alcoholic beverages, picnicking, and sleeping on the grass or benches. Sometimes even taking pictures requires a special permit.

The public space offered in the corporate downtown is to be viewed passively. Settings are organized and programmed as orchestrated spectacles, where visitors are invited to watch but not interact, to admire but not change or appropriate. The only active experience encouraged is conspicuous consumption (Crilley 1993). Retail is sanctioned but has to follow rules and regulations that guide the operation of the business and the appearance and type of merchandise. Design means such as strategic placement of entrances, escalators, and elevators and zigzagging of paths bring the user-shopper past the maximum possible number of retail establishments on the premises (Loukaitou-Sideris 1991).

While commercial activities are promoted in the new downtown, political or civic uses have atrophied, if not disappeared altogether. Political gatherings, picketing, and protests either are not allowed or need special permits. According to a book published by the International Council of Shopping Centers (Carpenter 1978, 87), the following uses in public settings within private property can disrupt business: pickets in labor disputes, social demonstrations, political campaigns, charitable solicitations, and obstreperous juvenile frolics. Owners of shopping malls and plazas have fought a series of legal battles that focused specifically on the public/private nature of their properties (International Council of Shopping Centers 1974; Kowinski 1985; Free Speech 1986). The courts have been called upon to decide whether the rights of freedom of speech and assembly—including the distribution of leaflets, solicitation of support for initiatives, petitions, and referendums, public debates, and picketing—apply to shopping centers and corporate plazas.

Up until the 1970s, the courts extended public rights to private properties, reasoning that the owners of these places were assuming public roles and functions. In the Supreme Court's words, "the more the owner, for his advantage, opens up his property for use by the public in general, the more do his rights become circumscribed by the statutory and constitutional rights of those who use it" (*Marsh v. Alabama*, 326 U.S. 501, 90 L. Ed. 265, 66 S. Ct. 276 [1946]). In 1968, the Supreme Court ruled that a labor union could picket a supermarket in a shopping center, despite the "no trespassing" signs posted by the management. In the same year, a California state court permitted antipollution petitioners to enter a San Bernardino mall reasoning that "in many instances the contemporary shopping center serves as the analogue of the traditional town square" (*Diamond v. Bland* 1968).

Later, however, the balance tilted towards conservatism. A Supreme Court decision in 1972 banned political activists from distributing antiwar leaflets in a Portland mall (*Lloyd Corp. v. Tanner*, 407 U.S. 551, 33 L. Ed. 2d 131, 92 S. Ct. [1972]). Supreme Court decisions in 1975 and 1976 also favored arguments promoted by owners and allowed them to limit activities normally permitted in public spaces. Noteworthy, however, was the dissent of Justice Thurgood Marshall, who in 1976 wrote, "It would not be surprising in the future to see cities rely more and more on private business to perform functions once performed by government agencies. . . . As governments rely more and more on private enterprise, public property decreases in favor of privately owned property. It becomes harder and harder for citizens to find means to communicate with other citizens. Only the wealthy may find effective communication possible" (in Kowinski 1985, 357).

In 1979 the California Supreme Court used the state's constitution to protect free speech on private property used as public space in malls, corporate plazas, and private university campuses (*Prune Yard Shopping Center v. Robbin* 1979). The decision was upheld by the United States Supreme Court when appealed. This left the states to settle the issue according to their constitutions, which has led to different rulings all across the country.

Picketing and demonstrations have been rare and "abnormal" uses in the

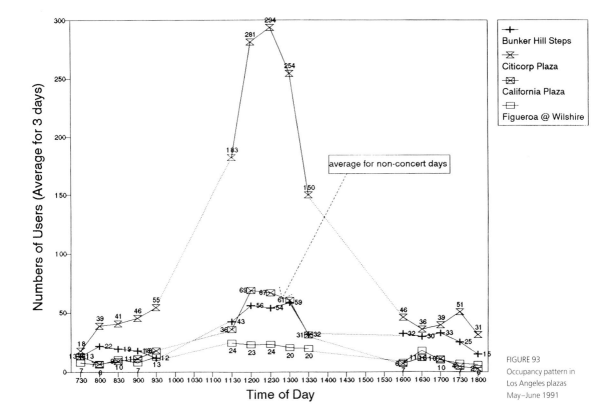

FIGURE 93
Occupancy pattern in
Los Angeles plazas
May–June 1991

1980s and 1990s. In general, uses of the new public settings are limited and predictable. Our activity count showed nine types of activities in the corporate plazas of Los Angeles and San Francisco (eating, standing, sitting, walking, meeting friends, reading, working, taking pictures, and feeding pigeons). A similar count found a much greater number of activities (more than twenty-five) in Pershing Square and Saint Julian Commons in skid row.[4]

Uses of downtown plazas are limited and temporal. Lunch time on weekdays is the peak time. As William H. Whyte (1980) has argued in his well-known study of New York plazas, food is a major attractor of people in open spaces. Our studies also showed that plazas closely linked to retail and food establishments (Citicorp Plaza in Los Angeles, and Crocker Center and Rincon Center in San Francisco) enjoyed much higher levels of use (see figures 93 and 94).

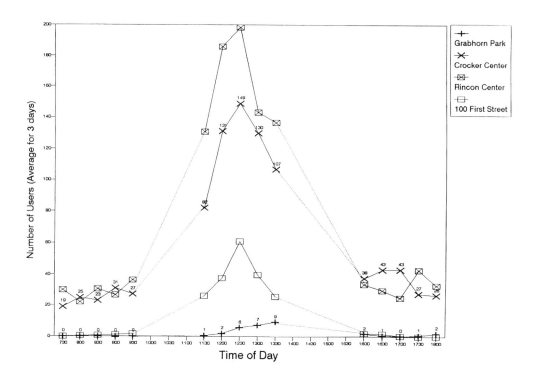

FIGURE 94
Occupancy pattern in
San Francisco plazas
May–June 1991

But even these plazas were not successful in drawing large numbers of people on weekends. Scheduled events and performances typically draw more people than usual, as illustrated by the example of California Plaza, where noontime concerts in summer months increase the use drastically. The majority of Los Angeles users we surveyed visited the same plaza once or twice weekly (see figure 95). In San Francisco, we found a greater number of frequent users (people who used the plazas once or twice a week or more) than we did in Los Angeles (compare figures 95 and 96). Visits were usually short; in both cities few users stayed more than an hour on the plaza grounds (figures 97 and 98).

Just a couple of blocks away from the new Los Angeles downtown, Broadway Street enjoys very high levels of use. On most days, and especially on Sundays, thousands of Latinos stroll down this retail corridor—the "Latinoway" of the west—to shop, to eat, to see and to be seen (Roseman and Vigil

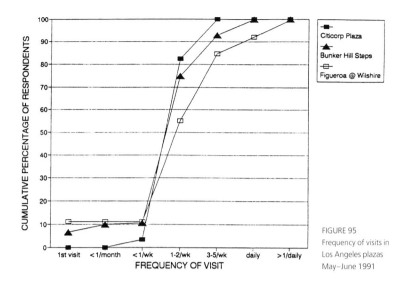

FIGURE 95
Frequency of visits in
Los Angeles plazas
May–June 1991

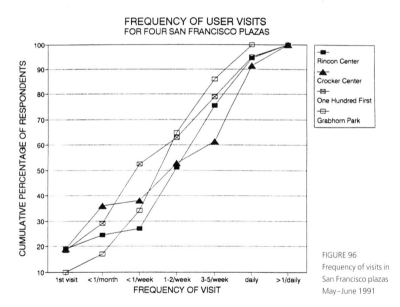

FREQUENCY OF USER VISITS
FOR FOUR SAN FRANCISCO PLAZAS

FIGURE 96
Frequency of visits in
San Francisco plazas
May–June 1991

1993). Catering to a different clientele, the skid row park witnesses a daily cramming of the downtown homeless and drug dealers into its 0.3-acre space. Before its renovation, Pershing Square was a hangout for Latino teenagers and young African Americans. Absent from the public spaces of the old downtown are office workers, business executives, secretaries, and professionals, who feel

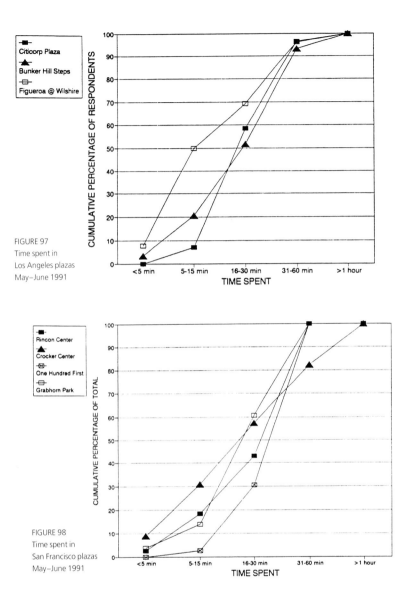

FIGURE 97
Time spent in
Los Angeles plazas
May–June 1991

FIGURE 98
Time spent in
San Francisco plazas
May–June 1991

out of place here and are more comfortable and protected in the corporate plazas. Public open spaces were once perceived as capable of bringing together people from different social strata. Today, both corporate plazas and traditional public spaces are often as segregated as any other part of the American urban form.

USERS' FEELINGS: BOURGEOIS PLAYGROUNDS

In a critique of downtown gentrification, Neil Smith and Michelle LeFaivre (1984, 60) argue that the restructuring of urban space that is now taking place produces "bourgeois playgrounds" in the downtowns of the American and European cities. Indeed, the new downtowns provide abundant settings for yuppies: espresso bars and French restaurants for gourmet dining, upscale retail outlets (Guccis, Calvin Kleins, and Laura Ashleys abound) for shopping in style, and amphitheaters for jazz concerts and outdoor plays. Our survey has shown that these are exactly the settings that affluent users appreciate. We found that many of the elements that people liked closely followed William H. Whyte's (1980) prescriptions: food, water fountains, outdoor seating, landscaping, and a sunny environment. Very often the location of a plaza was its most likable attribute, a fact which suggests that often people may use a plaza because of its convenient location and not because they have a particular attachment to its space or design elements.

Complaints about downtown open spaces were context specific. People did not like the type of food available (at Citicorp Plaza and Bunker Hill Steps), the lack of retail establishments (at Figueroa at Wilshire Plaza and Bunker Hill Steps), the windy environment (at One Hundred First, Grabhorn Park, and Crocker Galleria), the crowded environment (at Citicorp Plaza and Rincon Center), the lack of adequate landscaping and greenery (at Figueroa at Wilshire Plaza and Grabhorn Park), and the type of shops (at Crocker Galleria). And there were specific grievances about the design of Citicorp Plaza and Bunker Hill Steps.

Our survey showed that the plaza users appreciated their exclusionary environment. Up to 45 percent of the visitors in some plazas claimed that the most appealing characteristic of the space was the solitude that it offered. Safety, order, and the absence of undesirables ranked as positive attributes among users. One hundred years ago Frederick Law Olmsted argued that one of the social roles of public space was to enable contact between the upper and lower classes (Todd 1982). Today the users of the corporate downtown spaces go there not because they want a sense of togetherness or communality or because they wish to mix with different people, but because they desire solitude and privacy. Our observations confirmed a very solitary and private use of these spaces.

Our survey also showed that plaza users feel comfortable and safe in these homogeneous and exclusionary settings. Respondents often praised the cleanliness, order, and security of the new public settings. These feelings and perceptions are clearly recognized by the private sector, which creates these spaces to serve the needs of its clientele.

The meaning of public space is being redefined in the new American downtown. With the help of private security forces, design features, and rules and regulations, the public landscape provides protection by becoming "defensible space" (Newman 1972) that insulates the gentry from the unholy and unwashed. Right of passage in this landscape derives from the ability to pay for the services, space, and merchandise offered, and by appearance (dress and racial characteristics). Admittedly, there have been clashes between the upper and lower classes (the elites and the masses) over the rules of behavior in public spaces of the past (Mozingo 1995). But the "selling of downtown" in the 1980s and 1990s has led to the creation of "heterotopic" landscapes and has resulted in the exclusion of some segments of the public from the corporate enclaves of the new downtown.[5]

PART THREE

THE

POETICS

OF

FORM

7

THE POETICS OF CORPORATE OPEN SPACES

American architects and urban designers have long romanced the squares, open spaces, and pedestrian streets of the medieval and baroque cities. The appreation of classical plazas and squares—their form, design, scale, proportions, arrangements—is part of the initiation rites of the design profession; it is inculcated by readings from Camillo Sitte to Albert Peets and, ideally, supplemented by a semester in Athens, Barcelona, or Rome. The early romance with a Piazza della Signoria or a Piazza San Marco or the Campo of Sienna continues through the professional life. They remain idealized models of good urban spaces.

As we have discussed in chapter 2, during the early stages of downtown rebuilding, parks, plazas, and grand avenues were created out of this romantic longing for the European-style civic design. Although the era of grand public design has long ended, even today this romanticism with the "European motherland" (see Dyckman 1962) nourishes the poetics of place-making in downtown urban design, albeit on a different scale.

We should note, however, that the themes used to promote an office or a shopping complex may not always reflect the poetics architects use to explain their designs. Although architects are occasionally nudged and sometimes challenged by their clients to create a certain type of setting, the poetics of architects often remain private, and may not be the theme that the developer ultimately uses in the marketing brochure. For example, a basilica may inspire a designer's layout of a mixed-use office-cum-retail complex, but it is hardly the kind of theme that a developer will choose to promote a downtown office building. Nevertheless, today's developers, who have a sophisticated sense of urban design, openly indulge the poetics of place-making in the production of the various increments of the built form.

In this chapter we focus on the poetics of design and how it shapes the organization of space and the visual form of the new urban centers. For example, in San Francisco, architects of Crocker Center described it as a combination of galleria and garden; "oasis" and "room" were the metaphors for Grabhorn Park; the cruciform atrium of Rincon Center represented "a basilica, filled with the Zen of raindrops"; the plaza at One Hundred First was simply a "sun terrace." In Los Angeles "grotto" was the term for Citicorp Plaza; "vertical plaza" was the concept for the Bunker Hill Steps; the metaphor of "court"— spiral court, water court—dominated the design concept of the California Plaza complex. In defining the essence of Horton Plaza in San Diego, the designers invoked the term "urban theater" (while privately referring to the Italian hill towns as a source of inspiration).[1]

In this chapter, we will argue that these metaphors—the poetics—of design essentially create a collage of disjunctive postmodern urban design, driven mainly by privately initiated property development. This design seeks to justify itself by inventing a poetics of form, but the invented poetics itself is arbitrary and idiosyncratic, lacking a sense of context or history. If the urban design of postmodern cities is a non sequitur, it certainly befits the evolving urbanism of the market economy and the global economic order.

Our arguments rest on several case studies of the poetics of place-making in rebuilding downtown environments. We have organized these cases into three categories on the basis of their scale: sub-block, super-block, and multi-block projects. We will demonstrate later in this chapter that the poetics of place-making is not independent of the scale of the project, since the size of investment, financing, the politics of implementation, and most importantly, the degree of public subsidy are all related to the scale of the project.

THE SUB-BLOCK SCALE

First, we will present four cases of project design at the sub-block level—that is, projects built on small blocks or on parcels smaller than a block. The examples in this category are Grabhorn Park and One Hundred First in San Francisco; the Bunker Hill Steps and the Figueroa at Wilshire Tower (commonly known as the Sanwa Bank building) in Los Angeles. None of these projects involved direct public subsidy in any form.

FIGURE 99
Grabhorn Park, 1992.
Photograph by Anastasia
Loukaitou-Sideris.

An urban oasis   Landscape architect Andrew Butler used the metaphor "oasis" to describe his concept for Grabhorn Park. The challenge for him was "to create a space that would be an oasis . . . a respite from the high-paced downtown and the somewhat crumbling Chinatown."[2] Today, it is indeed a small oasis, only two thousand square feet, of tranquillity and great charm (see figure 99). An old building on the north side of Commercial Street—a quiet back street, more of an alley (see figure 100)—was taken down to make room for the park. Edwin and Robert Grabhorn (hence the name) operated a printing press in that building between 1933 and 1942. The park is less than two short blocks away from the busy and all-important California Street, with its noisy cable cars, and about a block away from Chinatown's historic Portsmouth Square. Located almost in the middle of the block bounded by Montgomery and Kearny, both rather busy streets, the park and the street lie in the seam between the financial district and Chinatown.

Although neither is visible from the other, Grabhorn Park and the expansive

FIGURE 100
San Francisco, sketch of
Commercial Street. San
Francisco Department of
City Planning.

and spacious Bank of America Plaza nearby offer an interesting counterpoint. Famous for a giant granite sculpture (dubbed by locals as "the banker's heart," more for its metaphorical significance, we suspect, than for its anatomical resemblance), the plaza is infamous for its shaded and inhospitably cold and windy microclimate. In a city where sunlight is zealously protected, this plaza's callous disregard for sunlight is not forgiven by the locals, and the plaza is constantly used by planners and urban designers as an example of what not to do.

The quiet respite that Andrew Butler sought in his design was reinforced by the alleylike character of the street. Isolated, almost hidden from public view, the park is a pleasant surprise. There is little hint of its presence from the Kearny or the Montgomery end of the block. One stumbles on it almost accidentally, like Paley Park in New York (captured rather dramatically in William H. Whyte's documentary, *The Social Life of Small Urban Places*). Indeed Martin

Brown of the Empire Group, the original developer of Grabhorn Park, spoke about Paley Park as an inspiration in the early stages of design.[3]

When the idea of the park was first being explored, there was some talk of providing play equipment for children, presumably for the benefit of the Chinatown neighborhood. Andrew Butler disagreed; he did not think that a play area belonged in the financial district at the edge of a Chinatown populated mostly by senior citizens and poor residents. Eventually the park was designed both for adult users from the financial district and for the Chinatown elderly. According to Andrew Butler,

> I wanted to create something in scale with Chinatown, but somewhat new and clean. I wanted an oasis quality with plants that would be tough enough to survive intensive use. My intention was to create a sense of entry, a set back from the street. That was to be done in three ways: one was with lath fences on the sides, two was the trellis over, and three was with the trees. So you essentially create a room which is separate from the street and invites you to get into it. . . .
>
> I did some shadow studies. Over the summer you get some shadow. Chinese elderly don't tend to like full sun—they like to sit in shady areas. So we wanted the park to be partly in shade. So we tried to create a variety of sunny and shady spaces.[4]

Here he introduces another metaphor—"room." The formal but unpretentious entry does set the park apart from the street space, like a room off a building corridor. The rendering by artist Jim Gillam captures the spirit of Andrew Butler's design (see figure 101). Although the rendering ignores the stark textures of the three surrounding walls, and especially the windows and balconies of the old apartment building, with hanging laundry, planters, and other paraphernalia (see figure 57, in chapter 4), Andrew Butler's clients wanted him to hide as much of this backdrop as possible. And yet it is this very context, and the visual juxtaposition and irony it offers, that make the park so dramatic, so effective. It is more than a public amenity; it is a commentary on the change, continuity, and contrast that characterize a corporate downtown.

In another time Grabhorn Park probably would have been called a "vest pocket" park.[5] Today it is officially recognized as an urban garden. A plaque by the entrance reads—in English and Chinese, and as specified by the City Planning Department—the following statement:[6]

This Urban Garden is provided
and maintained for the Enjoyment of the Public
By MITSUI FUDOSAN 433−4555
OPEN 8 A.M. TO 6 P.M.

A sun terrace   It was no accident that the open space requirement for the building on the southwest corner of First and Mission, known as One Hundred
First, was conceived as a sun terrace (see figure 102). By the time negotiations
got underway, building shadows and solar access (and street level microclimates
in general) had become major public issues in San Francisco. The popular initiative (Proposition K) passed in 1984 had added the "no new shadows" rule.
Furthermore the concept of "view and sun terrace" had already been codified
in the 1983 proposal for a downtown plan as one of the six categories of open
space. This particular category was defined as "(S)unny wind-sheltered area on

upper-level for enjoyment of city views and for relaxation" (San Francisco Department of City Planning 1983, 54). As the first test case of the downtown
plan ("we were guinea pigs," architect Richard Keating would later observe),[7]
One Hundred First complied with the open space requirement by creating a
sun terrace twenty-five feet above street level.

It was worthwhile for developer Michael Barker to dedicate for this purpose
the roof area of an existing three-level (one level is below grade) parking structure that he acquired adjacent to the original one-acre site on the corner of
Mission and First. It was fortuitous that this parking structure was to the west
of the main building site and that the adjacent building on the other side was
only sixteen feet higher than the roof of the parking structure, thus casting
very little shadow during the peak afternoon hours. It also protected the space
from wind. So the concept for the sun terrace essentially emerged from this
opportunity. Public access to the sun terrace was provided by means of a grand
staircase from the Mission Street side (see figure 65, chapter 4). Another access
is from the building directly at the terrace level. The Mission Street frontage
of the parking structure was altered to create street-level retail.

The location of the sun terrace to the west of the building was consistent with the developers' aim from the very beginning to locate the building as close to the eastern edge of the site as possible and without any setback. According to Michael Barker, "We wanted to push the building as far to the east as possible, and leave the parking garage as is and create this park. That's basically what we ended up with. We just added another deck to the parking structure and then created landscaping."

While a debate over the size and shape of the building was to ensue, the location of the open space never became an issue. Richard Keating, the original architect, and Jeffrey Heller, the mediating architect, both agreed with Michael Barker that given the sunlight requirement and the financial constraints, the terrace's present location was ideal. And of course the planning department consented as well.

A vertical plaza   The Bunker Hill Steps are an elegant outdoor stairway that connects the new Bunker Hill redevelopment area to the city's Central Library—a drop of seventy feet. Wedged between two modernist high-rise towers, the Steps are reminiscent of a celebrated urban landmark: the Spanish Steps in Rome, an all too obvious resemblance that was immediately picked up by the local media. Like its Roman counterpart, which was built to link a public piazza to a church on the summit of a hill, the Bunker Hill Steps are also designed as a connector.

The curved surface of the First Interstate World Center, the city's tallest building, forms the backdrop for the Bunker Hill Steps. Water cascades down the middle of the curvy stairway in a raised channel (hand-sculpted by the designer himself), which forms the centerpiece of this open space (see figure 103). A carefully paced sequence of steps with three landings is designed to allow a slow, enjoyable walk. But most pedestrians prefer the convenience of an escalator which flanks the west side of the Steps. The grade changes have been masked by lavish plantings, which partially hide the escalator from the stair users.

The Bunker Hill Steps, however, have yet to become a "people's place" like the Spanish Steps.[8] Even though they are situated at what the developers proudly call the "one hundred percent location for Los Angeles," the Steps

FIGURE 103
Bunker Hill Steps, 1996.
Photograph by Anastasia
Loukaitou-Sideris.

have yet not been able to attract any major users other than the lunchtime passers-by.[9]

Lawrence Halprin, the well-known landscape architect and designer of the Bunker Hill Steps, resists comparison with the Spanish Steps. Dismissing it as a journalistic fanfare, he commented: "Naturally if you are confronted by similar problems physically, often you end up with similar forms."[10] The Steps project uses baroque architectural elements, imagery, and motifs, which are popular in postmodern architecture. Halprin, however, vehemently opposes the characterization of his project as postmodern. In his words, he is more of a romanticist, driven by the desire to create an intimate people's place that had less of a "stainless steel feel" and had warm tones rather than cool, and plenty of plantings—an oasis enlivened by the sounds of gurgling water.[11]

In designing the Steps, Halprin was driven by his vision of a "linkage system"—the development of a series of interconnected open spaces that would follow the north-south axis of downtown Los Angeles. As he explained,

> This kind of networking and linking is one that I believe in very deeply, and I have devoted a lot of time to the idea that it is really not the building as an object that makes urban spaces important, but rather the creation of a continuum of movement, because that is the way one experiences things. The shape of the Steps is one that encourages movement. If I had designed steps that went straight across instead of being curved, it wouldn't respond to the way people move around. My whole idea was to encourage people to pass through, using it as a place for choreographic movement, both up and down and transversely into the building and out, with its three landings, each linked to an entrance to the building. In addition to that I expected—and still do—that this flight of steps would become a place for many different kinds of activities. My vision for the Steps is that of a vertical plaza, an amphitheater.

In an effort to transform the Steps into a destination space, Halprin extended all three landings into patios for outdoor dining. But the privacy of the patios is functionally and symbolically underlined by colonnades that mark the separation of the restaurant space from the pedestrian traffic along the Steps.

A fire and water paradox: an urban amusement   Figueroa at Wilshire plaza was designed by A.C. Martin Associates. According to David Martin, the principal designer, the work of William H. Whyte (1988) strongly influenced his design for the plaza. He tried to include in the design all the elements that Whyte prescribes as the ingredients for a successful plaza: water, food, adequate seating with movable chairs, street-level access, and adequate sun exposure.

The L-shaped plaza is designed to complement the office tower and provide relief for the four thousand or so people who work there. The expensive materials (granite, marble, brass) used in the hardscape of the plaza reflect its corporate milieu. The street corner is the obvious focal point of the plaza. There, on a low circular base of gray granite, stands the most exciting element of the landscape: a thirty-five-foot-high water-and-fire art piece designed by sculptor Eric Orr (see figure 104). Two slender rectangular blocks release a sheath of water that magically disappears at the base. Every twenty minutes the upper

FIGURE 104
Figueroa at Wilshire Plaza,
1996. Photograph by
Liette Gilbert.

portion of the sculpture lights up in flames. The paradoxical coexistence of fire and water creates an intriguing effect for the spectator. David Martin predicted that "The art object is going to be a tourist attraction, a bit of urban amusement that everybody will be able to understand. Fire and water do not mix. This is a crazy thing, just right for Los Angeles. I imagine people will be hanging around the plaza waiting for it to blow off."[12]

The Figueroa and Wilshire corner of the plaza (where the sculpture stands) is very accessible to pedestrians. Although the public realm of the street fuses into the corporate plaza, the Orr sculpture remains a strong territorial reminder of the corporate domain. Up the hill along Wilshire Boulevard, the westerly arm of the plaza appears sunken below the street. A hard edge defined by a food kiosk, a pool with streams flowing from a wall, and a rectangular planter separates the plaza from the sidewalk. A twelve-foot-high, terraced cascading fountain adorns the back wall of the plaza. This more protected and private area serves as an eating place with marble tables, movable chairs, and patio umbrellas. Colin Shepherd from Gerald Hines Interests, the company that manages the building and plaza, emphasizes, "We are maintaining this space for anyone's use, even for brown-baggers, though there was no require-ment for that. We wanted a place where office workers could go buy their food and sit, or people who have brought their own lunch could come and sit." [13]

The eastern wing of the plaza along Figueroa Street is a twenty-five-foot-wide hardscaped promenade, divided into two parallel strips by a series of planters. The strip adjacent to the building is three steps above street level and serves as a somewhat private walkway for the building's tenants. The second strip is formed by the extension and widening of the sidewalk and is punctuated by a double row of trees.

Even though the sidewalk promenade is designed to encourage a relaxed walking pace for the passer-by, the adjacent ground floor does nothing to gen-erate or support sidewalk activity. Furthermore, the setbacks detract from the formation of a continuous retail edge along Figueroa, which could contribute to a more coherent downtown environment. As David Martin recognized, "It would have been nice if the front of the building was lined up with shops. If you have plaza and retail you can have more people. But we couldn't do that on Figueroa because of the setbacks. Also the developer did not want retail. I wish we had legislation that encourages ground-level retail, like in San Diego, where ground-level retail is not included in the FAR requirements, so it is easy to get theaters, shops, and restaurants along the street." [14]

It should be apparent from these examples that design at the sub-block scale usually emphasizes spaces between and around buildings. The task is often to mediate between adjacent sites, or to negotiate the transition from the public to the private realm, or to establish linkages between areas not connected be-fore. The poetics of form is still significant, even at this scale.

THE SUPER-BLOCK SCALE

The second category of examples involves super-block scale projects. These projects involve areas larger than a block and require consolidation of several adjacent properties. Examples in this category are Crocker Center and Rincon Center in San Francisco and Citicorp Plaza in Los Angeles. Projects of this scale typically require some public contribution, usually in the form of vacating a public right of way (an alley in the case of Crocker Center or a street in the case of Citicorp Plaza) or financing a parking structure.

FIGURE 105
Rincon Center, 1997:
Atrium. Photograph by
Tridib Banerjee.

The Zen of raindrops in a basilica   Rincon Center is a short walk from Embarcadero Center, a block south of Market Street, and a short block west of the
waterfront. The project occupies one complete block and used to be the most
significant redevelopment project south of Market, before Moscone Center
and the San Francisco Museum of Contemporary Art were completed.

The genius of the project lies in the preservation and conversion of the shell
of a historically significant post office structure into a successful mixed-use
complex of office and retail. The project includes a new structure consisting of twin residential towers sitting atop a six-story base of apartments and
more offices. Combining the old with the new, in architectural form, textures,
fenestration, access, circulation, and organization of open space, was a major
challenge.

The most significant and talked about space of Rincon Center is a covered
interior space, an atrium with a glass roof (see figure 105). During the day the

space is filled with filtered sunlight. The atrium is a circular space roughly ninety feet in diameter, a dimension that is limiting for making eye contact and is considered optimal for theater viewing. This was a carefully chosen scale, for architect Scott Johnson wanted a certain level of user involvement in the space (Frantz 1991). At the center is the most distinctive feature of the atrium, a "rain column" created by an incessant shower of water plunging eighty-five feet from the top of the atrium within a tight circle of about fifteen feet in diameter. A part of the public art requirement, the rain column was designed by Douglas Hollis, a San Francisco artist. The sound of water is soothing white noise; it muffles voices and conversations. The overall sonic ambiance of the atrium is subtle but memorable. Scott Johnson commented, "The rain column everyone was excited about. The idea was a transparent pan with twelve thousand holes and water in it. So what you've got was sections of rain. He [the artist] wanted raindrops. I liked the idea because it was organic and spontaneous. . . . The sound of twelve thousand raindrops is a Zen kind of sound." [15]

The perimeter of the atrium is devoted to food and retail. It serves as a food court, a feature typically found in shopping malls and gallerias. Appropriately stocked with tables and chairs, the eating areas are raised platforms that essentially define a larger circle surrounding the rain column. They are separated from the retail and food outlets at the outer perimeter by a wide walkway. The atrium is full at noon on a weekday, and the tables are all taken. The hum of conversations of the lunch crowd competes with the patter of the rain column. A lone pianist plays, courtesy of the management. Occasionally in the evening there are office parties and receptions.

The monumental volume of the atrium resulted from the gutting of the concrete slabs of the two upper stories of the old post office structure and removing the heavy columns and girders that supported them. Although the shell of the original building remained intact, two new floors of office space were added on the top of the existing three levels. The interior of the structure beyond the atrium area was also "busted out" to create a linear glass covered galleria. It connected the atrium to the opposite entrance at the southern face of the original building. The galleria space is crisscrossed by new columns and girders that tie the new structural changes to the original skeleton of the old post office. These new structural elements, however, are reshaped and sculpted with great care to reflect the original Art Deco interior.

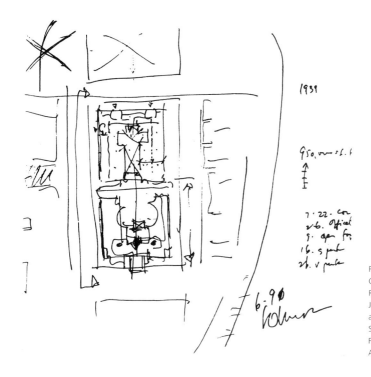

FIGURE 106
Conceptual sketch of
Rincon Center by Scott
Johnson (drawn for the
authors). Courtesy of
Scott Johnson, Johnson
Fain and Pereira
Associates.

In order to create the galleria, the old south wall had to be torn down, a major coup for the developers. Preservationists do not like to modify the exterior of historic buildings. The reconstructed south facade of the old building now overlooks an outdoor plaza—another element of the overall public space. This plaza is essentially the transition between the old and the completely new parts of the Rincon Center complex. It is like an interior court, enclosed completely to the south by the U-shaped building footprint of the six-story base of the two curved and symmetrical apartment towers, with some affordable housing units. The main entrance to the apartment towers faces this outdoor court.

Access to the outdoor plaza is roughly at the midpoint of the long sides of the block. These side entrances are well heralded by banners and canopies seemingly free-floating between the old and new structure, a gap left mainly for seismic reasons.

In plan view then the configuration of the indoor atrium and galleria opening into this outdoor plaza is that of a cruciform (see figure 106), which, according to Douglas Frantz (1991, 74), "reflected two of the forces that had shaped Scott Johnson's vision as an architect." He elaborated,

> Johnson had developed a strong interest in classical form during the year he spent studying in Italy, and it had been nurtured by frequent trips back to Europe and voracious reading. Growing up and attending college in the Bay Area also had exposed him to San Francisco's architecture. Over the years, the buildings and places in the city that he felt endured were those that had been designed in the 1910s and 1920s by a handful of American architects who had trained at the Ecole Nationale des Beaux-Arts in Paris. Among his favorite Bay Area sites were the Civic Center complex designed by Arthur Brown, Jr., John Galen Howard's schemes for the University of California at Berkeley, the early commercial buildings of Willis Polk and Julia Morgan, and the formal city gardens of Union Square.
>
> So the final design concept for Rincon Center was, at its heart, a Beaux-Arts plan that paid homage to the classical forms in which the style was rooted. Indeed, viewed in its simplest terms, the final design was a crucifix, one of the oldest and sturdiest of architectural foundations. . . . (Frantz 1991, 73–74)

Scott Johnson affirms today that his idea of a cruciform was a simple concept—"too simple to believe"—yet one that helped to organize a complex redevelopment project. He also uses the metaphor of the basilica to refer to the central design concept—the atrium and the cruciform layout of the circulation space. And this metaphor is not entirely accidental. When asked whether his design was inspired by any model, Johnson responded, "I thought of basilicas. I know this sounds rather mundane. Not that basilicas are mundane, but as a model it may be. I lived and traveled in Italy a lot. I go there all the time and I like the old churches, their intimacy, the fact that it's all compressed enough that there is contact, there is society. At the same time they are uplifting and public."[16]

When asked about his philosophy on the public quality of the space and how Rincon Center serves the overall urbanism of San Francisco, Johnson commented,

> We had a program that comes from the financial part of the deal that generates what the rents are and the economics of that. Public space is an inevitable thing. People want to sit and talk or whatever. It is like movie-making in a way. The heart of it,

the thing that makes it work or not work is completely unquantifiable. It is this certain essence. I am told that during lunch on an average day there are over three thousand people at the atrium. This suggests that people enjoy it for one reason or another. In my view of things it looks like an opportunity, because the nature of the historic building and the new construction created an indoor and an outdoor room. . . . [17]

Today Rincon Center is a secular "basilica" of commerce and trade. As a mixed-use project, however, it is more than just that. People live, shop, work, congregate, and take their children to day care—all within one city block.

A galleria between two gardens   A November 23, 1982 Crocker National Bank press release claimed that Crocker Galleria was the most elegant shopping environment in San Francisco, offering "everything from croissants and Italian ices to the latest in European fashions and publications." The press release included the following statement from David A. Brooks, vice chairman of the bank: "We believe we have to fulfill our dream of giving the city an architectural delight which will become a treasured landmark during the years as it serves San Francisco's downtown and shopping community."

Today Crocker Center is considered an exemplar of successful mixed-use development and urban design. It is a creative jigsaw puzzle of new structures and refurbished old spaces, rather cleverly shoehorned into a block packed with historic buildings. Even before the project was built the block already had some critical pedestrian and visual linkages to the adjacent blocks. Its location is strategic, bounded by Sutter to the north, Montgomery to the east, Post to the south, and Kearny to the west. The southeast corner of the block almost touches historic Market Street at the point where the entrance to the Montgomery Street BART station is located.

The southeast corner of the Crocker Center block is occupied by a two-story structure of considerable architectural distinction. This building is richly featured with high-arched openings, tall columns, decorative friezes, and a rather impressive porticoed entry at the corner of Post and Montgomery (see figure 107). Now occupied by Wells Fargo Bank, this structure is the original base of a thirteen-story building once owned by Crocker National Bank, developers of the Crocker Center project. As the salvaged remains of an earlier era, the building is a critical link to San Francisco's past.

FIGURE 107
Crocker Center, 1992:
Base of the original
historic building.
Photograph by Anastasia
Loukaitou-Sideris.

If one examined the top of this building one could see an unbroken bank of shrubbery and lush foliage above its ornate parapets, the only hint that there might be a roof garden there (see figure 108). The roof garden itself is rather quiet and peaceful, used mainly during lunch hours like most other open spaces in downtown San Francisco. The decor of the garden is vaguely reminiscent of a baroque garden surrounding a French chateau, presumably an attempt to maintain continuity with the classical architecture of its host. The roof garden has four main semicircular clusters of seating on two sides of an aisle marked by a row of trees in huge freestanding planters, with smaller benches located between the planters, surrounded by shrubbery (see figures 109 and 110). This formal axis leads to the galleria in the back. A modest structure shelters the elevator and the stairs, and separates a smaller sculpture court from the main area.

There is another smaller, if less formal, roof garden located on and accessible only from the other side of the galleria. This space is used much less frequently and intensely; the air here is thick with the smoke and odors emanating from the exhaust fans of a lower-level restaurant. This cholesterol-redolent ambiance

FIGURE 108
Above, left: Crocker
Center, 1992: Roof
garden on top of
the old bank building.
Photograph by Anastasia
Loukaitou-Sideris.

FIGURE 109
Left: Crocker Center,
1992: The roof garden.
Photograph by Anastasia
Loukaitou-Sideris.

FIGURE 110
Above: Crocker Center
roof garden, 1992: Lone
user. Photograph by
Anastasia Loukaitou-
Sideris.

is a paradoxical setting for occasional noontime joggers and a retreat for workers who like to eat lunch in solitude.

The design of the galleria was clearly influenced by the clients' desire to create a European ambiance (see figure 111). The press release mentioned previously pointed out that "the Galleria has a spaciousness, an atrium-style atmosphere, and a natural lighting influenced by Milan's famous Galleria Vittorio Emmanuelle." Architect David Larson of SOM concedes that the design of the galleria was inspired by the Italian and British arcades, and that he was also quite impressed by the attractive arcades of Australia. One could also add to this list the late-nineteenth-century arcades of Paris, which became symbolic of the material culture of the era (see Buck-Morss 1989). The rhetoric of architecture here coincided with the marketing aims of the developers.

An upscale grotto   Jon Jerde, architect and urban designer, describes the multilevel subterranean shopping complex of Citicorp Plaza in downtown Los Angeles as a grotto: "a surprise within the city that you come upon through discovery." Jerde, who by his own account is inspired by European public spaces, spoke of Park Güell in Barcelona: "Park Güell influenced the choice of many of the design elements that bring a high contrast to the corporate-tailored nature of other parts of the complex." [18]

Citicorp Plaza advertises itself as one of the most visible landmarks in downtown Los Angeles. It includes 1.9 million square feet of luxury office space "situated in a park-like setting where wide benches and shade trees provide a quiet respite from a busy day" (see figure 112). A three-acre landscaped park surrounds the subterranean retail complex, while a special food court is located at the lowest level. A steel trellis over the shopping court defines the focal point for the whole project. Open escalators and elevators connect the three levels of shopping.

To Jerde, who designed the open space and retail element (but not the office towers), the biggest challenge was to "marry the world of corporate business and populist retail in a way that the buttoned-up executive would not necessarily have to interact with the retail environment." Taking advantage of the natural gradients of the site, he was able to separate commercial from office uses and strike a balance between a conservative corporate image and a more populist retail image. Jerde wanted "retail to become the 'park-part' of the city,

FIGURE 111
Sketch of Crocker
Galleria. San Francisco
Department of City
Planning.

FIGURE 112
Citicorp Plaza, 1996:
Figueroa Street entrance.
Photograph by Anastasia
Loukaitou-Sideris.

and with all its variations, including the shops and restaurants, an important pole that would attract people." In his experience, Jerde has found that retail can effectively encourage communality and bring people back into the center.

Jerde admitted that he had to fight many battles throughout the development process. He lost some, but also won some. For instance, he insisted on creating an outdoor plaza. He commented, "I wanted the place to be a big contrast to what people do all day long. Downtown Los Angeles is dissociated from the outdoors completely. The developer was afraid that by having an outdoor space you expose the user to the 'polluted outside.' In the end, we created a filter, we put a steel trellis over the top, thus addressing some of the developer's concerns."

Originally, Jerde had hoped that flowering vines climbing up the trellis would form a green canopy "screening the buildings and the city outside." He wanted it to create a "truly refreshing difference in the daily life of the city and a high contrast to its buildings, pavements, and sidewalks." Fire department regulations prohibiting plant growth beyond a certain height ultimately precluded the greenery.

Jerde's penchant for an environment unique in its surroundings—amplified by the developer's explicit intentions for inward orientation, enclosure, and control—produced a space with a strong sense of territoriality, a space disconnected from the existing city fabric. Jerde admits that "There is a gap from the corner [the busy node of Seventh and Figueroa Streets] to the entrance of the project, where in essence it is a no man's land. Yet, the place is more outward-oriented compared to what you normally get, because it is all there; but you have to go to the edge of the open space to find it."

Although the plaza is visually open along Figueroa Street, a series of planters, semicircular steps, and decorative cylindrical and pyramidal elements serve as territorial markers between the plaza and the street's public realm. A strip of metal embedded in the paving further reinforces the legal claim to this territoriality (see figure 113). There are two other pedestrian entrances along Seventh and Eighth Streets, but they are low-keyed, almost hidden. After all, Citicorp is a destination point, not a passage.

As noted previously, projects of this scale require significant land assembly and private appropriation of public easements and rights of way. But more fundamentally, these projects represent a transformation of the urban fabric

FIGURE 113
Citicorp Plaza, 1996:
Property line on Seventh
Street. Photograph by
Tridib Banerjee.

from a finer to a coarser grain. Such consolidation of urban space under a single
corporate ownership is almost always a product of the urban redevelopment
process, and the available powers of eminent domain. What emerges also is an
expanded sense of corporate territoriality, with diminished possibilities for
public access and circulation. Inevitably this results in some shrinkage in the
effective public realm. The rhetoric of design in these instances is an attempt
to temper this consequence.

THE MULTI-BLOCK SCALE

Finally, we present two cases of what can be called multi-block projects, that is, projects involving several city blocks. These two projects, California Plaza in Los Angeles and Horton Plaza in San Diego, are truly megadevelopments. Both are urban renewal projects that have involved substantial public contribution in the form of land write-down, underwriting parking, and the like.

A system of courts   California Plaza constitutes the largest segment of the Bunker Hill redevelopment project area. Today it is a premier corporate office complex that is mixed with arts and cultural facilities. Occupying over 11.2 acres of land, the design of this complex features three office towers, three residential high-rise buildings, the Museum of Contemporary Art (MOCA), a luxury hotel, a dance gallery, and parking facilities, all of which are linked through a series of open spaces, courts, and landscaped plazas. Many of these structures are already in place, with the completion of the project's second phase of construction.

This sprawling complex covers five unified city blocks. The logic of the development is explained by Don Cosgrove, former deputy director of the Community Redevelopment Agency (CRA), as follows:

> We [the CRA] came to the realization that these parcels were the last remaining contiguous parcels in downtown. This was fairly unprecedented in a developed downtown. Previous development in Bunker Hill was on a piecemeal, block-by-block basis. So we felt that this was a potential we should try to capitalize upon, to offer this land to a developer as a single offering—to make this the place in downtown Los Angeles, a focus, a center. The vision was that once it was completed anyone coming to the city would naturally know that this is the place to go to.[19]

The master plan, prepared by architect Arthur Erickson, utilizes the superblock concept. Erickson gave form to CRA's vision of monumentality by creating two axes emanating from a central open space, which is the focal point of the organization. Three high-rise office towers and other residential structures were located along this axial arrangement. Known as a "pure modernist architect,"[20] Erickson wanted to create a completely unified scheme, with the towers as pure geometric objects in the middle of open-air plazas. The two

FIGURE 114
California Plaza,
1996: The Watercourt.
Photograph by Liette
Gilbert.

towers constructed so far have the same modernist corporate architectural features: smooth and geometric forms, absence of ornamentation, flat rooftops, and the like. Here the Miesian modernist vision is revisited thirty years later.

The heart of the California Plaza is an open-air space, designed as a performance plaza. It has been recently renamed as the Watercourt (see figure 114). According to the developers, "the Watercourt is destined to become the compelling centerpiece of Downtown and the city's artistic community." The Watercourt spans over Olive Street like the hanging gardens of Babylon. The developers call the space an "urban garden." It has a lush landscape with water cascading down stepped terraces into a pool, seventeen feet below its highest point. The water feature apparently models an ocean wave, taking on a variety of forms "as it moves along the California coast."[21] The renderings show a futuristic landscape with elaborate domed pavilions and circular stages constructed of ornate metal frames. This is a landscape quite different from all other plazas. It is symbolically and functionally a non sequitur in its surrounding urban reality. The poetics of design is often oblivious of the context.

Erickson's original scheme included a 1.5-acre park along Grand Avenue, in front of the residential units. As Erickson explained, in the original concept the hotel was placed at the north end, the residential units were along Olive Street, and the office buildings were located at the south end. However, the park site became the site for MOCA, and the hotel was pulled southward because the developers decided that it was too isolated at its original location. Performance specialists brought in by the owner required a closed theater. Later a multistage concept was developed with the city's Cultural Affairs Department. Faced with these unexpected changes, Erickson had to adjust his design. His idea was to make the stages a water feature when they were not in use. Thus, the Watercourt became a focal component of the project. As Erickson stated, his intentions regarding the space did not coincide with those of the developers:

> When I was asked to change and adjust my drawings, I developed the idea of a major open space for performances. I felt that this space along with the museum could be a major attraction to the site. In downtown Los Angeles, in Bunker Hill more specifically, you don't have much pedestrian activity. You have to try and bring people in. So if this space for performances existed it could bring artists and spectators to the site. The developers were quite skeptical. Sometimes developers can be quite narrow-minded! They were skeptical about the museum, but now that it is the major attraction to the site they are very happy. They learn down the line. In the Watercourt they were skeptical about the performance space. We finally suggested the space as is [with water], but the idea is that the water can be drained very quickly and the space can serve for performances.[22]

Metropolitan Structures, the managing partner of the development group, pointed out that the developers wanted the Watercourt to be more "orchestrated," rather than free-form, and more inward-oriented. Although they saw the complex as "an oasis for entertainment and relaxation," they felt that the performance area in the original plan would, when not in use, cause people to loiter. In the final design, the Watercourt is much less accessible and is insulated from the public realm of the adjacent street.

Although the Watercourt is the dominant feature of the complex, a smaller and more intimate open space was the main amenity California Plaza had to offer in the first phase. Known as the Spiral Court, it is designed as a four-hundred-seat amphitheater. Situated along Grand Avenue, between MOCA, the hotel, and the office towers, the space was designed by Erickson as a circle within a square. A wide, relaxed spiral staircase along the perimeter of the circle descends to the lower level. Steps inside of the arc form the amphitheater, with a stage at the lower level. This lower level, which has shops and restaurants, is hidden and protected from the street. This space is more public than the Watercourt. Its street edge, although partly protected by shrubbery and a low wall, is soft, and the space bleeds into the street realm. The design seeks to convey serenity through the use of natural elements: greenery and water. A waterfall cascades down to the lower level, drowning out all street noise. The seating area inside the circle is also surrounded by rows of trees and lush vegetation. The Spiral Court is a popular site for weekday lunches and summer concert programs.

An urban theater   When Horton Plaza first opened one weekend in 1985, a quarter of a million people showed up in downtown San Diego.[23] People came mainly to experience a new kind of shopping mall. A nine-block redevelopment project, it was one of the several elements of a concerted effort to revitalize downtown San Diego. A lazy, meandering street of gentle curves and changing levels cuts diagonally through the six-block complex. It is the central organizing feature of the project, connecting many interlocking levels of parking, shopping, food, and entertainment. It is flanked by four department stores and four staggered levels of shopping arcades. This is an "invented street" par excellence (Banerjee et al. 1996).

Architectural observers consider Jon Jerde's design of Horton Plaza unorthodox (see figures 115–117), because, as Witold Rybczynski (1993, 106) points out, it "turned the tables on the now-traditional enclosed mall and put all the public area outdoors." Commenting on the design of Horton Plaza, Rybczynski further observes, "Horton Plaza is a tour de force that includes bits and pieces of almost every stylistic period in history—Egyptian, Renaissance, Moorish, Art Deco, Victorian, Mediterranean. The result resembles a Cecil B. DeMille backlot."

For Jerde, designing Horton Plaza was an opportunity to apply urban design ideas based on a notion of "urban fields." This mode of design, according to Paul Sachner (1986, 130), "focuses less on individual buildings than on the

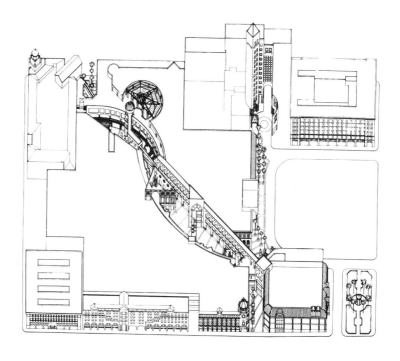

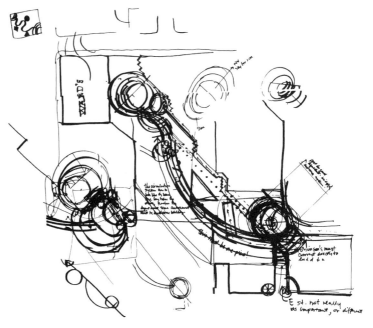

FIGURE 115
Opposite, top:
Axonometric sketch of
Horton Plaza. Courtesy of
The Jerde Partnership, Inc.
(The Jerde Partnership
1992, 12).

FIGURE 116
Opposite, bottom:
Conceptual sketch of
Horton Plaza by Jon
Jerde. Courtesy of The
Jerde Partnership, Inc.
(The Jerde Partnership
1992, 11).

FIGURE 117
Horton Plaza, 1995.
Photograph by Tridib
Banerjee.

creation of mixed-use districts—that Jerde had first encountered as a student traveling through the hill towns of southern Europe."

Jerde himself has called Horton Plaza an "urban theater." Indeed this is a place designed for what the French call *flânerié* (Buck-Morss 1989; Friedberg 1993)—"to stroll, to loaf, to saunter, to lounge" (Sachner 1986). The intent was to develop the kind of urbanism commonly found in European cities—particularly those of southern Italy—that had inspired him for so long. In commenting about the eclectic and ersatz mix of architecture that Rybczynski described as a Hollywood backlot, Jerde observes (The Jerde Partnership 1992, 10),

The underlying principle of this kind of a project is that it precisely signatures the host place . . . the social, cultural, and phenomenological essence of what San Diego is, as place: subtropical, Hispanic in origin, deep shadow, color.

In some way we are talking about memory and distillation. We composed the project out of fragments of buildings already existing in San Diego; it was composed of the city that was pre-existent. . . . The initial thing was to de-code the language of the city . . . to discover its fantasy.

While Jerde has seen his design as one that reinvented the original city ("It . . . completely knits back into the city as the district re-emerges out onto its pre-existent grid pattern" [The Jerde Partnership 1992, 10]), some believe that it suffers from the "shopping-mall tendency to focus inward" (Sachner 1986, 130). This introversion is similar to that of several other projects we reviewed earlier. There is little doubt, however, that the complexity and novelty of its "internal reality" stand in sharp contrast to the bland, commonplace, and predictable architecture of office towers of the adjacent blocks.

In a piece entitled "The Aesthetic of Lostness," written as "a conceptual design for Horton Plaza in San Diego," author Ray Bradbury (1991, 47) captures the essence of its design:

That even in our interior malls, we can plan in such a way that, for a brief if not lengthy time, we can enjoy a few sensations of lostness. To build into these arcades twists and turns, and upper levels that by their mysteriousness draw the eye and attract the soul: That can be the subliminal lure of all future architectures.

Hell, why not, at the very top level of some future mall rear an entire floor labeled: THE ATTIC? Up there stash all your antique shops, antiquarian booksellers, Victorian toy merchants, magic shops, Halloween card and decoration facilities and little cinemas running "Dracula" fourteen hours a day, or name another half-dozen specialty stores that wouldn't mind being half-lit and fully exciting. Do you mean to tell me that wouldn't be the first place the kids would rush, hurling themselves and their parents onto escalators headed up among the fireflies and dingbats?

Projects of this scale represent a wholesale rearrangement of the urban fabric. They involve big decisions, major public and private investments, and usually complex and lengthy negotiations between many stakeholders. They are promoted as pivotal projects, ones that become catalysts for additional development. Horton Plaza was seen as such a project, and seemingly it has had a significant role in revitalizing downtown San Diego. Although similar in scope, the circumstances of California Plaza are different, and it has yet to reach the level of success enjoyed by Horton Plaza. Nevertheless, they are both promoted as major destinations. Their design and the associated rhetoric reflect such aspirations.

RHETORIC OF DESIGN

The poetics of open space, as should be apparent from the above examples, not only may vary with the scale of the project (and, therefore, with the degree of public involvement in the process) but also may depend on the configuration and location of the open space within the complex. Terms like "room," "terrace," "court," "garden," and "grotto" are inherently private and personal. They indicate repose, withdrawal, control, enclosure, separation, and more than a whiff of aristocracy and exclusiveness. In the design imagination, the potency of the metaphor is linked directly to the form of the space. Thus when Jerde invokes the metaphor of grotto to describe his subterranean shopping space, or when Andrew Butler describes his little park as a "room," they not only articulate the physical form of the space but also invoke the meaning commonly associated with it.

As the scale of the project increases, the space becomes more Dionysian and less precise and controlled; open-ended edges easily fuse into the public realm of the street. The poetics accordingly changes to reflect the publicness of the open space. Thus, a space may be called a court (more private) or a plaza (more public) depending on its configuration and design. In part this differentiation can be seen as a reflection of the increased public "equity" that comes with the increased scale of projects, and thus the increased public claim over the space. In table 3 we show a generalized relationship between the degree of public control—ranging from incentives to equity—and the scale of development. As we see in table 4, the rhetoric changes according to the scale of the project. Rooms, gardens, courts, and terraces give way to basilicas, gallerias, plazas, theaters, and the like. The rhetoric of privacy, repose, and exclusivity changes to that of communion, congregation, and community.

Table 3. Degree of Public Control and Scale of Development

Degree of Public Control

Private	Incentive	Requirement	Small Equity	Large Equity	Ownership	Public
	Sub-block					
		Super-block				
				Multi-block		

Table 4. Scale of Projects and Poetics of Space

Scale	Project	Design Metaphor	Official Designation
Sub-block	Grabhorn Park	Oasis, room	Urban garden
	One Hundred First	Sun terrace	View/sun terrace
	Figueroa at Wilshire	Plaza	Plaza
	Bunker Hill Steps	Vertical plaza	Steps
Super-block	Crocker Center	Galleria	Galleria
	Rincon Center	Basilica	Galleria
	Citicorp Plaza	Grotto, market	Plaza
Multi-block	California Plaza	Water court, cultural complex	Plaza
	Horton Plaza	Urban theater, village	Plaza

Beyond this rough correspondence between the scale and form of urban spaces and their poetics, there is also the more profound question of the dialectic of the urban design of a postmodern downtown. It has been suggested that the very act of design involves mediating between, on the one hand, a set of arguments that represent, say, the purity, sustainability, and community of a site and, on the other, a different set of arguments involving property rights, market forces, and internal rates of return. Any new increment of change in the urban form sets in motion a whole new set of arguments and counterarguments. The process of city design and city building is, thus, an incessant dialectic (see Cuff et al. 1994, 141). Since the dawn of market liberalism in the nineteenth century, urban design has always encountered the dialectic of public interests versus private property rights. But as urban design has become more dependent on the private sector, it has come to represent several parallel dialectics. The poetics of urban space described here can be seen basically as rhetorical attempts to mediate between these dialectics.

One such dialectic, and perhaps the central theme of our enterprise here, is the tension between the private realm of corporate ownership and the public domain. Architects and urban designers who are working for private clients are caught in the dilemma of, on the one hand, following the directives of the immediate client—which are intended to produce greater control, safety of users, and exclusion of incivilities and undesirable elements of the public life—and, on the other hand, following their own romantic views of the good city, historic models of public places, and the like. The rhetoric of design grows out of this dialectic and is reflected both in the design and in the poetics of the urban space.

The parallel dialectics we referred to are subtexts of this main theme: they are the tensions between outside and inside; alienation and identity; exclusion and inclusion; change and continuity. Thus when Andrew Butler referred to Grabhorn Park as an oasis, he attempted to legitimize the private control of the space by invoking its function of offering shelter and respite to the individual from the din and bustle of the anonymous urban environment. The roof gardens of Crocker Center and the sun terrace of One Hundred First also have similar intentions. Recall also Jerde's attempt to shelter his users from the "polluted outside" and to screen the larger urban context. In invoking the image of basilica in Rincon Center's design, Scott Johnson was suggesting a purity in the domain of space—an inside space protected from the city outside, almost a sacred space protected from the profane (see Eliade 1959). At the same time the metaphor asserts the greater public claim and access that a church implies. Jerde's metaphor of urban theater, and his vision of promoting flânerié, also reflect an effort to assert the public and populist aspects of the place while creating a physically introverted space that maintains private control.

8

■

An important component of the new downtown urban design is the provision and orchestration of what is commonly referred to as "public art." Frequently linked to the requirement for open space, public art has become an important part not only of individual building design but also of overall urban design. Consider the design of the open space in front of the Japanese Cultural Center in Los Angeles' Little Tokyo redevelopment district. When the Los Angeles CRA invited sculptor Isamu Noguchi to design a sculpture for this space, Noguchi declined, saying that the space was too small to provide appropriate viewing distance for the scale of sculpture he had in mind (see figure 118). Determined to have a Noguchi sculpture, the CRA planners made the space larger by eliminating one of the buildings originally proposed for the site, even though it meant losing a nontrivial amount of tax-increment revenue. This episode might sound like the tail wagging the dog, but in fact it establishes the importance an agency like the CRA places on acquiring a piece of signature art. In this case not only urban design but also the redevelopment program for the site itself was dictated by the art decision.

The public agency's remarkable gesture is comparable in scale only to the bidding of rich art collectors at Sotheby's. With the stroke of a pen (actually an eraser in this instance), the agency expended millions of dollars of future tax revenue to acquire a piece of public art. What makes it particularly noteworthy is that the days of statues of figures on horses are long gone, and we no longer celebrate national heroes or moments of national glory by commissioning public art of monumental scale (such as the monument in downtown Detroit pictured in figure 119), much less by celebrating a piece of art. A Piazza Navona with Bernini's *Four Rivers* is not very likely these days what with shrinking public coffers. But as Karen Halbreich (1988) points out, these days we have found ways to convince downtown developers—although they are not quite

FIGURE 118
Above: Little Tokyo, Los
Angeles, 1996: Sculpture
by Isamo Noguchi.
Photograph by Liette
Gilbert.

FIGURE 119
Above, right: Monument
in downtown Detroit,
1995. Photograph by
Tridib Banerjee.

the Medicis of our time—that patronage of public art is good for business and good for the welfare of society.

In spite of this success, questions about the role of public art remain. Does public art enhance urban aesthetics and contribute toward a higher quality of urbanism or public life? Why is public art so integral to downtown urban design? Does public art have any role to play in achieving urban design objectives? In this chapter we consider these questions.

PRIVATE PATRONAGE OF PUBLIC ART

Over the last four decades there has been an explosive growth in public art. The arts community sees this growth as a result of almost thirty-five years of activism and concerted efforts that began with government support for and patronage of the arts. Yet, despite earnest efforts by the arts community to define "public art," the term remains ambiguous, if not a contradiction in terms.[1] There are lingering questions about what constitutes public art and about who can create, commission, or choose such art. There are always questions about taste and the public purpose of or public interest in such art. To the chagrin of the arts community, public response to major works of art has often been controversial, and vulgar. Picasso's sculpture at Chicago City Hall has frequently been likened to a baboon or an Afghan dog. In Seattle, Isamu Noguchi's *Landscape of Time* and Michael Heizer's *Adjacent, Against, Upon* were compared to the "pet rock" craze. Richard Serra's *Tilted Arc* in New York's Federal Plaza was considered dangerous, and it ultimately required relocation (Senie 1992; Balfe and Wyszomirski 1986). The Vietnam Veterans Memorial in Washington touched an emotionally charged controversy over its meaning and symbolism (Hubbard 1984; Griswold 1992).

Critical discourse and practice in the arts community place equal emphasis on "public" and "art" (Halbreich 1988). Discussion of "public" usually involves consideration of the audience and purpose of the piece and of the participation of the public in the process of obtaining an art object. In this chapter we focus on the critical issues of ownership and placement of such public art pieces, and how these issues affect the potential viewers' access to and knowledge of the pieces. These issues arise because, as we will discuss in the following text, public art is increasingly being provided by private funds. The private funding is sometimes inspired by philanthropy (for example, Herbert Bayer's sculpture in the ARCO Plaza in downtown Los Angeles) or enlightened corporate interest,[2] but it is usually a result of coercion, if not legal mandates. The public art so produced is often not owned by the public or even situated in the public domain. Public access to such art is at worst controlled, at best privileged.[3]

True, there are examples where public art is unambiguously owned by the public and in the public domain: the "Chicago Picasso"; Calder's initially controversial *La Grande Vitesse* in Grand Rapids, Michigan (Allen 1988; Senie 1992);[4] the Vietnam Veterans Memorial in Washington; murals in Boston's metro rail stations; murals on the retaining walls of the Harbor and Hollywood freeways in Los Angeles in commemoration of the 1984 Olympics,[5] and the like. Examples of such publicly sponsored and owned public art, however, are becoming few and far between. More commonly, purveyance of public art has become a responsibility of corporate America, especially in the downtown setting.

Perhaps the most significant aspect of the burgeoning of public art is that such art is now required by the city authorities as a part of the permit process. It is relatively common today to see redevelopment agencies requiring a percentage of the construction cost set aside for public art. Developers oblige by locating art pieces in the downtown office plazas and corporate open spaces.

ONE PERCENT AESTHETICS

The first percent for art ordinance was passed in 1959 authorizing the Philadelphia Redevelopment Authority to collect 1 percent of private development funds for promoting art. By 1985, more than twenty cities in the United States had an art requirement for public projects or private projects on public land (Jones 1986). Of the major cities, Atlanta and Baltimore (in addition to Philadelphia) had a 1 percent art requirement for all developments. In 1985, a 1 percent art requirement was included in San Francisco's new downtown plan. That same year the Los Angeles CRA introduced a mandatory 1 percent art requirement on all development costs for downtown commercial projects.[6]

One percent of the construction cost is not an insignificant amount of money, either for the developer or for the arts industry. A fifty million dollar office building can produce one-half million dollars of public art. Nevertheless, developers and their corporate clients do not seem to mind the cost because proper selection and display of the public art can add to the appeal and prestige of the building. Plazas and forecourts to these buildings are often designed around a centerpiece art object. As we will discuss later, in Los Angeles the well-known Museum of Contemporary Arts (MOCA) designed by Arata Isozaki was paid for entirely by the percent for art requirement.

Specific rules and mechanisms for percent for art funding can vary among cities. In Los Angeles developers are required to contribute 1 percent of the project cost (exclusive of land). Of this amount, at least 40 percent is to be deposited in the Downtown Cultural Trust Fund. Developers can use the other 60 percent toward their obligation to provide on-site artwork. However, the on-site art requirement can be waived if a developer makes a donation of

0.8 percent of the project cost exclusively to the trust fund. This policy is clearly designed to give the CRA greater control of the art fund in terms of both the location and the selection of artwork for the purpose of beautification of ugly urban spaces. Interestingly, developers continue to have on-site artwork, even though it costs them more.

The broad aims and the stated public purpose of this requirement also vary from city to city. For downtown Los Angeles, the CRA's aim is to develop an art in public places program "that is diverse and of the highest quality; that will, over the decades reflect the City itself and the minds of its citizens; that will improve the quality of life in the downtown area and be a source of pride to all City residents" (Community Redevelopment Agency 1985).[7] Some cities take a prescriptive approach to public art without necessarily making explicit underlying policies or purposes. A case in point is San Francisco's planning code, which includes detailed specifications about the types of art and the materials that are acceptable, as well as their location, visibility, and maintenance. Other cities focus on overall policies and processes. In cities like Dallas, Phoenix, and Seattle, public arts programs are institutionalized in the form of detailed master plans.[8]

Must public art be situated in the public realm? Metropolitan Dade County ordinances seem to suggest that public art belongs only in public spaces—beaches, parks, squares, streets, and the like—that are under public ownership. In most cities, however, public art is located in sites under private ownership but with a presumption of public access and visibility. The Los Angeles CRA, for example, has developed operational guidelines to broaden the eligibility of public art. It defines eligible locations for public art as follows:

> Spaces that are accessible to the public a minimum of 12 and preferably up to 18 hours a day, either on private or public property, may be considered suitable locations for public art. Such facilities include commercial and residential buildings and adjoining plazas, parks, sidewalk, traffic islands, public buildings, power stations, etc. Spaces may be interior or exterior. Locations can include surface treatments of buildings, retaining walls and bridges. . . . However, the primary objective of visual or interactive public accessibility must be realized for the specific number of hours per day. (Community Redevelopment Agency 1985, 7)

This definition does not, however, involve any presumption of public domain. Any private space, whether outdoor (courts, plazas, gardens) or indoor (lobbies, foyers, atriums), is eligible if the exposure criterion is met. This rule also allows developers to meet the public art requirement by locating the artwork off-site and in such public domains as sidewalks, parks, traffic islands, public buildings, and the like. What is more, the agency uses the broadest definition of art and "encourages imaginative interpretations of media" to include such categories as sculpture, murals or portable paintings, earthworks (or fiber works, neon, glass, mosaics, and so on), and such standardized fixtures as gates and streetlights (Community Redevelopment Agency 1985). Because of the broad definition of art allowed in Los Angeles and in most cities, the design of a plaza itself could be considered public art.[9]

In Los Angeles, the CRA has creatively defined the scope of the 1 percent art fund to include not only on-site art but also broader cultural programs within downtown. Even the scope of the on-site projects has been expanded to include such cultural programs as performance arts (theater, dance, music), literary arts (poetry readings and storytelling), media arts (film and video, screenings, and installations) and education (lectures and presentations about art).

Let us then consider some notable examples of public art—in its widest range of interpretations—that have been created by the percent for art movement. These examples are selected to emphasize the urban design implications of such public art.

The Museum of Contemporary Art   Clad in red sandstone brought from India and considered an architectural jewel by many, MOCA stands along the Grand Avenue edge of California Plaza, immediately north of the Spiral Court (see figure 120). The 1 percent for art program was being formalized at about the time that the competition for California Plaza was taking place. The CRA wanted to devote 1.5 acres to an open park area. Discussions between the CRA and the committee appointed by the mayor to identify a location for a contemporary arts museum led to the idea that MOCA could find a home in California Plaza. The developer would have to contribute 1.5 percent of the project cost (instead of the usual 1 percent) toward the construction of the museum. Canadian developers Cadillac Fairview (one of the two competition finalists) offered to carry the entire construction cost of the museum, in order to en-

hance their chances of winning. According to former CRA Deputy Director Don Cosgrove, this gesture weighed significantly in the agency's final decision.

In architect Arthur Erickson's original concept, the museum was incorporated into the base of a residential building, and it opened out onto the park along Grand Avenue. It featured two-story-high, transparent art galleries, with huge canvases to capture the attention of automobile drivers. However, the museum's board did not like Erickson's design and were offended by what they perceived to be a "billboard approach" to the display of fine art.[10] Although Erickson started modifying his design to address the board's concerns, the chairman of the board announced a design competition for the museum.[11] Out of this competition Arata Isozaki was chosen as the architect. Erickson had to revise his master plan, which led to difficult negotiations between the developers and the museum's board.

According to Don Cosgrove, the issue of the museum became extremely important, and especially important were questions about where to locate it and how to integrate Isozaki's design into Erickson's concept. The whole issue of the museum's height was sensitive. The developers did not want to have the

views of the housing blocked, or to have the ground floor retail concealed from the street. Another issue was the museum's coffee shop; developers were concerned that it might compete with the project's restaurants. The developer wanted to make the museum building as small, compact, and low as possible. The inclination of the MOCA board was quite the opposite: the board wanted to make a statement.

Eventually an agreement was reached about the placement and footprint of the new museum: it would consist of two low blocks separated by a sculpture court. Erickson designed the open space, a linear park behind MOCA, which links the museum to the upper level of the Spiral Court (see figure 121). This linear open space, with its axial placement of pools, trees, planters, and benches, provides a clear transition from the museum and office buildings to the hotel and residential towers.

The museum is an example not only of how the percent for art program can be used to develop major cultural facilities but also of how the art object itself, like the Noguchi sculpture we discussed earlier, can influence the overall urban design. We will return to this theme later in this chapter.

FIGURE 121
Opposite: Museum of
Contemporary Art in Los
Angeles, 1996: Outdoor
art. Photograph by Liette
Gilbert.

FIGURE 122
Corporate Head, public
art in Citicorp Plaza,
1996. Photograph by
Tridib Banerjee.

Poet's Walk   Poet's Walk at Citicorp Plaza is a good example of how corporate America takes its role as a purveyor of art quite seriously. Here Prudential Property Company, the developer of Citicorp Plaza, responded to the percent for art requirement with enthusiasm. Instead of installing a single piece of monumental art, they commissioned creative work from many artists and poets. Most of the pieces are scattered throughout the open space, on the surface of buildings and the outer edge of the property next to the public sidewalk. The artwork is an integral part of the hardscape of the site and is strategically located throughout the plaza to dramatize its impact on the viewer. Most of the pieces are quite small and unobtrusive, and they require close examination. The subjects are often humorous, and many deprecate the downtown culture. Perhaps the most striking of the lot is Terry Allen's life-size bronze of downtown businessman with his briefcase in hand and his head buried in the granite wall of the base of an SOM-designed office tower (see figure 122). Titled *Cor-*

FIGURE 123
*Pigeons Acquire
Philosophy*, public art
in Citicorp Plaza, 1996.
Photograph by Tridib
Banerjee.

FIGURE 124
Water and fire sculpture
by Eric Orr, Wilshire at
Figueroa Plaza, 1996.
Photograph by Liette
Gilbert.

porate Head, the sculpture captures the stress and alienation of the downtown work environment. "He appears to be a tall man having 'one of those days,'" reads one caption. David Gilhooly's bronze replica of pigeons pecking at a fried egg on some abandoned newspapers (accompanied by the captions "The Public Abandons Philosophy" and "Pigeons Acquire Philosophy") is an example of what the developers see as "a means for uniting urban and artistic culture" (see figure 123).[12]

What is noteworthy about this collection of commissioned artwork is not only the novelty and intrigue of the pieces and their relation to everyday life, but also their overall choreography within the site, almost like that of a museum. The management wants its public to explore and view this art, to discover the not so obvious pieces, to read the verses that accompany them. The whole presentation is designed to make people spend time in the plaza. The management now has a special guide, entitled "Art Walk," to all of the art pieces scattered throughout the plaza, just as a museum might have a guide for its exhibits or collections.

The fire and water paradox The arts obligation for the Figueroa at Wilshire Tower a block north of Citicorp Plaza, was met in a very different manner (see figure 124). A single art piece installed at the corner of the property essentially defines the plaza and separates it from its otherwise seamless transition from the sidewalk. The L-shaped plaza is the residual space, the difference between the building footprint and the site area. It is defined by forty-foot and twenty-five foot setbacks from Wilshire and Figueroa, respectively, by pushing the building back to the northwest corner of the site.

The street corner is the focal point of the plaza. There stands the thirty-five-foot-high water-and-fire art piece designed by sculptor Eric Orr, which we described in chapter 7. Before the sculpture was put in its place, architect David Martin commented, "I want the sculpture to be perceived from an automobile as well as by pedestrians. The only regret I have is that I wanted it to be a fountain. But it is a very intellectual piece with a very populist end result. Few art pieces can accomplish that kind of trick." [13]

Art in a basilica San Francisco's Rincon Center is a redevelopment project, and it began before the 1985 downtown plan was approved. Technically it was outside any of the linkage requirements, but as we have seen elsewhere, it was eventually overrun by a "creeping Downtown Plan." [14] Nevertheless the arts requirement was inevitable and was met creatively with several elements integral to the architectural design of both the interior and the exterior spaces.

The inspiration for the art came from the original art treasures of the Rincon Annex—its famous murals covering four hundred feet of wall space in the old post office lobby. These murals were painted by the famous Russian immigrant painter Anton Refregier between 1940 and 1948. The commission was awarded by the section of painting and sculpture of the Treasury Department on the basis of a national competition. According to one account, "The murals are important in the history of American mural painting, not only for their size, but for the sweep of their narrative power and for the controversy caused by their treatment of the subject matter" (San Francisco Department of City Planning 1979, 3).

FIGURE 125
Rincon Center, 1992:
The rain column, with
decorative friezes in the
background. Photograph
by Anastasia Loukaitou-
Sideris.

The murals—with their theme of the hardships and struggles of California's early settlers—became the focus of a major political controversy in the fifties. At the height of McCarthyism they faced serious threats of removal. The murals survived the political storm, and they became steeped in special meaning and significance and continue to be a major tourist attraction today. On November 1, 1978, the Landmarks Preservation Advisory Board designated the interior lobby, which includes the murals, and the exterior of Rincon Annex as historical landmarks.

In the friezes surrounding the atrium, above the eating areas, there is a different style of mural, in bas-relief and more muted color (see figure 125). Since access to the atrium, which is located inside the shell of the old post office, from Mission is through the lobby of the old post office, the artistic continuity created by the new murals is self-evident and probably appreciated as a nice gesture by most visitors. The new murals in the atrium were done by Richard Haas, a New York–based muralist of considerable fame.

The second art element, also a part of the public art requirement, is the "rain column" described in chapter 7 and depicted in figure 125. A third art element in Rincon Center is an outdoor art piece that is located in the transitional open space between the historic post office and the new residential towers atop commercial spaces. As it turned out this art piece is more user friendly. People perch on its various levels during lunch hours eating lunch, and children like to climb on it.

The examples above are but a few vignettes of how the corporate plazas of downtown America are now being transformed into private art galleries of nominally public art. These art pieces have replaced the mimes, the jugglers, and the fire-eaters of the earlier public squares. Public performers have not, however, completely vanished from American cities. Amateur opera singers, troubadours, folksingers, jazz musicians, saxophonists, and violinists are still commonplace on the concourse of the Harvard Square subway station in Cambridge or on the sidewalks around Union Square in San Francisco. But these public performers are not likely to be allowed in the corporate plazas. They are considered riffraff, or worse, and are seen as engaging in a form of solicitation. It remains unclear, however, where in a free market economy selling (of entertainment in this instance) ends and solicitation begins.

A plaza for performance   To the promoters of percent for art programs it was clear that art in itself was not going to create the kind of social life in small urban spaces that William H. Whyte (1980) so eloquently described. This realization led to a broadening of the scope of percent for art programs. Los Angeles is one of the cities that required some of the developers to not only provide the setting but also produce specific cultural events such as noontime concerts in summers and evening and weekend performances on a fairly regular basis.[15]

The California Plaza development was one of the projects that was dedicated to the staging of such public events and performances. It will be recalled from our earlier discussion that Cadillac Fairview had committed to building

FIGURE 126
California Plaza, 1996:
Amphitheater in the
Watercourt. Photograph
by Liette Gilbert.

MOCA. The provision of cultural programs was an additional requirement, one that was not necessarily a bane. As we will see in the next chapter, all downtown developers are looking for a theme or a selling point to remain competitive in the office leasing market. A cultural theme was convenient for product differentiation. Because it is close to the civic center cultural facilities and includes MOCA in the complex, the California Plaza complex can promote itself as a culturally oriented development—a stage set for arts and culture.

The overall organization of California Plaza is based on a system of courts. The function of the courts was seen mainly as accommodating various types of performing arts and their spectators. The Spiral Court, built during the first phase of development, is exclusively designed as an amphitheater with stepped seating. The Watercourt, built several years later as part of the second phase, is a much more elaborate and lavish affair, with fountains, gazebos, pools, an amphitheater with a floating stage, and the like (see figure 126). It appears more like a garden court of a Las Vegas casino-hotel than that of a downtown office complex.

As expected, there is a limit to what can take place in California Plaza. The developers will not allow unplanned events, speeches, and so on. Rather they try to program a wide variety of theatrical entertainment. Indeed Metropolitan Structures, the owners of California Plaza, already have an active cultural program for the Spiral Court area, which includes weekend evening performances and weekday noontime concerts during the summer months. In 1990, they even hired a full-time artistic director who now plans and coordinates such events, sometimes in collaboration with the city's Cultural Affairs Department.

In the Watercourt, the water can dry within an hour, and the space can be used for scheduled performances, for a philharmonic orchestra, for example. The space can seat about four thousand people. The developers expect the Watercourt to be used for office parties and receptions, and even private wedding parties. This latter use is not unique to California Plaza; office lobbies and courtyards are being used for such receptions in other downtowns also. As the representative of the developer further explained, the cost for the Watercourt (roughly 5 percent of the project's total cost) can be fully justified, as this focal open space helps attract tenants. Scheduled performances and cultural activities draw people and give recognition to the project. The plaza's maintenance and operation costs are passed back to the tenants.

THE CUMULATIVE EFFECT

We began this chapter by arguing that the emphasis on public art and open spaces is an important element of the new downtown urban design. As we have shown in the selected examples from Los Angeles and San Francisco, there are many forms and interpretations of the public art requirement today. Individual situations and sometimes creative deal-making make the implementation of arts requirement quite varied. We want to conclude this chapter by addressing the questions that bubble to the surface:

- Why public art? What is public art? Does public art serve a public purpose? How are these purposes served? Have they succeeded?
- Why has public art grown so much in recent years? What explains this investment in aesthetics in the face of worsening urban poverty and social problems?

- Does public art add up to or supplant urban design? Is this use of public art a trait of postmodern urban design in the sense that it mimics classical urban design? Is it simply urban ornamentation? Is it a tacit attempt to redeem poor architecture and urban design?

As we have discussed earlier, the arts community is still wrestling with the first set of questions, the why and what of public art. Attempts to define the "publicness" of public art are usually limited to procedural criteria—which type of art, which artists, public participation, selection process, and the like—rather than functional criteria, that is, access, audience, exposure, benefits, ownership, and the like. We suspect that the latter criteria are not often explicitly considered because the vast majority of the art results from corporate patronage and remains on private property and under private ownership. Under these circumstances, applying the above functional criteria to judge publicness of the public art becomes an untenable prospect.

If the purpose of public art is to educate the uneducated or to serve an economically disadvantaged public, who are usually deprived of opportunities to appreciate art, it is not clear that the public art produced by percent for art programs actually reaches these segments of the public (children, teenagers, or residents of poor neighborhoods). As figure 127 shows, even within the downtown environment public art is concentrated predominantly in the white-collar corporate downtown, or at best in the more public civic center, but not in the older and poorer section of the downtown.

There is also the sense that these pieces of public art are not truly in the public domain; that is, despite invitations to the public, such as that in Citicorp Plaza's attractive brochure for Poet's Walk, access to such art is always privileged, courtesy of the management. As explained in chapter 6, people could conceivably be excluded because of their clothing, appearance, or behavior. Even in a city like San Francisco, which has a strong legacy of being a "public city" (Ethington 1994) and where the planners emphasize the public's right to such art or open spaces by requiring the owners to post a sign, it still remains a contrived right under a presumption of public domain.

Is this diminished publicness of public art a serious problem? What is lost

FIGURE 127
Map of public art in
downtown Los Angeles.
Drawing by Liette Gilbert.
Closed dots represent
sculptures; open dots,
murals.

after all? If what is lost is the right to what are generally considered public annoyances and incivilities—skateboards, "boom boxes," and pigeon feeding—is that a real problem? No public art gallery or museum would allow such incivilities. All public art galleries are carefully monitored by the security. No gallery or museum would allow visitors to bring food and drink to the galleries, but, in fact, a brown-bag lunch crowd is quite commonplace in most plazas.

So why shouldn't the rules that apply to museums and galleries apply also to corporate plazas, which can be seen as open air museums? We believe that the exclusion of certain segments of the public results not from the enforcement of some implicit code of public decorum (although that always remains a possibility) but mainly from the highly selective and concentrated location of public art within the downtown and the larger city.

The second set of questions, those concerning the recent growth in public art, is easily answered. The growth is mainly a function of the percent for art programs promoted vigorously in many cities. Of all the linkage requirements, open space and public art are the least objectionable to the development community. When cities like San Francisco tried to add other linkage fees to mitigate such social problems as the lack of affordable housing, the development community resisted such requirements, calling them a form of exaction. But the attitude of developers toward the public art requirement is very different. As we have discovered from our interviews with various downtown developers, they not only do not mind these requirements but actually see them as opportunities to showcase their projects and remain competitive. Because the developers have considerable leeway in choosing, commissioning, and locating the specific art objects within the site, they prefer to include the art requirement in their overall project design rather than simply donating the money to some trust fund for arts, as many cities allow. From the developer's point of view, art is a permanent investment that is likely to appreciate at a much higher rate than the building itself.

The overall outcome of this process is that most of the public art is becoming concentrated in the downtown—even where there is a citywide program such as that in Seattle—since most large projects are typically located there. Downtowns have now to some extent become "aesthetic ghettos" (Goldin 1974).

This then brings us to the last set of questions, those concerning the public art nexus of downtown urban design. Does this accumulation of public art contribute to or supplant urban design? Is it a sign of vulgar postmodernity in urban design in the sense that it mimics classical civic design? Is public art a form of urban ornamentation, a form of window dressing? Is public art an attempt to redeem poor urban design, declining urbanism, and the poor quality of urban life? Some art critics have suggested that the benefit and purpose of

FIGURE 128
Public art embellishing
glass-and-concrete in
downtown Los Angeles,
1996. Photograph by
Liette Gilbert.

public art are derived from its palliative effect on the contemporary built form (Allen 1988). The modernist glass and steel box architecture of contemporary buildings is so repetitive, ubiquitous, banal, and sterile that it has intensified the public alienation with contemporary cities (see figure 128). Whether public art has managed to humor, intrigue, captivate, or inspire the public in a way that diminishes the collective sense of alienation is difficult to say. Some critics feel that it is unreasonable to expect art to compensate for the banality of the built environment. According to Allen (1988, 248),

> The public art movement of the last quarter century had its origin partially from an impulse to correct these urban design problems. The question is, how successful has this effort been? It is not an easy question to answer. . . . Its detractors refer to it as

"plop art" (as in, architect designs plaza, artist plops down sculpture). It seems clear that this approach to public artmaking, however well-intentioned, has cured few of the ills of modern architecture. Even Henry Moore . . . has deplored the use of art as costume jewelry, pinned on a building as an embellishment, as an afterthought. We cannot expect public art to atone for, or cover over, bad architectural design or shoddy urban planning. That aesthetic challenge is simply too great.

What we have seen in our examples, however, is that public art is expected to not only atone for the architecture and urban design but actually dictate the planning and design of the larger context. It is not clear if that has led to a successful urban design.

Perhaps the aim of public art is to revive the social life of privatized public spaces, but that too may be an untenable proposition, wishful thinking. As Spiro Kostof (1992, 181) has argued, "the social world of cities that played itself out in the old town square is dying; we will not bring it back by designing imitations of Piazza San Marco or the Hauptmarkt of Nuremberg." In contemporary "designer squares," Kostof argues, public space is seen as an "artist's canvas"—a medium for "signature designs" of architects, artists, landscape architects, and sculptors. This is the essence of the art and urban design nexus in the design of contemporary downtowns. Can aesthetics or contrived public events substitute for a true public space? Answering that question is one of the challenges of contemporary downtown urban design.

9

There is another side to the story of downtown urban design that has often eluded conventional models and theories of design: the particular way in which downtown building complexes and their accouterments are conceived, produced, promoted, and eventually managed. Our discussion in the previous two chapters focused on two important aspects of the story—the rhetoric of architectural design and the growing imperative of public art. In this chapter, we focus on the production and promotion of several modern mixed-use and office complexes. In these processes the development industry draws on the skills of many different specialized professions: the arts consultant, the media consultant, the theme designer, the facilitator, the negotiator, the event manager, and so on. As expected, the production and promotion of corporate real estate are guided by the private sector's concerns about marketability, competition, and high returns. In some cases the planners and urban designers working for the city are looking after the larger public goals, with an eye for the cumulative effect of the projects on downtown urbanism. More frequently, however, the development of the script for specific downtown projects is an exclusively private responsibility. The public good may then become co-opted completely by the developers' predilection, philosophy, and vision.

THEMING AND STAGE SETTING

Production, promotion, and management have become distinguishing features of contemporary downtown urban design because many downtown spaces are being seen as stage sets or even, to use Michael Sorkin's (1992) term, "theme parks," or some variation thereof. Contrived, Disneyland-like theme parks—privately produced, controlled, and managed—are considered indispensable for promoting, reinventing, and gentrifying older and declining districts of the city: including old industrial waterfronts, historic districts, languishing Main Street shopping districts, and the like. Critical writings on contemporary urban design (Sorkin 1992) have offered insights and interpretations of this burgeoning phenomenon.

Here we will argue that attention is increasingly given to developing a theme for downtown spaces, in promoting a theme park setting, in packaging and advertising the product, and finally, in managing and maintaining these places true to the script. In fact, as we have discussed previously, once the stage sets are created, the corporate owners sometimes hire full-time program managers to organize and schedule public events. These spaces are created to attract and entertain a limited and chosen clientele. Thus, for example, the elderly couple across the street may be welcome, but not the kids on skateboards from the local neighborhoods. Amenities are created to help spaces compete with others within a particular downtown and, collectively, with other downtowns. The downtown developers and their architects and urban designers are the leading actors in creating these stage sets and theme parks.

Disneyland has shown that it is possible to construct epitomized versions of environments that we have read about in history books, seen in movies, or visited in our travels, to construct environments that represent settings of the past, of a different land, and even of the future—all in a slightly edited, miniaturized, or exaggerated form. Disneyland, for example, offers a quaint but sanitized New Orleans square, a seven-eighths scale rendition (to create a subtle "Gulliver" effect for the visitors) of a U.S. Main Street, and a Tomorrowland, a Frontierland, and a Fantasyland, playing upon our fascinations with technology, wilderness, and childhood romanticism. Even the everyday urban world becomes the object of emulation. Walt Disney World in Florida has recreated Hollywood itself, and the EuroDisney in Paris and Disneyland in Japan come complete with urban settings from different countries. Significantly, people like to visit these contrived environments, and they pay good money for these make-believe experiences.

The theme park metaphor is particularly applicable to the larger downtown complexes that have relied on architectural leitmotifs to make the complex look quintessentially local, regional, or generic. Because of the differences in their size and design, however, not all downtown developments can be so characterized, as we have discussed in a previous chapter. After all, theme parks are very large enterprises—the EuroDisney theme park outside Paris consists of five thousand acres, and the proposed Disney's America in rural Virginia will take up three hundred acres of land. In contrast, the downtown spaces we have considered so far are parts of projects that range in size from several blocks to a part of a block. The theme park metaphor may seem malapropos for several other reasons: one does not have to pay a fee to enter the premises of a modern downtown office complex, nor is one drawn to any of these spaces purely for entertainment or fun. In fact, one is not expected to be there unless one is a worker, a client, or a customer. Nevertheless, they can still be seen as stage sets with a carefully crafted script for the kinds of activities that can or may occur.

We therefore use these metaphors advisedly. The term "theme park" has pejorative connotations—inauthenticity, contrivance, and speciousness—in the critical reviews of contemporary design. Yet, the obsession with theme-based design—the historic, the exotic, the phantasmagoric—is so widespread in architectural practice today that architecture critic Brendon Gill (1991, 96) has argued that architects are all suffering from a type of "Disneyitis." Others have argued that theme parks and so called tableux vivants and heritage experiences (Museums, Theme Parks 1991) are not creative expressions but trivialization of history and geography. According to one specialist in popular culture, they threaten "to compromise the values of literacy and history" (King 1990, 60). According to Sorkin (1994, 67) theme parks represent bad taste: "Taste is the battleground of history, and theming tests the limits of taste." Furthermore, others see theme parks as essentially an architecture of spectacle (Buck-Morss 1989; Foster 1985).

It seems, however, that the concept of stage set may be a more acceptable metaphor for the designers. Architect Jon Jerde, who bristles at any reference to his work as "theme park," finds the notion of a stage set quite appropriate for much of his work, including Horton Plaza. For a stage set, although contrived, representational, and ostensibly temporary, serves a larger purpose of supporting a drama, an event, or a performance. Not all of these downtown corporate plazas, however, have formal events. While California Plaza actually holds noontime concerts and summer evening performances, in other places the stage set is only there to provide props for everyday uses and activities. Jerde spoke of designing for the "common man" and serving his needs.[1] The central axis and the corridors of Horton Plaza may be seen as a stage set mainly for the purposes of flânerié and shopping, much the way the central space of Rockefeller Center was designed for such uses as skating or eating outdoors. To use Roger Barker's (1968, 17, 18–35) nomenclature for "behavior settings," a stage set is a synomorph for the behaviors—the acts—that occur in that location. We should note that anthropologist Erving Goffman (1969, 39), in describing behavior in "public places," uses the stage metaphor also, referring to the "backstage" and "front stage" components of spaces designed for public events. Similarly, although William H. Whyte (1988) does not explicitly use the stage set metaphor, he nevertheless enumerates a number of performance characteristics for public places as essential props for a successful public setting.

THE STORY OF PRODUCTION

In some sense, creating a major downtown office complex is not unlike making a film. While it may be difficult to draw exact parallels between all of the steps involved, there is a similarity in spirit that seems to resonate with recent observations of designers, developers, and writers about the changing nature of urban design and development. Consider, for example the following statement from a *Los Angeles Magazine* story about Two Rodeo Drive, a new shopping center in downtown Beverly Hills: "It's a $200 million haute shopping village, *written, produced and directed* almost entirely by developer-hyphenate Stizel . . . " (McNamara 1990, 106, emphasis added).

The fact that we are borrowing terms from the media and entertainment industry to talk about the design and production of urban spaces should not come as a surprise to anybody. The parallel between place-making and movie-making was drawn, and hinted at, not unexpectedly, by the architects and developers themselves. "It is like movie making in a way," commented architect Scott Johnson, in describing the intangible side of creating a successful public space. When asked to comment on this parallel, Jerde exclaimed: "It's exactly like making movies."[2] A similar response came from architect Herbert MacLaughlin, designer of the Two Rodeo Drive development and Colorado Place in downtown Pasadena, when he argued that the aim is to create a place where people would come back again and again, in the same way that they might want to see a successful movie over and over again. When Witold Rybczynski

FIGURE 129
Horton Plaza, 1995.
Photograph by Tridib
Banerjee.

(1993) refers to Horton Plaza as a Cecil B. DeMille backlot, the movie-making metaphor is apparent once again.

In the following text we draw from our case studies to highlight the less visible aspects of production and promotion of downtown settings. The story of downtown urban design will remain incomplete until we fully understand the uncertainties, risks, and idiosyncratic choices involved in the production and promotion of modern office and commercial complexes.

The intangibles: producing Horton Plaza   The design and development of Horton Plaza in San Diego took a long time to evolve into its present form (see figure 129).[3] The idea of a large retail complex downtown as an ingredient for revitalizing San Diego's languishing central district was proposed in the early seventies by Pete Wilson, then mayor of the city. He approached Ernest Hahn of the Hahn Company, the well-known shopping center developer, with the idea of redeveloping the area next to historic Horton Plaza park to bring retail back to downtown. Hahn was not sure, because the company had just taken all the major retailers out of downtown when they developed the Fashion Valley shopping complex, not too far from downtown.[4] But the mayor insisted, saying that he was truly committed to revitalizing downtown and felt that retail was an important ingredient in its revival. Furthermore, he wanted to know how to get the retailers to come back downtown.

In response to the mayor's request, the Hahn Company hired a planning group called Archisystems and along with ROMA, another consulting firm working with the city, proceeded to do a master plan for downtown San Diego. This plan was not limited to the small area around the Horton Park but encompassed about three hundred acres of downtown properties. The master plan included those elements that major retailers like Robinson's and Mervyn's had indicated, in their preliminary conversations with the Hahn Company, as preconditions for their anchoring a major retail complex downtown. These included new hotels, a new convention center, a marina, a residential development, and a light rail system.

Much to the surprise (and concern) of the Hahn Company, the mayor came back to them having more or less fulfilled all of the requirements, forcing the company to deliver its part of the deal. The company's initial proposal for the Horton Plaza development was a suburban shopping center in the urban core. It was an enclosed shopping mall surrounded by surface parking. The initial design of the retail complex received considerable public criticism for its unimaginativeness and the threat to wipe out the now successful Gaslamp district in order to meet the surface parking requirement. According to John Gilchrist, the president of the Hahn Corporation,

It was not that exciting. . . . We were being subject to some fairly decent criticism as it relates to the architectural solution. And also, as we started to take a harder look at the market, we realized that there wasn't sufficient daytime population to make the thing work. There wasn't sufficient tourist activity to make it work alone. There wasn't sufficient number of people living within a close radius to make it work. So there had to be something to attract those three constituents, as well as the pull from San Diego County. And what that meant was that pull by suburban centers, most of which we had developed in San Diego. So we knew the market, and we knew the competition, because for the most part, the competition was us.[5]

Having realized that they needed a special type of retail complex, one that could compete with existing regional malls, the Hahn Company finally called Jon Jerde, who had a long association with the firm and had designed many of their shopping centers. Jerde, who considered Hahn his mentor, had been urging for a chance to make shopping centers that were different from the standard formula, to design them as "people's places" like Italian hill towns. As Gilchrist recalled,

> But through the years, Jon had always talked to us about the hill towns of Sienna, people places, and Mr. Hahn and I would always say, "That's great, Jon, but we're not really ready for that yet." Well, lo and behold, we were finally ready for it, because we knew that it had to have a special feel to in fact work. . . . And the goal that we gave him was to make something that didn't look, taste, or feel like a regional shopping center, but one that had to have the practical aspects of one that could function. We said, "That's the ground rule. Plus, you can take the roof off."[6]

Finally given the chance to design a shopping center according to his own ideas, an invigorated Jerde assembled a team of designers and went to work immediately. He had very little time to produce the overall concept for the center. Nevertheless, he built a large model of the six-block area that is Horton Plaza today.

Theatrics were involved from the beginning. Since he wanted to impress the client, he put together a dramatic show choreographed with his architectural assistants. As Jerde recalls,

> We built a thirty-foot square model. The project is more like a Casbah, a district of a city; it is not a building. . . . We added to that every known special effect—smoke, music, light, drapes in black velvet. All of my people were dressed in black Ninja outfits running around the rafters with spotlights, because we didn't have any sophisticated equipment. The mayor, the city council, the redevelopment agency, chairmen of all the department stores, all the Hahn people, all showed up in one day. No one had seen the project. Hahn hadn't seen it. . . . This was the drumroll day of my life.[7]

It was the defining moment for the project. According to Jerde, they all left without speaking a word, leaving his team stunned and puzzled. Three days later he got a call from Jerry Trimble of the San Diego Redevelopment Agency saying that they hadn't seen anything like this before, but they were impressed and ready to move.

The design and development of Horton Plaza continued to evolve with insights and impulsive decisions from both the designer and the developer. Hahn himself played a critical role in making the place very distinctive. According to Bernard Frieden and Lynne Sagalyn (1989), who chronicled Horton Plaza's development, Hahn's decision to build a mall without enclosure, and air-conditioning, was a money saver and made the parking structures possible. It was also perhaps one of the most innovative elements of the design. According to Bernard Frieden and Lynne Sagalyn (1989, 192),

> Hahn recalled waking up at two in the morning and thinking, "We're going to take the damn roof off this thing, and we're going to make it look like part of the city, and we're going to make it exciting. . . . " He called Jerde in the middle of the night and said, "Take the damn roof off of it and see what you come up with." Jerde yelled with excitement, according to Hahn, because "he hated to be restricted to designing the toothpaste tube sort of air-conditioned environment prevalent in the normal suburban center, and suddenly his imagination and his talent took off."

The design team that Jerde assembled included Deborah Sussman, a color and graphics consultant, who had just finished working with Jerde on the design of the many venues of the 1984 Los Angeles Olympics. According to Frieden and Sagalyn (1989, 194), "they recreated the pastel shades and the stagelike settings of the Olympics, emphasizing soft blues and blue-greens, mauve-violets, aquas, magentas, peach, coral and rust." Although the forty-nine shades present a major challenge for the maintenance crew today, they are an important part of the visual excitement of Horton Plaza (see figure 130).

The script of Horton Plaza, however, was continually evolving even after major design elements were finalized. According to Gilchrist, the Hahn executives were literally looking over Jerde's shoulder as he was designing. To fine-tune the design, they were constantly expressing practical concerns about as-

FIGURE 130
Horton Plaza, 1995.
Photograph by Tridib
Banerjee.

pects such as space layout from the leasing standpoint or truck access from the servicing standpoint.

The other part of the evolving script was finding the right mix of tenants and merchandise. According to Gilchrist, "Great architecture and great space can attract the customer one or two times, but if you need them on a continual basis, you have to make sure you have a spectrum of merchandise."[8] Hahn himself played a major role in persuading the department store executives about the originality of the center. Similarly he urged the mall tenants to be creative and depart from their conventional store design. The Hahn organization developed a set of design guidelines that nudged the tenants to come up with new and innovative storefront design (Frieden and Sagalyn 1989).

When Mayor Pete Wilson wanted retail as a major ingredient in the down-

FIGURE 131
Model of the Metropolis
project. Courtesy of City
Centre Development.

town revival, there was widespread skepticism. In retrospect, the success of Horton Plaza was not at all certain. It was only after the script was completely rewritten and a team of creative designers and technical experts was assembled that the project became a financial success. The end result, what we know today as Horton Plaza, is the outcome of a process that seemed risky at the outset and ultimately required considerable imagination and creativity.

Writing the script: the Metropolis project   The Metropolis project in Los Angeles, which is described by its developers as a city within a city, was designed by Michael Graves (see figure 131). The developers plan to build it on a 6.3-acre site immediately west of the Harbor Freeway and to the south of the Citicorp complex. The project has been on hold for several years, mainly because of the depressed real estate market. It is conceived as a mixed-use development—

office, hotel, and retail—containing up to 2.7 million square feet of floor area. Its principal open space feature is a 90-by-550-foot garden court with a major amphitheater and a galleria connecting it to the street to the west. According to Leon Whiteson (1990, E1), the architectural form of the project "resembles a contemporary Karnak, a giant logo model created by a playful Pharaoh."

Some of the basic requirements for public amenities—open space, for example—were set by the Community Redevelopment Agency (CRA) in the early stages of the project. According to John Vallance, executive vice president of City Centre Development,[9] the project owners and developers and architect Michael Graves had no problem with that requirement: "Michael Graves wanted open space, we wanted open space, the CRA wanted it too."[10] In fact the guidelines set by the CRA with respect to the height and the massing of the buildings, a moderate height limit of thirty stories, were quite compatible with the overall program and the design approach of the architect.

Nevertheless, some basic theming needed to be done to make the project distinctive and competitive in a very soft office market. Coming up with a theme required some systematic thinking about the special public purpose the project could serve. Vallance commented, "I basically spent this time going around doing a needs assessment of the downtown area—talking to existing institutions, major but also informal and small, about what the cultural needs are in Los Angeles, in the downtown area, that are not served, and trying to find support. That's when we came up with a much larger list than we anticipated." Ultimately, the developers felt they needed an outside expert to develop the theme for the project. They hired an independent arts consultant, Helen Fried, who specializes in advising developers of office and mixed-use complexes on their themes and programs. For the Metropolis project, a major civic facility such as an art museum has been considered as a key thematic attraction that could distinguish this complex from its competitors. Citicorp Plaza had already established the Seventh Street Market as its principal theme, and California Plaza, the Watercourt.

Fried's role was to give advice about the "package" itself and to consider the tenant base and the demographics. According to Fried, her role was to determine "what else exists in the city and what can be supported over a long period of time."[11] The trick was packaging a theme without being redundant or trendy. From the leasing point of view, the amenities would need long-term appeal. Commented Fried, "There are certain things that will exist in all open spaces: the need to have relief from an office environment, the need for the occasional visitor, the pedestrians, the residents, to feel comfortable to come to a public open space, when they are not working in the building. But beyond that how to distinguish these open spaces, how to give them a sense of character, is really the task at hand." [12]

The expertise of the arts or event consultant is directed toward not just advising the architect what to design but also considering how the life of these places will be sustained in the long run. In a way, this process is similar to that involved in developing a program for a building, which many architects are called upon to do these days. The task here is to design the program for the place. As Fried explained, the quality of an enduring experience of the place is a function of more than just the physical design of the space: "If you look at the plans of all those projects you see . . . they all have the required seating, the required public art, the sunshine. But twenty years from now the projects that will really work usually will be the ones in which the owner-developer will stay . . . and the tenant is an active participant."

While Michael Graves's design for the complex includes an amphitheater, a major garden, and a connecting shopping arcade, the search for an enduring theme that will seal the long-term distinctiveness of the complex still continues. At the time of our discussion with John Vallance and Helene Fried, the idea of a multicultural center that would reflect the diversity of the Los Angeles area and could serve as a regional attraction was very much under consideration. According to Fried,

> In LA what we decided on this project is to take the clue from the cultural entity. Although we have an amphitheater designed and planned for, we will look at what will be the eventual use. We are looking at everything from a cultural center about LA, about the history, the art, the architecture, the culture. We are talking to people as diverse as Latino, the new Latino Museum of Art History and Culture, the Shakespeare Festival, . . . the Theater Center Group to expand an existing distinguished program.

If the developers decide to accept the consultants' recommendation, it could ultimately determine the long-term programmatic character—the final script—of the open space.

The screenplay of public design: Crocker Center   In the cases of Horton Plaza and the Metropolis project, we have seen how the various members of the development team collaborated on the theming and stage setting of the complexes. While the team had to fulfill certain public requirements, the themes of the projects were not dictated by the public sector. Under certain circumstances, however, the imperatives of the public sector can essentially determine a particular design outcome (though admittedly, it does not happen frequently). Crocker Center in San Francisco is a case in point.

In chapter 4 we reviewed the politics of negotiation and deal-making, between a major bank and a planning department with a strong sense of a public mandate, involved in the approval process for the Crocker Center project. Here we will focus on the details of the urban design negotiations that we touched upon only briefly in chapter 4.

With the passage of time institutional memory becomes hazy, but former San Francisco Planning Director Rai Okamoto recalled that the Crocker Center proposal was presented toward the tail end of the incentive zoning regime. The scope of the project was immediately subject to scrutiny, even though the existing bonus provision would have allowed what was being proposed. In a September 7, 1972, letter to Ed Abrahamian of A.C. Martin & Associates, Alan Lubliner, a planner from the zoning administrator's office pointed out that "[A]lthough the subject site could be developed with an extremely high gross floor area given the various bonuses that might be applicable to the site, we do not believe that maximum development would be appropriate" because, he continued, "the City Planning Commission adopted a policy a number of years ago to review under its discretionary powers all building permits for sites on or generally viewable from Market Street." [13] The Crocker site was in the viewshed of Market Street and therefore subject to such discretionary review. This then led to an in-house urban design analysis of the site by the City Planning Department and its urban designer, Richard Hedman. The department made several recommendations for the design of the building. The analysis emphasized the importance of maintaining the historical base of the original Crocker Bank building. It stressed the importance of the view of the Hallidie and Aetna buildings from Lick Alley. It argued against constructing a plaza at the northwestern side of the site so as to not weaken the pleasing Aetna building and

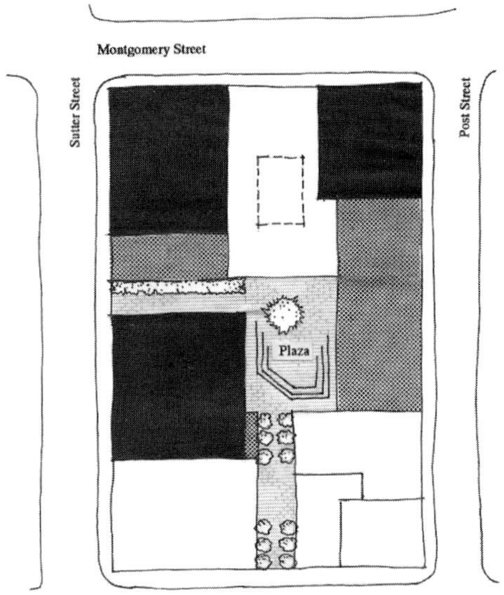

FIGURE 132
Sketch of proposed
Crocker Center by the
planning department:
Alternative 1. San
Francisco Department
of City Planning.
Redrawn by Liette Gilbert.

outlined the possibilities for the main banking room of Crocker Bank. Thus, the first draft of the plot was already written in the urban design directives!

These main points were illustrated in a sketch showing the locations of various buildings and the constraints on and possibilities for the site. The urban design study by the Department of City Planning went even further to propose three schematic alternatives. The first, and most preferred, scenario was the creation of a small, 85-by-110-foot plaza to the west of the main banking room and literally at the center of the larger street block bounded by Post, Montgomery, Sutter, and Kearny (see figure 132). This scenario would have connected Lick Alley with Ver Mehr and created a pedestrian connection between Sutter and Kearny inside the block. A fountain was to be located asymmetrical to the sides defining the plaza but at a critical intersection of two visual axes linking important buildings and vistas. This was all very medieval in spirit— almost a primer on Camillo Sitte—except that the buildings surrounding this plaza and the pedestrian walkways were to be of different scale and proportion than those that bordered medieval squares. This scheme proposed a tower of twenty-five to thirty floors replacing the original building (but retaining the facade of the lower two levels), and with a ten- to fifteen-story wing extending

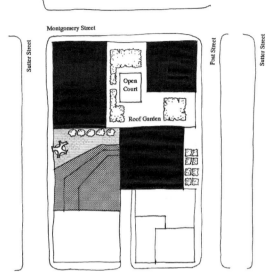

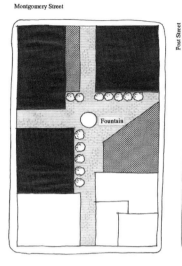

FIGURE 133
Sketch of proposed
Crocker Center by the
planning department:
Alternative 2. San
Francisco Department
of City Planning.
Redrawn by Liette Gilbert.

FIGURE 134
Sketch of proposed
Crocker Center by the
planning department:
Alternative 3. San
Francisco Department
of City Planning.
Redrawn by Liette Gilbert.

out along Post. Another office tower was located west of Lick Alley and north of the plaza, "as high as FAR and dollars permit."[14] Another tower replacing the existing building on the corner of Montgomery and Sutter was seen as possible. The ground level of the buildings was to be devoted to retail to make the plaza active and lively, and sunlight studies were to be conducted to determine the final height of the building along Post.

The second scheme (see figure 133) featured a triangular plaza opening toward the Hallidie building, with a smaller plaza on Post. Three major towers were proposed. The lobby of the office tower located along Post and in the middle of the block was considered to be a hub connecting various pedestrian walkways. A rooftop garden was conceptualized as a space that would connect the office towers on the upper level with an open-air restaurant overlooking Aetna Plaza.

Finally, the third, and the least preferred, scheme was to have a central plaza with pedestrian walkways radiating from the center in all four directions (see figure 134). This scheme would have made the plaza accessible at midblock on all four sides of the larger block. The main banking room and the building at the corner of Montgomery and Post were to be removed and replaced by an office tower. Another office tower was to be located diagonally across the plaza, at its northwest corner. The shape of this plaza—and the sense of enclosure—were much more ambiguous than those of the plaza in the first scheme, although both plazas were located roughly in the same spot and adorned by an off-center fountain. The third building located on the middle third of the Post frontage was not fully defined.

It is interesting to note that the urban design study provided by the planning department was predicated on maximizing available FAR. But there was no explicit mention of any kind of bonus. Of course one would not expect the planners to broach the subject first; usually it would be up to the developers to ask. However, that it was not mentioned might suggest that the idea of granting bonuses for public amenities may already have been dead by then.

It is also worth noting that vestiges of these exploratory schemes did endure, albeit significantly transformed. As we have seen, these initial ideas—saving the existing facade of the original bank building and the main banking hall, keeping the corners of the street block intact, creating a system of interconnected pedestrian spaces, including historic Hallidie and Aetna buildings in the visual domains of the new pedestrian space, providing a roof garden for public use, and the like—would ultimately influence the final design of Crocker Center.

It was almost ten years before all the issues were fully resolved. More than a year after he did the urban design study, Richard Hedman met with Richard Foster of SOM, the projects' design firm, to discuss the design issues. Hedman emphasized the findings of his urban design study and urged Foster not to make the tower thirty-eight stories tall but limit it to thirty stories. Foster mentioned the potential for a 20 : 1 FAR in view of possible bonuses derived from plazas, access to rapid transit, and the like. He also thought that the building might exceed the diagonal dimension of 150 feet stipulated under bulk control even if it stayed within the maximum 120 foot facade dimension.

From the bank's point of view, locating the new tower on the corner of Post and Kearny resolved many of the concerns about saving the facade of the old building, the banking hall, and the building at 111 Sutter. An urban design study prepared during the environmental impact review explained the key aspects of the new design concept in the following manner:

The property enjoys the presence of two handsome and important older buildings: the Crocker Branch at One Montgomery and the adjacent 111 Sutter; buildings of considerable functional value to the Bank but of even greater historic and sentimental importance to both the Bank and the community. Often such buildings fall victim to the need for growth when lack of space offers no alternative but that of demolition and replacement, but in this case, the purchase of additional land permits allows the new office structure to be placed at the corner of Post and Kearny Streets, thus enabling both buildings to survive as useful and handsome parts of the urban scene. There were further, equally important benefits: our design studies demonstrated immediately that the new tower enjoyed an excellent relationship with the adjacent large buildings and conversely, that the same building placed directly at the corner of Post and Montgomery was an urban disaster. We found too that the relationship became even better when the existing Headquarters was removed because the Aetna Building, 111 Sutter, and the new tower were suddenly revealed in a fresh and dramatic relationship, and that the absence of the smaller building created a kind of a great urban room, opening to the east and south towards Market Street. It seemed sensible to place a garden in this room, a planted terrace above the street, sheltered from northerly winds and facing into the midday sun.[15]

The last reference was to the roof garden to be created on top of the original banking room after the upper nine stories of the twelve-story bank building were lopped off. This particular outcome was directed by the planning department to achieve the public aims of historic preservation and public open space creation. A set of detailed and prescriptive guidelines ultimately determined the design solution. Although Crocker Bank produced the building, with the help of SOM as the main actor, the project was fundamentally scripted and directed by the urban designers of San Francisco's City Planning Department.

THE STORY OF PROMOTION

The Figueroa at Wilshire Tower in downtown Los Angeles was still under construction when Hines Interests Limited Partnership, a well-known Texas development firm, moved into several floors of the building on the corner of Wilshire and Flower, almost kitty corner from the site.

The firm had a contract from the Mitsui Fudosan Corporation of Japan to oversee the entitlement, construction, and leasing of the office tower. Designed by A.C. Martin Associates, the new office tower was to be available for occupancy in the summer of 1991. Leasing of office space seemed a formidable task. The glut of office space that began in the late eighties had already produced a 15–20 percent vacancy rate in the downtown office market. Moreover, two other office towers, the First Interstate World Center and the Gas Company Tower at the edge of Bunker Hill, were also about to come on line at the same time. Clearly, the situation called for aggressive and innovative marketing.

The technique chosen by the Hines group to promote the Figueroa at Wilshire Tower was quite novel. As the prospective clients came through the door, they were first shown a short film about the development of the project; then they were taken to a room with several scale models of the building. Perhaps the most spectacular display was a model of a cutaway section of the interior floors and the entrance lobby. The model was made on a rather large scale so that a viewer could actually insert his or her head inside the lobby to appreciate the decor and finishing—the popular neo–Art Deco look with gilded metal trim and expensive Italian marble tiles—in a miniaturized version. The overall effect was a sort of "virtual reality," different, however, from the recent creations of high-tech computer wizardry. If the average viewers were vaguely aware of a "Gulliver" effect, of being inserted into the Lilliputian world of the model, it only added to their enjoyment of this simulated environment. It was indeed a very effective marketing tool.

After the tour of the models, visitors were ushered into a small conference room. As they sat down still savoring their virtual reality trip through the building, the drapes along the back wall opened suddenly and dramatically to reveal the real building in its full glory across the street, still under construction. The whole presentation was so stunning that, according to one senior staff member, a prospective tenant was ready to sign the lease agreement then and there.

While this was a unique form of marketing a building, architectural renderings and scale models are routinely used in the packaging and selling of modern office buildings and other speculative projects involving significant investment (see Banerjee and Loukaitou-Sideris 1992). Scale models of projects under development are strategically displayed in the leasing or sales office. Reproductions of renderings or images of scale models are included in multicolor bro-

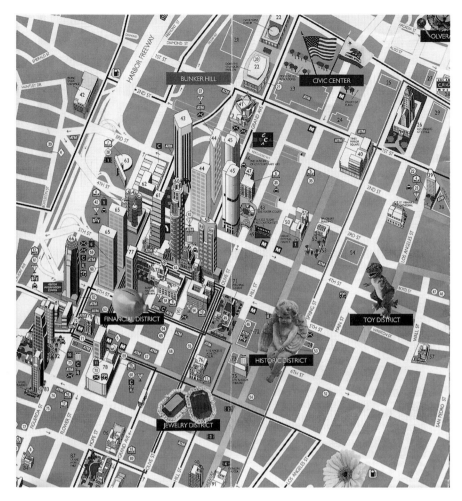

FIGURE 135
Promotional map
of downtown Los
Angeles. Community
Redevelopment Agency
of Los Angeles and the
Downtown Marketing
Council.

chures printed on glossy card stock. These are often supplemented by other promotional materials produced by public agencies (see figure 135). Well-known architects are prominently featured in these efforts, especially if the project is labeled as a signature building. Developers of the proposed Metropolis project in downtown Los Angeles asked architect Michael Graves to design the interior of the project development office, which now features not only the furniture designed by the architect but also his well-known stylistic renderings hanging on the wall.

Not only do corporate clients and developers use architectural representations to market the buildings, but also architects themselves rely heavily on representation to market their services—as designers and as corporate entities—and to sell their ideas to clients. Today formal representation is so important a tool of the trade that secondary industries have emerged to support the representation needs of the design profession, from reproduction technologies to model building. Indeed building of scale models is now such a specialized activity that it is a thriving cottage industry of its own. With the explosion of CAD and GIS software and the dawn of CD-ROM and virtual reality technologies, possibilities for design representation and environmental simulation are limitless today (Sheridan and Zeltzer 1993).

The Hines approach to promoting an office building admittedly was unusual, but almost all downtown developers find ways of advance billing their project. This often includes signs or large billboards announcing the groundbreaking or the opening of the project. Like a movie premiere, the opening of a major downtown building is associated with considerable glitz and hoopla. When Citicorp Plaza opened in downtown Los Angeles, a major party was given by the building owners. The guest list, which included Mayor Tom Bradley and the members of the city council, was a who's who of the downtown community. Similar fanfare marked the opening of Horton Plaza on August 9, 1985. In fact the opening itself was a major stage show. Recalled Gilchrist, the former CEO of the Hahn organization,

> But I have to tell you, the day we opened the center, August 9, 1985, we had the obelisk that sits out in front of the Lyceum Theater . . . the whole thing was so unique, that for the ribbon cutting we needed something unique. So our marketing people talked me into bringing Philippe Petite, who is a wire walker, who has walked the wire between the spires of Notre Dame and the World Trade Center. So we ran a wire from the corner where Marie Callendar's is over to where Robinson's is. So he walked across the wire, he would get halfway, and then he'd sit on the wire, and then he lowered the key down for the center. And I was sitting on the dais next to then Senator Wilson and he looked at me and said, "How did you let them talk you into this? I can see the headlines tomorrow—'Philippe Petite is impaled on the Obelisk—ominous start for Horton Plaza.'" [16]

As it turned out, Philippe Petite was not impaled. Far from being ominous, the opening weekend of Horton Plaza drew a crowd of 250,000 people, signaling a successful future. In the summer of 1995, it celebrated its tenth anniversary with some pomp and circumstance.

The opening of Horton Plaza got mostly rave reviews from such professional journals as *Architectural Record, Progressive Architecture*, and *Architecture;* it also drew some positive coverage from the national media including the *Los Angeles Times*, the *New York Times*, the *Wall Street Journal, Sunset, California Magazine, Connoisseur*, and the like. Like movie producers and distributors, developers look for positive reviews from the national media—the equivalent of a Siskel and Ebert "two thumbs up!" Good reviews mean good promotion and good news for leasing agents.

Advance reviews are even better. Skilled marketing people and salespeople want to have extensive press coverage as soon as the project is approved. It helps to have the project designed by a well-known, trendy architect. It is not surprising that the Metropolis project was featured prominently in the March 23, 1990, issue of *USA Today* long before the project went to the city council for approval (Brackey 1990). A day earlier Leon Whiteson (1990) of the *Los Angeles Times* had done an extensive review of the same project and had interviewed Michael Graves.

Marketing and promotion are inexorably linked to the concept of selling in a market economy. In a competitive marketplace, product differentiation is important, and mythification of added value is critical. Good reviews and media coverage help to establish the myth. Developers depend on them in the same way producers of films, plays, and shows depend on the critics and reviewers.

Stage setting and theming are part of selling finished and packaged space and together are the initial step toward establishing this myth of added value. The process of production and promotion begins with the selection of an architect, but it is not just about architects or architecture. Jerde captured this idea when he commented, "The days of solo virtuosity are spent."[17] The process is a collaborative effort of many agents, and as we have seen, it is deliberate, yet sometimes contingent on certain public demands and imperatives. The financial success of any downtown project depends not just on the design of the buildings but also on the marketing, packaging, and promoting of the concept of the place in its totality.

10

Throughout this book we discussed the urban changes that have remolded the form, character, and social functions of the North American downtown. Some of these changes had to do with the transformed nature of the economy, others with the way that people live, and still others with the way that the built environment was produced (Sudjic 1992).

As we saw in part 1, the classic city form had a semantic unity; it was organized around a center within which the social practices of politics, religion, business, and culture were exercised (Gottdiener 1986). As the urban center progressively lost its role in daily life (Jackson 1980), and as its primacy ceased to be the important prerequisite for many activities, the downtown lost its significance as the unifying heart of the metropolis. Later, in response to a restructuring in the early 1970s (Soja 1989), the downtown tried to resurrect its original importance. The center became the command post of a global economy (Abbott 1993) dedicated to power, money, and modern technology (Jackson 1980).

The rise of a service economy—in which finance, marketing, and the rendering of personal services have become the cornerstones of economic activities—brought about a downtown rich in signature buildings, upscale marketplaces, convention centers, and entertainment facilities. Advances in communication and information technologies in the late twentieth century allowed global mobility and flexibility in the accumulation of capital and reduced the importance of geographic location. Thus, in addition to the global cities of the United States (New York, Los Angeles, Chicago), second-tier cities also got involved in an unprecedented competition to attract corporate investment in their downtowns (Boyer 1992). As we explained in chapter 3, the active state involvement of the previous era declined in favor of the increased role and significance of the private sector. Policy makers turned overwhelmingly to market-based solutions. Privatization, commercialization, and deregulation became key words for a policy that led to an increasing polarization between the haves and have-nots (Hitters 1992). As some researchers have documented (Fainstein 1994; Sudjic 1992; Grönlund 1993; Deben, Musterd, and van Weesep 1992), similar socioeconomic processes occurred simultaneously in other parts of the Western world and led to similar spatial outcomes in downtowns.

As Henri Lefebvre (1971, 31) has argued, space is political and ideological, a product "literally filled with ideologies." If space is the product, urban design is the tool that shapes it. Urban design interprets, expresses, and legitimizes the socioeconomic processes that affect the building of cities and their spaces. In that respect, the contemporary American downtown is a product of purposeful design actions that have effectively sought to mold space according to the needs of a corporatist economy and to subordinate urban form to the logic of profit. A new urban design language has invented a new downtown urban form. Some (Jameson 1991) have argued that this language represents a complete break from modernism. Others (Harvey 1989; Berman, 1986) described it as an evolutionary and transitional phase of modernism, as reflecting a late modern rather than a postmodern discourse. But even if the new language represents an evolution and not a replacement, its vocabulary, syntax, and semantics are quite different from those of modernism. In the following section we will discuss the characteristics that distinguish postmodern design from its modernist predecessor.

POSTMODERN DESIGN

During the post–World War II period the modernist ideals of rationality and functionalism, modulated by concern for social welfare, overwhelmingly dictated the shape and form of downtown buildings and spaces. By the 1960s, however, it was clear that the modern movement's original imperatives had been replaced by the imperatives of an advanced capitalist economy. The legacy of the movement was not social housing for workers but flagship buildings for corporations. The building skyline of all major American downtowns was outlined by the flat rooftops of monumental glass boxes.

In the late 1960s a new design ideology appeared as a commentary and a reaction to the primacy of the modern movement. Interestingly, the postmodernist polemic against modernism concentrated more on issues of style rather than substance. Postmodernism advocated a selective revitalization of older styles (Jencks 1977), often leading to a pastiche of vernacular architectonic elements. The overall effect has sometimes been characterized as aesthetic populism (Dear 1986). Postmodernist writings were critical of the anonymity, standardization, and placelessness of the International Style. Reacting against the aesthetic austerity and purity of form that modernism had espoused, they called for an architecture of "complexity and contradiction" (Venturi 1966) that would draw from commercial and vernacular landscapes, as well as from the world of television and advertising.

While postmodernism seemed to concentrate on aesthetics, the construction of witty "decorated sheds" (Venturi, Scott Brown, and Izenour 1977, 87), some looked beyond the playfulness, depthlessness, and superficiality of this new design ideology. Fredric Jameson (1991) was one of the first to argue that rather than being a temporary stylistic fad, postmodernism represented the "cultural logic of late capitalism"—it was the product of and response to a historical reality, the third expansion of capitalism around the globe. A postindustrial economy, characterized by an internationalization of fictive commodities and based on financial and business services, required an architecture for the consumer, identified as the white-collar office employee (Lash 1990).

The idioms that compose the language of postmodernism intend to serve the same need: to make space all the more appealing for consumers. Many consumer experts argue that a product is more easily liked if it is familiar. Hence, while modernism often intended to shock its audience by using new materials and vocabulary and by breaking with the past, postmodern design uses familiar elements borrowed from older styles. Arches, columns, pilasters, and pediments are historical quotations, but they also provide visual references to beloved and popular settings of the world (Italian piazzas, country towns, European hill towns, and so on). Umberto Eco (1985, 166) has called this practice the "new aesthetics of seriality," where the repetition of known and expected patterns and themes aims to relax, entertain, and even amuse the viewer. Eco explains that postmodern aesthetics avoid interruption, novelty, or shock and instead value the repeatable, familiar, and expected.

Often a product has to be attractive or entertaining in order to sell. The minimalism and austerity of modernism are replaced by a pastiche of colors and by stylish and highly ornamental materials that intend to attract, impress, and at the same time promote the feeling of affluence in a materialistic, capitalist society. The aesthetic result blends well with the purposes of commercial enterprise. The appearance of the signifier is enhanced through decoration, packaging, and advertising, while the meaning and substance of the signified become fuzzy.

Sometimes a product needs to achieve some distinction in order to sell. The universality and standardization of modernism are replaced by designs custom-made for developers and their clients. Ironically, however, these designs do not show any particular sensitivity to the context, culture, or local history of places, but simply provide the decor for the act of consumption (Boyer 1992). Scott Lash has argued that this postmodernist idiom reveals a "de-semanticized historicity," since historical signifiers are utilized not for their relationship to the history of the setting but simply for their ability to produce an effect on the consumer (Lash 1990, 72).

A product should not scare its perspective consumers. In contrast to the political agenda of the early modern movement, postmodernism appears neutral and apolitical; it is interested in aesthetics rather than ethics, in the medium but not the message (Harvey 1989; Ellin 1996). Postmodern design eliminates feared and unwanted political, social, and cultural intrusions. Space is cut off, separated, enclosed, so that it can be easily controlled and "protected." This treatment succeeds in screening the unpleasant realities of everyday life: the poor, the homeless, the mentally ill, and the landscapes of fear, neglect, and deterioration. In the place of the real city, a hyperreal environment is created, composed by the safe and appealing elements of the real thing, reproduced in miniature or exaggerated versions.

The use of a postmodern urban design language has been the trademark of development in contemporary American downtowns. In what follows we will present the major themes that capture the tragedy of postmodern urbanism, and we will analyze their impact on the urban form of American downtowns.

FROM SYNOPTIC VISION TO A COLLAGE DOWNTOWN

"Make no little plans," urged Daniel Burnham, setting the pace for modernist town planning and downtown design. The modernist ideal of the "machine city" envisioned an urban environment broken down into functional segments that constituted the parts of a coherent whole. Downtown was one constituent part, and planners tried to homogenize it, unify it, plan for its totality. Grand plans and designs and large-scale urban models were the dominant tools of modernist planning and architecture.

Postmodernism advocated a very different approach to downtown design. The coherent canvas of modernism was now broken down into incoherent fragments. A collage of unrelated settings and spaces started appearing in downtown environments as a result of an urban design praxis that was commissioned by private entities. Because of its private nature, urban design became disjointed, episodic, incrementalist, and fragmented. When megablocks in downtown got developed, they composed self-sufficient environments instead of being pieces in a unifying master plan, as modernism had dictated. The postmodernist settings were not linked to the city; they excluded it instead. Horton Plaza in San Diego, Rincon Center in San Francisco, California Plaza in Los Angeles, and all the other cases that we have discussed in this book aspire to form miniature cities within their city. As will be recalled, the developers of the Metropolis project in Los Angeles promoted their project as a city within a city. The episodic nature of their development, combined with the public sector's lack of overall vision for downtown, prevents these increments of change from becoming integrated into the city's urban tissue. They remain incoherent fragments, and together they compose a collage of downtown spaces. This market-driven urbanism places more emphasis on aesthetic appearance and promotes the idea of space as a set piece designed to complement only the building, but not necessarily the rest of the city. This urban design is oblivious of its immediate context and the overall urbanism. Attention is given to the architectural style and form, the colors and texture (remember the forty-nine shades used in Horton Plaza), the seating and landscaping of specific buildings, but not to urbanistic objectives such as coherence, continuity, transitions, and pedestrian connections.

The difference between modernist and postmodernist urban design ideologies is well illustrated when we compare urban design documents of different eras. *Design for Development* (Community Redevelopment Agency 1968), produced by the Los Angeles CRA in the mid 1960s, provided the overall framework for the redevelopment of Bunker Hill in Los Angeles (see chapter 1). The *Los Angeles Downtown Strategic Plan* (Community Redevelopment Agency 1993) is the recent product of an advisory committee appointed by the CRA and composed of downtown businesspeople; developers; housing and social service providers; residents; cultural institutions; and consultants for urban design, historic preservation, economic planning, and transportation. The document discusses the future of downtown Los Angeles and recommends programs and projects.

The first document aspires to be a grand unifying plan. It strives to plan and determine the form and uses of all twenty-nine blocks of the Bunker Hill landscape. Its authors note that

> It is important to realize as essential to the overall concept, that the land uses, circulation system, and urban forms proposed throughout are immeasurably interdependent. The *Design for Development* is predicated on the total cumulative effect of complementary uses, integrated circulation patterns, and the structuring and interplay of urban forms. (Community Redevelopment Agency 1968, 1)

The rhetoric of the text attests to the urban designers' wish for unification, integration, and comprehensiveness. The major concepts of urban form, as described in the document, are:

> A carefully conceived interaction of building volumes and open spaces.
> A strategic arrangement of building forms.
> A project-wide organization which differentiates one zone of activity from another while expressing their necessary interdependence within the whole of the project and related Downtown area.
> An integrated organization of all open spaces.
> A pleasant landscape environment unifying public and private areas.
> A comprehensive design of public improvements. (Community Redevelopment Agency 1968, 4)

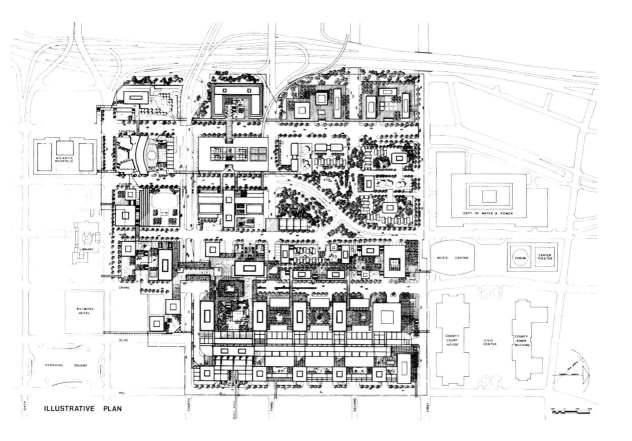

ILLUSTRATIVE PLAN

An illustrative plan included in the document clearly reveals the designers' intentions (see figure 136). The twenty-nine blocks are consolidated in twenty-four superblocks. The high-rise towers are connected with skyways, street-level connections, and midblock linkages. Planting and paving is provided to unify the whole. This is a master plan that, true to the doctrines of modernism, presumes that the whole Bunker Hill area can be uniformly designed like a building and that its environment can be shaped and controlled in an overarching manner.

There is no illustrative master plan in the downtown strategic plan (DSP) of the 1990s. An aerial map of the downtown projected for Los Angeles in the year 2020 shows only the proposed building sites: "actual locations and se-

FIGURE 136
Bunker Hill urban renewal project, 1968. Community Redevelopment Agency of Los Angeles.

1. Grand Central Square (Phase 2)
2. Market Square
3. California Mart Renovation and Expansion
4. Convention Headquarters, Hotel and Hotel District
5. 7th Street Retail District
6. Broadway Theater Entertainment District
7. Downtown Rail Transit Alignments
8. Eastside Truck Staging and Traffic Management
9. Broadway Circulator and Streetscape Improvements
10. Hill, Olive and First St. Streetscape Improvements
11. Broadway/Spring Arcade Building Renovation
12. San Julian Commons
13. South Park Neighborhood (Phase 2)
14. Plaza St. Vibiana
15. Bunker Hill Neighborhood
16. South Park Square
M Metro Portals/Stops

FIGURE 137
Map of catalytic projects
from *Los Angeles
Downtown Strategic Plan*,
1993. Community
Redevelopment Agency
of Los Angeles.

quences of development projects will depend on thousands of decisions made by public and private interests" (Community Redevelopment Agency 1993, 2). The document describes downtown Los Angeles as a collection of districts (the financial core, the markets, the civic center, the convention center, and so on). It discusses general "district strategies" but not downtown-wide physical plans. In the place of a unifying urban vision, designers talk about small-scale architectural intervention and a series of "catalytic projects" inserted into the existing districts (see figure 137).[1] But few of these projects address the specific social context, the history of the site, or the local cultures.

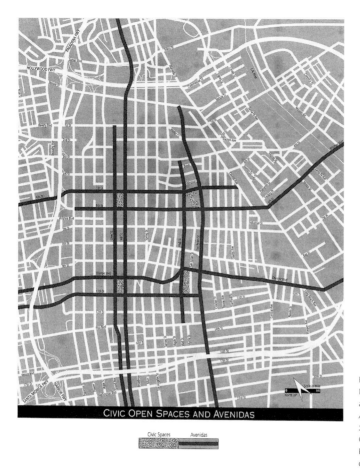

CIVIC OPEN SPACES AND AVENIDAS

Civic Spaces   Avenidas

FIGURE 138
Map of civic open spaces
and avenidas, *Los
Angeles Downtown
Strategic Plan*, 1993.
Community
Redevelopment Agency
of Los Angeles.

In an effort to selectively draw from an invented imagery of downtown's Spanish past, the DSP proposes four *avenidas* with planting and broad side-walks—seen as "corridors of power and commerce" in the new downtown (Community Redevelopment Agency 1993, 126); and four civic plazas: Per-shing Square, Market Square, South Park Plaza, and Saint Julian Commons (see figure 138). Pershing Square, redesigned by architect Ricardo Legoretta as a stage set, aspires to be the living room for the office district. The proposal for Market Square, envisioned as a covered urban mall in the tradition of Les Halles in Paris (Betsky 1993), seeks to "revitalize" the presently very successful and predominantly Latino Grand Central Market by providing an upscale and trendy shopping environment. In doing so, it colonizes a thriving Latino commercial district (Morton 1994). South Park Plaza is envisioned as an open space for a proposed housing district consisting of condominiums and upscale executive suites; while Saint Julian Commons is reserved for the denizens of the city's skid row district

The plan legitimizes a collage downtown composed of unrelated districts and privately initiated and financed projects. The districts are not given the same emphasis. The plan includes an extensive discussion of how the CBD (where all new private investment has concentrated) can become more "livable," but there is very little about the connections to and development of the "other" downtown.

THE VISIBLE HAND OF PRIVATIZATION IN DOWNTOWN DEVELOPMENT

Privatization, the extreme reliance on private initiative and investment, is to a great extent responsible for the uneven development of many downtowns. As outlined in previous chapters, even the design initiative has shifted from the public to the private sector. With declining fiscal resources, local governments have become increasingly dependent on private investments for improvements and amenities and are forced to rely heavily on regulations and entitlement processes to negotiate the outcome of design (Loukaitou-Sideris and Banerjee 1993). Design concepts have largely been dictated by the designers hired by the private sector. Governmental efforts to shape public environments through urban design and public policy have been largely abandoned in favor of private initiatives (Francis 1988). Private developers have become the city builders, and frequently it is private interest that determines what gets built where in downtown. It is only rarely that any strategic planning is done by the public sector regarding the form and character of downtown's public realm: on how much public space is needed, where it should be allocated, which models of public space can best serve the needs of different segments of the public. In the absence of a broader public vision or purpose, the private production of downtown settings remains a non sequitur in a shrinking public domain. This is the inevitable result of a weakened and passive public design and a total absence of public initiatives.

Privatization has also resulted in the weakening of downtown's public domain. Although corporate open spaces are presumed to be part of the public domain, there is considerable ambiguity about whether they actually are. Legally, the corporate open spaces remain private property. In San Francisco, the presumption of public domain is legislated: an official plaque that declares the publicness of plazas is required. In Los Angeles and many other downtowns, this presumption at best remains in the planners' visions, and is not an official requirement. But even in San Francisco, the formal requirement has not always succeeded in integrating plazas and other private open spaces into the public realm. These spaces are inward oriented, cut off from the street, detached, and isolated. They are created for the benefit of the office tenants and not for the general public.

We have seen that private interests have always played a role in downtown development, but the complete subjugation of urban design to market forces is a phenomenon of the last two decades. Downtown urban design, because it is determined by private interests, has become reactive and opportunistic rather than proactive. The public sector reacts to the initiatives of the private sector for downtown building. The developers' actions are opportunistic, predicated upon their expectations of market response. Their objectives are profit and good business—which are not always congruent with good city form and urban design. This philosophy is quite different from earlier urban design philosophies that relied on the strategic location and investment of public projects and improvements to stimulate civic pride, sense of community, and private investment in a desired pattern.

Finally, the lack of strategic planning and the dominance of the private over the public sector in the creation of downtown's public realm have resulted in some lost urban design opportunities for downtowns. For example, the inward orientation and fragmentation of most urban plazas and downtown open spaces are in conflict with urbanistic objectives for coherence, effective linking of districts, and pedestrian connections. Plazas effectively turn their backs on one another, closing the city outside. This tactic produces a noncohesive arrangement of open spaces and a fragmentation of the public realm.

THE POLARIZATION OF NEW AND OLD IN DOWNTOWN

In their effort to create exclusive settings and spaces accessible to some but not all, contemporary patterns of urban design serve only a limited public. This result has contributed to a polarization between the public, but old and derelict, downtown for the indigent, and the new, private, and glamorous downtown of the corporate America. Increasingly, the new downtown has come to be at odds with the traces of the old downtown, the Main Street of yesteryear. The public life of the Main Street downtown is vestigial at best and has been totally transformed by the culture of the poor, the homeless, and the new immigrants. What is left of the earlier downtown is ignored or forgotten as indeed are many of its denizens. This polarization is all too apparent in the segregated urbanism of contemporary downtown, and is a challenge yet to be addressed by most urban designs and downtown plans.

Reviewing the downtown plans of six cities (Cleveland, Denver, Philadelphia, Portland, San Francisco, and Seattle) in the 1980s, Dennis Keating and Norman Krumholz (1991) express skepticism that any of these plans can change the pattern of uneven development that insulates revitalized downtowns from all the socioeconomic problems that plague their ailing downtown frames. It can be argued that postmodern urban design contributes to the widening of the gap between the private downtown of corporate America and the public downtown of the poor. This gap is reflected in the distribution of downtown open space. Maps of the downtown areas of San Francisco and Los Angeles clearly show that the corporate plazas are not located in the high-intensity pedestrian and transit corridors (see figures 139 and 140). There are very few open spaces in and around the old downtown. Los Angeles is both an embarrassment of riches and an embarrassment of deprivation. Since the downtown rebuilding has systematically segregated the contemporary downtown from the historic core, corporate plazas normally do not have to worry about integrating different classes of users. But the contrast between the old and the new should haunt public policy. Should public priorities keep fostering investment into the new downtown while neglecting the poor and more ethnically diverse parts of the city?

Polarization of space in downtown happens also at the microlevel. In contrast to the modernist design scheme that placed buildings within a limitless

1.	Citicorp Plaza	15.	Biddy Mason Park
2.	California Plaza	16.	Onizuka Street
3.	Bunker Hills Steps	17.	Japanese American Cultural
4.	Figueroa @ Wilshire Plaza		and Communtiy Center (Noguchi Plaza)
5.	Manulife Plaza	18.	Japanese Village Plaza
6.	Union Bank Plaza	19.	Civic Center Mall
7	Bonaventure Hotel	20.	City Hall
8.	Arco Plaza	21.	East Mall
9.	Maguire Gardens/ Public Library	22.	El Pueblo Plaza
10.	444 Flower Street Plaza	23.	Olvera Street
11.	Security Pacific Plaza	24.	Alpine Recreation Center
12.	Wells Fargo Plaza	25.	Chinatown Plaza
13	Angel's Flight	26.	St-Julian Park
14.	Pershing Square	27.	Gladys Park
		28.	Grand Hope Park

FIGURE 139
Downtown Los Angeles
public and private open
spaces. Drawing by Liette
Gilbert.

and abstract public space, the postmodernist approach is to enclose public space, to drastically separate the fragment of new development from its context. In the examples that we studied we found that an array of architectonic elements is often utilized to produce the desired effect of seclusion. Developments are surrounded by blank walls and impenetrable street frontages. Frequently, plazas are sunken below the street level and, thus, separated from the life and activity of the city fabric. The exterior gives few clues to the space

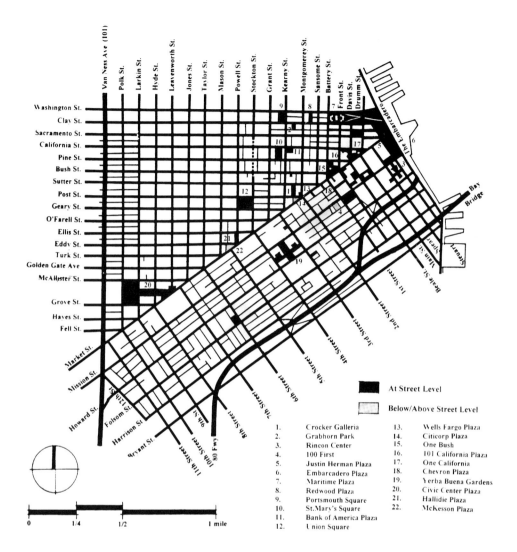

At Street Level

Below/Above Street Level

1. Crocker Galleria
2. Grabhorn Park
3. Rincon Center
4. 100 First
5. Justin Herman Plaza
6. Embarcadero Plaza
7. Maritime Plaza
8. Redwood Plaza
9. Portsmouth Square
10. St. Mary's Square
11. Bank of America Plaza
12. Union Square
13. Wells Fargo Plaza
14. Citicorp Plaza
15. One Bush
16. 101 California Plaza
17. One California
18. Chevron Plaza
19. Yerba Buena Gardens
20. Civic Center Plaza
21. Hallidie Plaza
22. McKesson Plaza

FIGURE 140
Downtown San Francisco
public open spaces.
Drawing by Liette Gilbert.

within the private premises. Major entrance points to plazas and open spaces are often through parking structures. Doorways and openings that provide a direct link to the street are de-emphasized. The intention of design is to create a break, a sharp contrast, between the gray exterior space and the bright interior courts and atria.

Interactive and creative uses of retail have not been exploited in the postmodern design of discrete projects and places. In the old days, street-level retail enlivened the downtown area and contributed to the vibrancy of the streets, but now postmodern urban design creates commercial projects that are islands. These developments, which usually occupy several consolidated blocks, deny the surrounding streets by placing retail around interior ways, plazas, and atria. Street vendors are perceived as a nuisance for corporate tenants and are chased away to their "proper place"—the dirty streets and alleys of the old downtown.

DOWNTOWN AS A COLLECTION OF SPECTACLES

The fragments that compose the contemporary downtown can be presented as a series of spectacles or as variations on a theme park. As we saw in chapter 9, a great deal of attention is given to developing a certain mood for each space, to promoting a theme park–type setting, to packaging and advertising the product, and finally to managing and maintaining the theme park environment. Postmodern urban design seeks to create catalytic projects in downtown and present them as a collection of spectacles. Sometimes the themes are imported from other parts of the world, as is the case with the Bunker Hills Steps in Los Angeles or Horton Plaza in San Diego. Other times the themes derive from glimpses into the city's past. South Street Seaport in New York and Inner Harbor in Baltimore revive and gentrify parts of older harbors; Ghirardelli Square in San Francisco renovates the shell of an old factory; Faneuil Hall in Boston adapts the structure of an old market to contemporary retail needs. A theme can also be devised by packaging together different settings and architectural pieces.

The theme park–like settings that have mushroomed in the American downtowns create an idealized image of the public realm, which in reality was never so clean, safe, or stratified. Postmodern urban design strives to screen out the problematic social and physical elements of downtown. As the developers of City Walk, an outdoor mall in Universal City, California, argued, "A new and improved Los Angeles is needed" because "reality has become too much of a hassle" (Wallace 1992, A1). The produced spaces are designed for passive viewers, tourists, conventioneers, and busy office workers who want to browse, safe and undistracted, through a collection of spectacles that tries to substitute for the real city center. This simulation of urbanity that combines the ideal with the real provides the stage set for consumption and is packaged so as to intensify the attraction of commodities (Boyer 1992).

PACKAGING DOWNTOWN SETTINGS

The majority of projects built in the new downtowns are associated with commercial activities. Their space is orchestrated so as to encourage and stimulate the act of consumption. Commerce has always been one of the primary uses of American downtowns. Markets and streets in downtown were characterized by their public nature. They often served as places for social encounters and as forums for public life and political activity.

Public debate and political controversy have no place in the settings of the new downtown. Owners and developers want their spaces to be apolitical. They separate users from unnecessary social or political distractions, and put users into a mood consistent with their purposes. The facilitation of consumption becomes the primary objective in the orchestration of space. At the same time the poetics of design is utilized to dress up downtown settings so that they stimulate the imagination and fantasies of tenants and clients. Built form becomes a marketable product, a commodity. As discussed in chapter 9, design becomes thoroughly integrated into the packaging, advertising, and marketing of downtown real estate. As David Harvey argues (1989, 87–88) the application of postmodern design creates a "veil" in downtown that entertains, but at the same time masks and diverts attention from pressing social problems that lie behind the veil.

Many have argued that there has been a shift to concerns that are politically benign and are cosmetic rather than substantive (Ellin 1996; Crilley 1993). The emphasis that postmodern urban design places on the aesthetics of settings, on the ornamentation, styling, and packaging of the signifiers, diffuses such political questions as: Who benefits and who loses from such design? Whose priorities and needs are followed? Whose history is represented? and What is the sociophysical context that should be respected?

THE CONTEXTLESS DOWNTOWN

Ironically, postmodernism has followed modernism in producing an acontextual downtown. Like postmodern architecture, postmodern urban design also tends to be context independent. Postmodernism criticizes the universality and standardization espoused by modernism and advocates instead the introduction of an eclectic combination of architectonic elements—sometimes whole settings from the past—as historic signifiers. The Spanish Steps of Rome find their way to the heart of downtown Los Angeles, and London's Burlington Arcade is recreated in a major commercial street of Pasadena, California. But these efforts are not attentive to the current realities and particularities or to the local history and culture of their context. As a result, they do not carry any particular meaning. Quite often, there is a recreation of an idealized past or present, a nostalgic selection of the safe and likable attributes, and an attempt to erase all the troubling elements. Spaces are created simply to impress their users. This attempt of postmodern urban design to reestablish historical meanings often results in deriding and trivializing those meanings (Lash 1990). The principal concern about this postmodern urban design is not one of style, which dominates architectural criticisms, but rather one of its missing connections, linkages, and continuity in space and time.

It is possible to explain postmodern urban form essentially as a true landscape of a market economy, where each project attempts to outperform its immediate competition in scale, scope, and novelty of themes, driven by imperatives of profit maximization and market success. Product differentiation is critical in a competitive environment. Autonomy from the context is the driving force behind such an urban design. Yet the architecture and imagery of contemporary downtown projects, urban malls, plazas, gallerias, and the like is characteristically similar in most American downtowns. This paradox can be explained by the fact that the goals of commercial or corporate developers are similar everywhere, and these are the goals that are expressed and served through design. Moreover, the superstar architects employed to create signature buildings in downtowns around the globe produce the same standardized form independent of the local context. This results in a franchise culture: an urban form created by multinational corporations, which incorporates popular and well-known elements and is reproduced at downtown centers in New York, Chicago, Los Angeles, London, Paris, or Tokyo (Zukin 1991).

PRODUCTION OF FORM AND PRACTICE OF DESIGN

Finally, we must consider the practice of design, which has been one of our major themes. In part 3 we have focused on several aspects of downtown design—from public art to the production and packaging of individual projects.

We have seen that in the absence of overall vision and direction, the public component of downtown urban design has become ad hoc and opportunistic. Because of their weakened fiscal position, cities have little leverage in influencing the location, timing, or direction of development. They don't have the resources to initiate the priming action that was common in earlier days. The public component of urban design has been essentially reduced to managerial and brokerage functions and, where feasible, to exaction of public benefits. Cities have essentially taken a reactive rather than a proactive stance. And because of this reactive position, the public sector has become more defensive and protective than it was in the past. Much greater emphasis is now placed on procedures, design and environmental impact reviews, and other such entitlement processes. It is as if urban design in the public sector has amounted to a "minimax" strategy—that is, one that minimizes "maximum" losses—for protecting the public good and interest. As we have seen from our cases in San Francisco, developers and property owners have considered such managerial oversight as authoritarian and meddlesome and, sometimes, counterproductive in terms of overall design outcome.

Even where the public sector has demanded public benefits from downtown developers and corporate clients, such as plazas and public art, these benefits have been presented mainly as ameliorative measures or reduced to bureaucratic formulas. Take public art for example. We argued in chapter 8 that public art has become an integral element of public urban design. Many downtowns have accumulated an impressive collection of art pieces—albeit located mainly within the privately owned plazas and courts—but their public purpose and their effect on the appearance of the city remain undefined and undetermined. At best they serve as window dressing that compensates for bad design or an ugly streetscape. Similarly when such money is spent on performing arts—outdoor concerts and shows—the benefit is only to momentarily enliven a plaza that otherwise has very little life of its own. Clearly these gestures have not served as the glue that connects and integrates the disparate pieces. But most importantly, as in the location of and access to corporate plazas, there is little equity in the distribution of this benefit. Like plazas, public art is also concentrated in the white-collar district. The art serves little educational purpose. We suppose this outcome has a Nietzschean logic—that is, you judge the welfare of society by looking not at the lot of the worst off but at how the elite class benefits from a policy. If downtown urban design is judged by this logic alone, there is no doubt the present outcome will score high.

If the public component of urban design is reduced to legislative, procedural, managerial, and opportunistic tasks, how much of the environmental quality concerns that have guided past urban design plans—structure and legibility, form, comfort and convenience, accessibility, health and safety, historic conservation, vitality, diversity, sociability, and so on (see Southworth 1989)—figure in the designer's thinking on individual projects for corporate clients? We tried to find an answer to this question in our discussion with the designers about their personal rationale and vision for various projects. We have discussed how each design scheme is guided by a poetics of form and place. Whether a design is officially adopted by the developer client or not, the rhetoric of design plays an important role in the way the designer identifies the problem, defines the constraints, and develops the scheme. But very little of this poetics concerns the larger public realm or a larger public good or includes any of the values implicit in earlier design plans (Southworth and Southworth 1973; Southworth, 1989). The poetics of design almost always finds some internal rationale—be it from the site, the building type, or the imperatives of the market. Even where the poetics is derived from some external referent, like Jerde's metaphor of an Italian hill town or an urban theater, the connection is abstract. The immediate context rarely figures in this poetics of form or in the legitimation of the immediate design proposal. We also sensed in several instances that the designer's instinct to serve a larger public purpose was squelched by the client's concern for cost, competition, or risk. In these instances the poetics of form seemingly has mitigated the cognitive dissonance between the designer's ideal and the imperatives of market.

While we have established that contemporary urban design has become an ad hoc collection of discrete projects with their own internal rationale, we are not quite ready to concede that these characteristics define postmodern urban design. If there is a postmodern ideology that includes an image of good society, it has yet to define the nature of urban design. What we have in fact is an urban design under a postmodern condition, or more appropriately an urban design of a market-driven landscape.

Still, there have been some deep and fundamental changes in how individual projects are conceived, designed, and promoted. We have found that contemporary project development is an open-ended process; the competition and approval processes are not finite. The projects carry a great deal of uncertainty and risk. It may take anywhere from five to ten years from the time a project is conceived to the time it is actually built. In the meantime, market demand may change, the state of the economy will inexorably fluctuate, and global economic trends or the federal deficit may influence availability of capital and the cost of borrowing money. The rules of the game—in terms of the entitlement process—may change as well. So the design process requires considerable flexibility.

Indeed the process of project development and design is, as we have pointed out, not unlike the production of a movie or a show. It is a collaborative process that involves many actors and experts. Even the end products—especially the open spaces, gallerias, and so on—are seen as stage sets where what matters is the design of the overall experience rather than the space itself. The script for the uses of an open space is equally as important as the design of the setting itself. We have seen also how the promotion and inauguration of a modern office complex resembles a Hollywood production and premiere. Ultimately the changing scope of design—the transformation from designing spaces to designing experiences—may define the scope of postmodern urban design. The real question is how the future urban design—call it postmodern or not—will address the social issues and meditate the conflicts and contradictions of a polarized city.

EPILOGUE:
CHALLENGES FOR DOWNTOWN URBAN DESIGN

In this book we have discussed the evolution of American downtowns, emphasizing contemporary times in particular, as we analyzed the production, poetics, politics, and packaging of contemporary downtown settings. The changes in the urban form and social uses of downtown are closely related to the evolution from a preindustrial to a postindustrial society; they are cultural and technological as well as endemic and anchored in the modern way of life.

There is no doubt that in the late twentieth century, the American downtown plays an important role in the nation's economy. It is, however, not a communal space, even though the gimmicks of design often try to emulate this feeling inside corporate atria and plazas. The users of the public realm in the new downtowns are determined by their ability to pay (directly or indirectly) for the private services offered. From the corporate perspective, the profitability of a setting becomes a major criterion for the determination of its design and terms of operation.

The character of the new downtown settings is determined by a postindustrial economy and reflects a collective apathy and reluctance to create a more inclusive public realm. The introverted, enclosed, controlled, escapist, commercial, and exclusive nature of these settings cannot be attributed simply to the whims of private enterprise or to the collective imagination of architects, planners, and urban designers. There is clearly a demand for the settings of the new downtown from the parts of the public sector that are threatened by the presence of other groups and are willing to pay for more privacy and seclusion.

But there is also a very serious and unmet demand for space for the less privileged members of our society. Witness the plight of the homeless at skid row, the packing of new immigrants into sweat shops in the downtown frame, the everyday struggle of downtown vendors to make a living in the old downtown, and the fight for territorial control among youth gangs in the inner city.

The increasing levels of affluence and prosperity exemplified in the new down-town contrast sharply with the deprivation and despair shared by the users of the old downtown. This is serious challenge for public policy and for urban design and planning.

We did not intend to conclude this book in a prescriptive vein. Indeed, given the complexity of issues, any design prescriptions would appear superficial. Yet we consider ourselves urban designers rather than social scientists; and although the literature is full of brilliant critiques of the contemporary built form, there are precious few visions of a good society or a good urban form. Although we have drawn widely from the critiques of the contemporary city, we have not been able to derive any normative criteria for city design. In fact, beyond Kevin Lynch's (1980) prescriptions for good city form, there are very few guides for contemporary city design. While we do not claim to have all the answers for questions we have raised in this book, we feel that we have some obligation to at least define what we consider to be the major aims and challenges for future urban design.

THE PRESUMPTION OF PUBLIC DOMAIN

Open spaces should be integrated into the public domain. While corporate open spaces will remain private property and will continue to be protected by such legislation as California Civil Code 1008, they could be treated as a part of the overall public domain in the sense Hannah Arendt (1959) discusses in *The Human Condition*. As we have seen, the presumption of public domain is legislated in San Francisco by the requirement for an official plaque that accepts that presumption. In Los Angeles, this presumption is not a formal require-ment; here the presumption is ambiguous at best, timid at worst.

Yet it is not clear that San Francisco's formal requirements have necessarily integrated corporate open spaces into the public domain any more effectively, because some of these spaces remain hidden and unannounced. While they are clearly marked and displayed on planners' maps, and while they represent some extraordinarily clever architectural and urban design solutions, the general public at large has no way of knowing that they exist. For many users these spaces are accidental discoveries. On the one hand, by encouraging innovative solutions San Francisco planners have created an intriguing diversity of open spaces and demonstrated their many possibilities. On the other hand, these complex form configurations involving many different levels and highly controlled access points have kept them detached and isolated from the larger public domain. So, for an urban design connoisseur the resulting urban form is exciting, but the question remains as to whether the lay public is adequately served. Many years ago Kevin Lynch argued, in an article entitled "The Openness of Open Space" (1972), that open spaces are not really open unless they are physically and psychologically accessible. This argument applies to contemporary corporate spaces as well.

A few simple rules could amend the future design and management of these open spaces with the goal of achieving greater integration into the public domain. First, all open spaces should either be visible from the surrounding public domain or conspicuously announced in the public domain if they are not visible, with clear instructions as to how they can be entered and used. Second, all open spaces should be available for spontaneous performances that have artistic merit and interest and are not objectionable to general public taste or established codes of public morality. This rule would be an important addition to the existing interpretation of public art (including performing arts), especially in Los Angeles. Third, appearance or clothing should not be the basis for exclusion of any potential users. This rule would still allow the corporate managers of space to exclude undesirable activities such as playing loud radios or panhandling, while increasing the publicness of these spaces.

CREATIVE USES OF RETAIL AND THE INFORMAL ECONOMY

Open spaces that are part of a mixed-use complex with a retail component appear to be more successful in terms of intensity of use than those that are not linked to retail activities. Crocker Galleria, Rincon Center, and Citicorp Center are all cases in point. In a city like San Francisco, where the demand for downtown retail is quite high, there may not be much of a difference in leasing rates for offices and retail; provision of retail may not be an issue. But where the office rental rate is higher than the retail rental rate, developers are hard pressed to justify allocating portions of allowable FAR to retail. In this instance public policy can promote street-level retail by not including retail space in FAR calculations. Such a policy in Los Angeles could certainly prove beneficial in making street-level plazas more effective.

Simple measures to integrate the informal economy and small businesses into the corporate business district—where there is considerable demand for such services as food, drinks, small merchandise—should be encouraged. Simple revision of vending laws could accomplish such changes. New projects could be required to creatively address such land-use and class-integration issues.

INTENSITY VERSUS DIVERSITY

There is, however, a trade-off between intensity of use, which is seen as desirable, and overall diversity in the types of open spaces and behavior settings that can be created within the downtown environment. No two spaces need be alike, and certainly not all spaces should contain or should be linked to retail activities. There is a need for intense, bustling, engaging, and inclusive spaces with a variety of behavior settings, like the spaces in European or Latin American urban places where people go for the ritual of watching others and for being watched. There is also a need for small and quiet spaces like Grabhorn Park. A space like this may be seen as "underutilized," but its underutilization may be its strength: it offers a space for people to withdraw in solitude, to brood, or to reflect. There is a need for such islands of tranquillity—like Chinese Gardens—in the middle of urban bustle and bedlam.

ATTENTION TO CONTEXT AND DISTRIBUTIVE JUSTICE

Cities like Los Angeles have been described as postmodern (Dear 1989; Soja 1989), although what constitutes postmodern urbanism remains a matter of debate. We have suggested earlier that as in postmodern architecture, urban design in the postmodern condition also tends to be context independent. Much of the urban design of downtown Los Angeles—especially the contemporary, self-contained theme park variety—attests to this claim. Citicorp Plaza and California Plaza in Los Angeles and Rincon Center and Crocker Center in San Francisco are notable examples.

The principal concerns about this trend in urban design have to do with connections and continuity, both in space and time. Lawrence Halprin's Bunker Hill Steps may be postmodern from a stylistic point of view,[1] having been sandwiched between two very different styles and regimes of architecture, but at least they attempt to connect diverse elements and parts of the historic core. Questions remain, however, as to whether the Steps project has adequately connected the adjacent corporate plaza or the West Lawn of the Central Library across the street. In any event the Steps are a departure from the postmodern urban design typical of Citicorp Plaza or California Plaza, which are designed as disjunctive and discrete pieces in the urban fabric, in the emerging patchwork quilt.

Whatever the reasons for the emergence of postmodern architecture, the urban design outcome is a reflection of a "market landscape." Product differentiation is critical in a competitive environment. Autonomy from the context—which is the sum total of competitions past, present, and future—is the driving force behind the market-driven urbanism and urban design.

In the face of this trend it might be a romantic notion to urge connections and continuity. Yet the challenges of making such connections must be met for the aggregate urbanism to make sense and for each project to work successfully, and meeting them will require anticipatory, strategic city design and effective public policy.

STRATEGIC FRAMEWORK FOR CITY DESIGN

San Francisco has a downtown plan; Los Angeles has just completed a strategic plan. Yet there is a significant difference between the two plans: the former is prepared by a planning department, the latter by a redevelopment agency. As we have noted earlier, to a large extent this difference is a reflection both of the difference in the planning cultures of the two cities and, perhaps more important, of the differences in the characters of the two institutions. Planning departments tend to alternate between a synoptic and a reactive mode, while redevelopment agencies tend to be opportunistic and proactive. Yet both approaches have a mission to develop integrated open space systems. Although the San Francisco plan has established some general principles and a framework by identifying a pedestrian network system, areas deficient in open space, and the like, it lacks the specifics about the location, size, and functions of nodal open spaces that can be functionally and visually linked to each other. While we do not expect either San Francisco or Los Angeles to create grand city design concepts like Sixtus V's Rome or William Penn's plan for Philadelphia, a more comprehensive framework for downtown design using open spaces as an organizing system that would stitch together disparate pieces of downtown development could be a strategic mission for both downtowns. Indeed, Lawrence Halprin suggested the beginning of such a concept in his proposal for the Hope Street corridor, which was designed to connect Bunker Hill Steps, the library, and the Olympic Park. Such strategic vision is needed for both cities. In the absence of such a framework it is difficult to guide the postmodernist theme park–style office developments to pay attention to the context.

REDISCOVERING THE STREET

We have already noted the shift in downtown urban design from the public street to the private plaza, from holistic strategies of downtown planning and design to specific project designs, from an emphasis on public systems and networks to discrete corporate open spaces. As we saw, this has created a downtown of isolated public and private realms. An essential link between these realms is missing. We believe that this link could be provided by softening the boundaries that separate territories (through design and policy), by making the relationship between the public street and private plaza complementary rather than antagonistic. The rediscovery of the street and alley network in downtown should be part of the strategic design framework discussed earlier. What we have in mind, however, is more than the treatment of the street as a channel for efficient movement (exemplified in the modernist era) or an aesthetic visual element (exemplified in the City Beautiful era). Postmodern urban design should rediscover the social role of the street as a connector that stitches together and sometimes penetrates the disparate downtown realms.

BRIDGING THE CLASS GAP

Perhaps the most significant challenge for downtown open space design is to bridge the class gap that exists in the distribution and use patterns of open space. Corporate plazas are not located where the high-intensity pedestrian corridors are, and there are very few public open spaces in or around the pedestrian districts and corridors. Since the downtown rebuilding has systematically segregated the contemporary downtown from the historic core, corporate plazas normally do not have to worry about integrating different classes of users. Indeed the corporate owners might even argue that it is not their responsibility to solve the disproportionate share of social problems that downtowns typically inherit. Nevertheless the awkward contrast must continue to haunt public policy.

In San Francisco, some planners are in favor of collecting an open space fee from the developers in lieu of tangible plazas. Presumably this fund then could be used to address specific open space deficiencies throughout the downtown. If this seems to be an additional financial burden on developers—some would surely argue that another linkage fee would be disastrous—perhaps a portion of percent for art fees could be directed toward developing open space and other public amenities in the needed areas.

PRESCRIPTIONS OF WILLIAM H. WHYTE

It would be inappropriate to conclude without returning to William H. Whyte's formula for successful plazas, which was effective and elegant. It is clear to us from some of our interviews that his work has significantly influenced the current thinking on plaza design, both at the level of public policy and in the form of a heightened design awareness among the architects, landscape architects, urban designers, and developers. The prescription seems to work. We might add two additional items to the list: retail and engaging public art. But any attempt to rigidly codify Whyte's prescriptions in terms of, for example, number of seats per linear or square foot is unlikely to produce desired results. Nor is it necessary to satisfy every item on the checklist to create a successful plaza. Many intangibles remain: good intuition about the overall chemistry of the place, what exists or might exist within a two-block radius of the site, the urbanism of the city, and the like. Obviously what works naturally within the context of the small-block, mixed-use, fine-grain urban form of San Francisco may not work for the segregated, large-block, coarse-grain urban form of Los Angeles. Thus, the Whyte formula can be fine-tuned on the basis of the large-scale urban design analysis and strategic thinking that we emphasized earlier.

TOWARD A FINER GRAIN DESIGN AND DEVELOPMENT

In tracing the history of downtown development, we have shown how the grain of development has become coarser: over time, smaller parcels and blocks gave way to larger, consolidated lots and blocks; narrow streets were replaced by wider streets; minor streets were closed; and alleys were eliminated altogether in this process. This outcome was preordained, in part, by the growth of modern skyscrapers and their ever expanding footprints and increasing height but also by the changing political economy and the emergence of corporate ownership and control of downtown real estate. It will be recalled that most high-rise buildings built in the later part of this century belonged to banks, savings and loan institutions, insurance companies, or multinational corporations.

The mechanism that brought about such consolidation was the urban renewal process, which allowed the public sector to assemble adjacent parcels within a designated area, by invoking eminent domain, and to reorganize the streets to accommodate a greater volume of traffic and parking than before. The process has increased distance and reduced adjacency between lots, buildings, and blocks. It has made these consolidated blocks exclusionary, introverted, and uncommunicative. This pattern has squeezed the public pedestrian spaces to a minimum and created large but exclusive open spaces that are privately owned. The diagram of the present Bunker Hill development pattern in figure 141 illustrates a case in point. Because these superblocks and consolidated blocks are part of large property holdings, their design has contributed to the modernist disjuncture in urban form we discussed earlier.

The result, as we have seen, has been disastrous for pedestrian life and social interaction. The disjuncture has contributed to the dualistic nature of downtown's shared space and created a rift between the residents and the workers of downtown. Yet where smaller grain fabric persists—as in parts of San Francisco—adjacencies are rich, uses are diverse, and the resulting street-life, punctuated by the aroma of espresso bars, is indeed still engaging and full of verve.

The challenge for future urban design, then, is to deconstruct this legacy of urban renewal. How can we return to the smaller grain urban fabric that once fostered a sense of place and community and an exciting street life? The next generation of design must revisit the street facades rather than interior open

PERSHING SQ.

1953

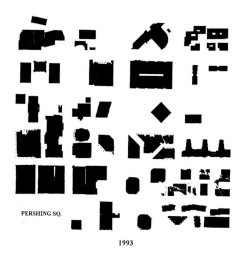

PERSHING SQ.

1993

FIGURE 141
Building footprints in
Bunker Hill, 1953 and
1993. Drawing by
Rebecca Liu.

spaces, and encourage small shops and buildings and a rich mix of land uses. The corporate obsession with tall buildings in the United States seems to be waning, although it is vigorously pursued by the nouveau riche corporations of Third World capitals. Michael Graves and the developers of the Metropolis project, for instance, have deliberately chosen not to build higher than thirty stories and have chosen to create a more modest scale for the complex (Whiteson 1994). The new design must also develop strategy for a smaller and incremental growth and change. Collective ownership of block interiors and faces may suggest the institutional changes that are necessary for implementing the process. Where such deconstruction is not readily possible in the form of ad hoc subdivision of existing built form, existing public spaces and the spaces between buildings can be the medium for humanizing the block if they make room for small businesses, multiple ownership with decentralized control of spaces, and mixed-uses. The task is not easy, and will remain a major challenge for the next phase of downtown urban design.

SPATIAL DIALECTIC OF A POLARIZED DOWNTOWN

We do not know for sure if any of the above prescriptions will improve what Brazilian geographer Milton Santos (1975) refers to as the "spatial dialectic" of the upper and lower circuits of economy. It is not clear whether urban design can ameliorate the deeper problems of cities. But short of liquidation, what then is the future for urban design? We feel that it is ultimately the tasks of managing and improving the spatial dialectic. Expanding the concept of an inclusive, democratic, and civil domain will remain the critical challenge for urban design; the process may begin with solutions that are incremental and marginal in scope, but it must progress with a larger vision of what needs to be accomplished. In this regard, the role and patronage of public institutions, which have shrunk dramatically in recent times, will have to expand and be sustained.

NOTES

Introduction

1. Downtown overbuilding has often been encouraged by state and municipal poli-
    cies: tax-increment financing, for example, allows cities to reserve for redevelop-
    ment purposes increments of property tax revenue accrued within the redevelop-
    ment areas (often within downtown districts). These increments in tax withdrawn
    from general revenue ultimately mean less money for other important social pro-
    grams in education, health, welfare, and the like. For this reason, charges of in-
    equity have been leveled against downtown developments in California because
    they have been mainly paid for by tax-increment financing. In the case of Los
    Angeles, the entire downtown was declared blighted and subject to tax-increment
    financing.

2. Market economists make a normative case for this centrifugal tendency, attributing
    it almost solely to market forces. Yet there is nothing inherently obvious about this
    tendency. For example, some earlier economic theorists have tried to explain the
    opposite phenomenon, that is, centripetal tendencies inherent in agglomeration
    economy principles. Metropolitan freeway development is probably the single
    most important trigger of this centrifugal force.

3. Ironically, political speeches in shopping centers remain a contested issue (see
    chapter 6).

4. The entitlement process is the process a developer must go through to acquire the
    right to develop a property. This may involve incentive zoning formulas, linkages,
    exactions, transfer of development rights, or owner participation agreements.

5. Most of the empirical research for this book is based on case studies involving in-
    depth interviews, field notes, archival research, and some limited systematic obser-
    vation and survey. In order to understand the intended purposes of downtown
    spaces and the processes through which they have been created, we have relied on
    extensive interviews with knowledgeable sources: city planners, architects, devel-
    opers, building managers, urban designers, and the like. Some of these interviews
    were project specific, others were broader in nature, involving overviews of design
    and planning processes. Our archival research was based on documents made avail-
    able by the various public agencies. Field observations and user surveys were con-

ducted to document how downtown spaces in Los Angeles, San Diego, and San Francisco are used and experienced.

6. We consider the CBD a part of downtown. We shall only make conscious reference to the CBD when discussing relevant literature—geography in particular—that has used that term.

Chapter 1

1. The recent literature on gendered spaces has pointed out that business districts were predominantly male domains (Spain 1992).

2. Similar socioeconomic trends produced department stores during the same period (from the 1840s to the 1890s) in France, England, and Germany (Barth 1980).

3. Chicago was devastated by a disastrous fire in 1871. For some time after the fire, city ordinances prohibited the erection of buildings exceeding four to five stories in height. With the invention of fireproof columns and beams, greater heights were allowed. So by the turn of the century, high-rise office buildings (ten to twenty four stories high) were quickly replacing the lower structures.

4. The term comes from walking tours of Seventh Street given by the Los Angeles Conservancy.

5. One notable exception was Rockefeller Center in New York, which had been envisioned during the boom years of the 1920s, but was actually completed in 1939. The next major downtown project, Gateway Center in Pittsburgh's Golden Triangle, opened in 1952.

6. The National Highway Trust Fund provided 90 percent reimbursement to the states for the building of a national limited-access highway net.

7. Municipal governments were often eager to designate areas as blighted so as to proceed with land clearance and urban renewal.

8. The Los Angeles Central City Committee was composed of forty businessmen appointed by then Mayor Norris Poulson to oversee a "co-operative effort between the business interests and the city" and to prepare "a basic guide for the immediate and long-range development of the Central City" (Hebert 1959a, 1).

9. Federal rules for urban renewal called for a sharp separation between the roles of private developers and public redevelopment agencies. The latter were responsible for land clearance. Developers were not involved during that stage but were selected later and were responsible for carrying out the project according to the redevelopment plan.

10. Kevin Lynch has used the terms "fine grain" and "coarse grain" to distinguish a land-use pattern that is characterized by a rich mixture of heterogeneous uses from one that is characterized by a single use that covers an expanded area (Lynch 1981).

11. This section of the book comes from an article on Bunker Hill redevelopment (Loukaitou-Sideris and Sansbury 1996, 394–407, 448–49).

12. The word "blight" first appears in the CRA's description of Bunker Hill in 1951 (Community Redevelopment Agency 1951). The CRA's annual report of 1953 (Community Redevelopment Agency 1953, 7) includes the following statement: "Intelligent citizens throughout the city know that Los Angeles cannot continue to support the blighted districts here indefinitely without grievous effects on the lives of those who dwell there and depressing results to property values and tax revenue. Redevelopment is good business for the city."

13. Litigation against the CRA in 1960 questioned some of the findings and procedures followed by the CRA and the city in adopting the redevelopment plan. Some points of the legal action dealt with the constitutionality of the urban renewal process, and these points prolonged the litigation process. On appeal, the Supreme Court of the State of California ruled favorably for the CRA in 1964, and the United States Supreme Court refused to review the decision.

Chapter 2

1. For Spanish settlements the Laws of the Indies required that the church be placed in its own space, at some distance from the plaza.

2. For a discussion of early American squares, see the chapter by Carl Feiss in Zucker 1959 (chap. 6).

3. New York was not the first major city to adopt a zoning resolution. In 1908, Los Angeles had enacted the country's first citywide zoning ordinance. But many historians perceive the 1916 New York City resolution as a landmark in zoning legislation because it combined, for the first time, districting by use with restrictions on the maximum building mass (Willis 1993, 1995).

4. The vertical height beyond which the setback started ranged from 150 to 200 feet for boulevards. It was 90 feet for secondary streets.

5. The RPA was formed in 1922 and represents the oldest regional planning organization in the country. The 1929 plan was the association's first plan for the New York region. In 1968, the RPA released its second regional plan, and in 1996 the third regional plan for the New York–New Jersey–Connecticut metropolitan area (Yaro and Hiss 1996).

6. For example in New York, as Stern, Gilmartin, and Mellins (1987, 45) inform us, "By 1933, when the volume 'From Plan to Reality' was published large scale progress had been made in implementing many of the 470 specific proposals advanced in 1929–1931. For example 555 miles of major highways had been built, rebuilt, or were under construction; 136 miles of new parkways and boulevards had been

built and another 130 miles planned and park acreage had been increased during 1928–1932 from 94,534 to 116,000 acres."

7. Welton Becket was one of the leading Los Angeles architects of the time.

8. In the end, only three freeways were built around downtown Los Angeles: the Santa Monica Freeway, the Harbor Freeway, and the Hollywood Freeway. The fourth, the proposed Industrial Freeway, was never built.

9. The concepts of nominal and substantive clients were introduced by Koichi Mera (1967). He also argued that there should be consumer sovereignty in urban design.

10. Incentive zoning allowed developers to increase the allowable FAR (and thus build higher) if in return they provided some amenities (usually plazas) on their site.

Chapter 3

1. Emanuel S. Savas served as assistant secretary of housing and urban development in the Reagan administration.

2. David Walker served as assistant director of the Advisory Commission on Intergovernmental Relations in the late 1970s.

3. The Allegheny Conference on Community Development, a group of prominent businessmen in Pittsburgh under the leadership of Richard King Mellon, was established in 1943 and initiated an ambitious effort that was called Renaissance I. This effort included various projects such as the reduction of smoke pollution, the removal of poor housing at the edges of the CBD, the creation of some office buildings, and the development of a park (Stewman and Tarr 1982).

4. The enormous and uncontrolled expansion of the Manhattan CBD provides a woeful example of what happens when "by right" development is left to run its own course. This was coined the "Manhattanization" of the environment and was referred to in negative terms by concerned citizen groups in various cities (for example, San Diego, San Francisco, Portland, Cleveland, Toronto) that were opposing uncontrolled growth.

5. As revealed in an article by Christopher Leo and Robert Fenton (1990) such development corporations have been formed by all major Canadian cities (Toronto, Vancouver, Montreal, Winnipeg, and so on) to oversee their downtown development. In the U.K. the London Docklands Development Corporation is engaged in one of the world's best-known downtown revitalization schemes.

6. California's Community Redevelopment Act allows localities to freeze the tax base of designated redevelopment areas. The future increment of taxes in that area from property improvement can only be spent in the redevelopment area for future planning and infrastructure development, subject to a pre-established limit or what

is commonly referred to as a "cap." This practice is known as tax-increment financing of local urban redevelopment work.

7. As an exception to this statement, we should note that Rockefeller Plaza in New York, built in the 1930s, is an urban plaza designed, built, and managed by the private sector.

8. This section of the chapter is a condensed version of Loukaitou-Sideris 1993.

9. In contrast to softscapes, which are grounds covered by grass or dirt, hardscapes are grounds covered with concrete, asphalt, cement, tile, and so on.

Chapter 4

1. Whyte argued successfully for the implementation of design guidelines that would define the minimum size of plaza space, the maximum permissible height of the plaza, the minimum number of trees, and the amount of seating (set as one linear foot of seating for every thirty square feet of plaza space).

2. Adopted, in a slightly abridged form, from Loukaitou-Sideris and Banerjee 1993.

3. Although some parts of downtown are still being developed under the authority of the agency, developers whose projects fall within the redevelopment area admit that the agency now yields to the guidelines established by the planning department.

4. The recession of the 1990s has had an impact on new building construction; as a result, there are not as many developers today willing to start major commercial projects, and competition is not as fierce as in the past.

5. In the 1970s the "pedway plan" was promoted by the planning department and studied by the CRA in an effort to link the different segments of downtown through an integrated circulation system. Pedways were envisioned as above-street-level pedestrian routes and connections between buildings. Elaborate people mover systems would link the most remote downtown activities. The plan was never realized partly because of lack of funding.

6. David Larson, interview by authors, tape recording, San Francisco, Calif., October 11, 1991.

7. Rai Okamoto, letter to Robertson Short, October 19, 1978, San Francisco Department of City Planning, San Francisco, Calif.

8. Martin Brown, interview by authors, San Francisco, Calif., October 11, 1991.

9. Ibid.

10. Frank Cannizzaro, interview by authors, tape recording, San Francisco, Calif., March 14, 1991.

11. Ibid.

12. Jay Mancini, interview by authors, tape recording, San Francisco, Calif., March 14, 1991.

13. Ibid.

14. Michael Barker, interview by authors, tape recording, Los Angeles, Calif., March 26, 1991.

15. Richard Keating, interview by authors, tape recording, Los Angeles, Calif., June 26, 1991.

16. Barker, interview.

17. Keating, interview.

18. Jeffrey Heller, interview by authors, tape recording, San Francisco, Calif., October 18, 1991.

19. Barker, interview.

20. Interview with a CRA planner who requested anonymity.

21. Rolf Kleinhans, interview by authors, tape recording, Los Angeles, Calif., March 11, 1988.

22. Jon Jerde, interview by authors, tape recording, Los Angeles, Calif., March 15, 1988.

23. Tim Vreeland, interview by authors, tape recording, Los Angeles, Calif., February 5, 1992.

24. Don Cosgrove, interview by authors, tape recording, Los Angeles, Calif., March 16, 1992.

25. The by-right FAR in this section of downtown is 6:1, and it can go up to 7.5:1 for rehabilitated buildings. Through transfer of development rights, a building in downtown Los Angeles can reach a maximum FAR of 13:1. The seventy-three-story tower proposed by MTP required an FAR of at least 20:1.

26. Jim Anderson, interview by authors, tape recording, Los Angeles, Calif., March 26, 1991.

27. Oki Komada, interview by authors, tape recording, Los Angeles, Calif., February 1991.

28. Jeff Skorneck, interview by authors, tape recording, Los Angeles, September 7, 1990.

29. Komada, interview.

30. According to Colin Shepherd from Hines Interests Limited Partnership, "The inclusion of the private property markers is a legal matter, nothing more. Owners are advised by legal counsel that the failure to include such signage will bring in to question the long term title relative to the property, and the ability to modify the property at a future time" (Colin Sheperd, letter to Anastasia Loukaitou-Sideris, July 3, 1996).

31. David Martin, interview by authors, tape recording, Los Angeles, Calif., March 1991.

Chapter 5

1. For detailed breakdown of the downtown residents in Los Angeles see Wolch/Dear Consultants 1992.

2. The *Los Angeles Downtown Strategic Plan, Final Draft* (Community Redevelopment Agency 1993) admits that the 26,000 people living within the freeway ring have little access to neighborhood services or basic amenities such as quality schools, recreational facilities, and local retail services.

3. In his book *Shared Space*, Milton Santos (1975) refers to the two circuits of the Third World economy as the upper circuit (the formal, modern sector linked to the global economy) and the lower circuit (the informal, traditional, peasant economy).

4. Wolch/Dear Consultants (1992), in a study conducted as background material for the Los Angeles downtown strategic plan, estimated the concentration rate of homeless for downtown as 116 per 1,000 people and the rate for the city as 2.21 per 1,000 people.

5. The following are examples of such recommendations: "Outreach [*sic*] to those who live on the streets to provide needed assistance . . . " and "On a trial basis, provide experimental and other alternatives to living on the street such as: 'maximum tolerance' facilities of various kinds for people who, for various reasons, tend not to use conventional shelters" (Community Redevelopment Agency 1993, 52).

6. For a detailed discussion of marginality, and a critique of marginality theory and policies based upon it, see Perlman 1976.

Chapter 6

1. Lyn Lofland argues for a trichotomous distinction. She introduces the concept of the "parochial realm," which is "characterized by a sense of commonality among acquaintances and neighbors who are involved in interpersonal networks that are located within 'communities'" (1989, 19).

2. A great deal of the literature on the loss of public life and space addresses urban contexts in the United States. However, some authors have argued that the same phenomenon can be observed in some Western European cities (see Grönlund 1993; Deben, Musterd, and van Weesep 1992; Archibugi 1992).

3. The field observations were conducted in a systematic way. During the months of May and June in 1991, photographs covering every corner and angle were taken at each of the eight sites (we will refer to this method as a "photo sweep" in our subsequent discussions) every half hour for two hours in the morning (from 7:30 A.M. to 9:30 A.M.), for two hours during midday (from 11:30 A.M. to 1:30 P.M.),

and for two hours at the end of the day (4 P.M. to 6 P.M.), on Mondays, Wednesdays, and Fridays. Only midday photo sweeps were conducted on Saturdays. The photo-sweep schedule was staggered and randomized for the total coverage. For the California Plaza site additional readings were taken for Thursdays because of the special noontime concerts scheduled on Wednesdays and Fridays, which were atypical uses of the space. The photos were used as a basic database to count the number of users for the various time periods. The photos were further analyzed to code the types of activities, the specific settings and locations used for different purpose, and users' gender and appearance (that is, whether formally or informally attired), as well as whether users were solitary or in groups. In addition to the photo-sweep documentation, a small sample of midday users was interviewed with a questionnaire survey in all but one site: permission could not be obtained to conduct interviews in the California Plaza area of Los Angeles.

4. Our observations took place before the recent retrofit of Pershing Square (see chapter 5), which has replaced the grassy areas of the park with extensive hardscape surfaces, has employed security forces, and has given this historic park a very corporate look.

5. Michel Foucault (1984) has used the term "heterotopia" to describe a society that has as common trends insulation and spatial dissociation. According to Foucault, when our understanding of public space excludes the notion of diversity the result is heterotopia.

Chapter 7

1. David Larson, interview by authors, tape recording, San Francisco, Calif., October 11, 1991; Andrew Butler, interview by authors, San Francisco, Calif., October 18, 1991; Scott Johnson, interview by authors, tape recording, Los Angeles, Calif., June 13, 1991; Jeffrey Heller, interview by authors, tape recording, San Francisco, Calif., October 18, 1991; Jon Jerde, interview by authors, tape recording, Los Angeles, Calif., March 15, 1988; Lawrence Halprin, interview by authors, telephone, November 1, 1991; Arthur Erickson, interview by authors, telephone, May 3, 1991; Richard Orne, interview by authors, tape recording, Los Angeles, Calif., December 12, 1994.

2. Butler, interview.

3. Martin Brown, interview by authors, San Francisco, Calif., October 11, 1991. Of course, the pedestrian volume on the streets adjacent to Grabhorn Park offers no comparison to that on the sidewalks of Commercial Street and East 53rd Street in New York, where Paley Park is located.

4. Butler, interview.

5. Vest pocket parks are small urban parks, often no larger than one lot. Many vest pocket parks were built in the 1960s (especially in New York City) in high-density inner-city neighborhoods.

6. The plaque was specified in an April 10, 1989, letter from George Williams, assistant director of planning, to Matthew Oliver of AMB Investments, Inc.

7. Richard Keating, interview by authors, tape recording, Los Angeles, Calif., June 26, 1991.

8. Halprin, interview.

9. Jim Anderson, interview by authors, tape recording, Los Angeles, Calif., March 26, 1991.

10. Halprin, interview.

11. Ibid.

12. David Martin, interview by authors, tape recording, Los Angeles, Calif., March 1991.

13. Colin Sheperd, interview by authors, tape recording, Los Angeles, Calif., March 1991.

14. Martin, interview.

15. Johnson, interview.

16. Ibid.

17. Ibid.

18. All of the quotes in the discussion of Citicorp Plaza are from Jerde, interview.

19. Don Cosgrove, interview by authors, tape recording, Los Angeles, Calif., March 16, 1992.

20. According to architect Tim Vreeland, who was a member of the design team during the initial stages of the project (Tim Vreeland, interview by authors, tape recording, Los Angeles, Calif., February 5, 1992).

21. Greg Schultz, interview by authors, Los Angeles, Calif., May 20, 1991.

22. Erickson, interview.

23. This section is taken from a study entitled "Invented Streets: Private Spaces in Public Life" by Tridib Banerjee, which was undertaken with an individual project grant from the National Endowment for the Arts, 1994–1995 (for a partial report on this study see Banerjee et al. 1996).

Chapter 8

1. Jerry Allen, director of the Cultural Affairs Division of Dallas, made the following comment:

> Indeed the very notion of a "public art" is something of a contradiction in terms. In it, we join two words whose meanings are, in some ways, an-

tithetical. We recognize "art" in the 20th Century as the individual inquiry of the sculptor or painter, the epitome of self-assertion. To that we join "public," a reference to the collective, the social order, self-negation. Hence we link the private and the public, in a single-concept or object, from which we expect both coherence and integrity. This is no idle or curious problem but is central to an issue that has plagued public art in modern times: the estrangement of the public for whose benefit the artwork has been placed. (Allen 1988, 246)

2. Corporations initiate public art projects for several reasons: to enhance the appearance of a corporate space; to increase corporate visibility and image; or simply, for investment purposes (see Cruikshank and Korza 1988).

3. According to Jerry Allen (1988, 246): "Much of what we call public art simply isn't. We must acknowledge that from the beginning. The overwhelming majority of public artworks are simply private artworks—gallery or studio pieces—'slumming it' on a plaza or in the lobby of some public structure."

4. *La Grande Vitesse* is considered to mark the revival of public art in the sixties.

5. The murals were sponsored by the California Department of Transportation.

6. Today, according to one recent inventory (see Cruikshank and Korza 1988, 288–95), the following major cities have similar requirements: Anchorage (1 percent); Phoenix (1 percent); Hartford and New Haven (0.25 percent to 1 percent); Orlando (1 percent); Honolulu (1 percent); Chicago (1 percent); Boston (1 percent); Detroit (voluntary 1 percent); St. Paul (voluntary 1 percent); Albuquerque (mandatory 1 percent); Buffalo (voluntary 1–2 percent); New York (mandatory 1 percent); Portland (mandatory 1 percent); Austin (mandatory 1 percent); Dallas (mandatory 1.5 percent); Salt Lake City (mandatory 1 percent); Seattle (mandatory 1 percent); Milwaukee (voluntary 1 percent).

7. Specifically, the CRA's objectives are the following:

    • Develop a public art program that is unique to Los Angeles.
    • Increase the understanding and enjoyment of public art by Los Angeles' residents.
    • Invite public participation in and interaction with public spaces.
    • Provide unusual and challenging employment opportunities for artists.
    • Encourage collaborations between artists and architects, and artists and engineers.
    • Encourage and support participation by women and minority groups that have been traditionally under-represented.
    • Support artist participation on design teams for planning public projects.

- Encourage and support Los Angeles' pluralistic culture.
- Encourage variety of art forms: temporary and permanent, object and event, single or dispersed locations. (Community Redevelopment Agency 1985, 2)

8. In the Dallas comprehensive plan, the uses of public art were explained in the following manner:

- Public art will give the city of Dallas a healthy, vibrant sense of place which will contribute to its prestige and identity for both its own people and for visitors.
- Public art will provide citizens with a means for dialogue through involvement in the public art process.
- Public art activates untapped resources. . . . A public art program gives artists a new source of income and an avenue for becoming involved in the city's functions. . . . Finally, citizens of Dallas assume a role as members of the team, contributing a new order and identity to their own visual environment. (Cruikshank and Korza 1988, 21)

    In Phoenix, a five-year arts plan contained specific objectives for public art: enhancing neighborhood identity; improving entrances to the city; obtaining "artwork of international significance, to serve as a centerpiece and symbol of the city" (Cruikshank and Korza 1988).

9. Indeed this broad definition has led to a considerable turf battle between different professions, for example, artists and sculptors, on the one hand, and landscape architects on the other (see Jones 1986).

10. As Don Cosgrove recalled:

    In the original request for proposal we [CRA] had the concurrence of the board of MOCA, when we said that the museum can be proposed as either a freestanding building, or it can be incorporated in one of the other buildings of the project. We went over this quite carefully with them beforehand and they took the high road and said "Yes, it can be incorporated in one of the other buildings. It is the art that is important. We are not interested in building a monument." However, when we got the competition entries the MOCA board took an immediate dislike to the Erickson proposal. When they became aware that the Erickson team was one of the two final contenders they began to lobby in opposition to his concept. (Don Cosgrove, interview by authors, tape recording, Los Angeles, Calif., March 16, 1992)

11.   As architect Tim Vreeland explained, the decision was quite rational from the board's perspective:

> The board made a predictable choice that in a big development such as this they only represented a small fraction, slightly more than 1.5 percent of the whole project. Imagine how much importance the developer would give to them. The museum was not a money maker but something the developer had to provide as part of the agreement. They would try to fit it in the best they could. So the board made the obvious choice to have their own architect, their own protagonist, since they believed that Erickson would be too much under the pressure of his developer. (Tim Vreeland, interview by authors, tape recording, Los Angeles, Calif., February 5, 1992)

12.   The quote in the text is from a pamphlet entitled "Explore" published in 1991 by Citicorp Plaza.

13.   David Martin, interview by authors, tape recording, Los Angeles, Calif., March 1991.

14.   Jay Mancini, interview by authors, tape recording, San Francisco, Calif., March 14, 1991.

15.   This requirement for cultural activities was written into the owner participation agreement of the California Plaza project and was a result of a series of negotiations with the CRA, which preceded the approval of phase two by the agency in 1986–1987.

Chapter 9

1.   Jon Jerde, interview by authors, tape recording, Los Angeles, Calif., December 20, 1995.

2.   Scott Johnson, interview by authors, tape recording, Los Angeles, Calif., June 13, 1991; Jerde, interview.

3.   This section is based on a research project entitled "Invented Streets: Private Spaces in Public Life" conducted by Tridib Banerjee funded by a grant from the National Endowment for the Arts, 1994–1995 (for a partial report see Banerjee et al. 1996).

4.   John Gilchrist, interview by authors, tape recording, San Diego, Calif., December 6, 1994.

5.   Ibid.

6.   Ibid.

7. Jerde, interview.
8. Gilchrist, interview.
9. City Centre Development is a private company of European investors with real estate interests in the United States.
10. John Vallance, interview by authors, tape recording, Los Angeles, Calif., April 5, 1991.
11. Helene Fried, interview by authors, tape recording, Los Angeles, Calif., April 5, 1991.
12. Ibid.
13. This review policy was stipulated in a June 29, 1967, resolution (no. 6111) adopted by the San Francisco City Planning Commission in view of an urban design plan for Market Street also being completed at that time. This resolution asserted that the design of Market Street was "a matter of utmost public importance to San Francisco" and resolved to establish a policy of reviewing under its discretionary powers all applications for new and enlarged buildings.
14. Richard Hedman, Design Terms of Reference: Crocker Citizen's Bank, internal memo, San Francisco Department of City Planning, August 4, 1970.
15. Internal memo, untitled, San Francisco Department of City Planning, undated.
16. Gilchrist, interview.
17. Jerde, interview.

Chapter 10

1. The emphasis on selected catalytic projects is quite typical of postmodern urban design and planning. Cleveland's downtown plan in the late 1980s also proposes a variety of catalytic projects, such as office space, commercial and entertainment facilities, sports stadiums, hotels, and theaters (Cleveland City Planning Commission 1988).

Epilogue

1. Halprin himself does not care for postmodern architecture and would probably cringe if his work was labeled as such.

BIBLIOGRAPHY

Abbott, Carl. 1993. Five Downtown Strategies: Policy Discourse and Downtown Planning since 1945. In *Urban Public Policy: Historical Modes and Methods*, edited by Martin V. Melosi. University Park: Pennsylvania State University Press.

Adler, Pat. 1963. *The Bunker Hill Story*. Glendale, CA: La Siesta Press.

Alexander, Christopher. 1967. The City as a Mechanism for Sustaining Human Contact. In *Environment for Man: The Next Fifty Years*, edited by William R. Ewald. Bloomington: Indiana University Press.

Allen, Jerry. 1988. How Art Becomes Public. In *Going Public: A Field Guide to Development in Art in Public Places*, edited by Jeffrey L. Cruikshank and Pam Korza. Amherst: University of Massachusetts Press.

Alterman, Rachelle, ed. 1988. *Private Supply of Public Services: Evaluation of Real Estate Exactions, Linkage, and Alternative Land Policies*. New York: New York University Press.

Amin, Samir. 1974. *Accumulation on a World Scale*. New York: Monthly Review Press.

Anderson, Martin. 1964. *The Federal Bulldozer: A Critical Analysis of Urban Renewal, 1949–1962*. Cambridge: MIT Press.

Archibugi, Franco. 1992. A Policy for New Public Spaces and Central Areas: The Recovery of the Urban Environment. *L'Archittetura* 38(3): 213–15.

Arendt, Hannah. 1959. *The Human Condition*. Garden City, NY: Doubleday.

Ascher, Kate. 1987. *The Politics of Privatization*. New York: St. Martin's Press.

Bacon, Edmund N. 1974. *Design of Cities*. New York: Penguin Books.

Balfe, Judith H., and Margaret J. Wyszomirski. 1986. Public Art and Public Policy. *The Journal of Arts Management and Law* 15(4): 5–30.

322

Banerjee, Tridib. 1993a. Market Planning, Market Planners, and Planned Markets. *Journal of the American Planning Association* 59(3): 353–60.

———. 1993b. Transitional Urbanism Reconsidered: Post-Colonial Development of Calcutta and Shanghai. In *Urban Anthropology in China*, edited by Greg Guldin and Aidan Southall. Lieden: Brill.

Banerjee, Tridib, Genevieve Giuliano, Greg Hise, and David Sloane. 1996. Invented and Reinvented Streets: Designing the New Shopping Experience. *Lusk Review* 2(1): 18–30.

Banerjee, Tridib, and Anastasia Loukaitou-Sideris. 1992. Private Production of Downtown Public Open Space: Experiences of Los Angeles and San Francisco. Report to the National Endowment for the Arts, University of Southern California, Los Angeles.

Banerjee, Tridib, and Michael Southworth, eds. 1990. Kevin Lynch: His Life and Works. In *City Sense and City Design: Writings and Projects of Kevin Lynch*. Cambridge: MIT Press.

Barker, Roger G. 1968. *Ecological Psychology: Concepts and Methods for Studying the Environment of Human Behavior.* Stanford: Stanford University Press.

Barnekov, Timothy K., Robin Boyle, and Daniel Rich. 1989. *Privatism and Urban Policy in Britain and the United States.* Oxford: Oxford University Press.

Barnett, Jonathan. 1974. *Urban Design as Public Policy: Practical Methods for Improving Cities.* New York: Architectural Record Books.

———. 1986. *The Elusive City: Five Centuries of Design, Ambition, and Miscalculation.* New York, Harper & Row.

Barth, Gunther P. 1980. *City People: The Rise of Modern City Culture in Nineteenth-Century America.* Oxford: Oxford University Press.

Beauregard, Robert. 1986. Urban Form and the Redevelopment of Central Business District. *Journal of Architectural and Planning Research*, no. 3:183–98.

———. 1993. Representing Urban Decline: Postwar Cities as Narrative Objects. *Urban Affairs Quarterly* 29(2): 187–202.

———, ed. 1989. *Atop the Urban Hierarchy.* Totowa, NJ: Rowman and Littlefield.

Benn, Stanley I., and Gerald F. Gaus, eds. 1983. *Public and Private in Social Life.* New York: St. Martin's Press.

Bennett, James T., and Manuel H. Johnson. 1981. *Better Government at Half the Price*. Ottawa, IL: Carolina House.

Bennett, Larry. 1986. Beyond Urban Renewal: Chicago's North Loop Redevelopment Project. *Urban Affairs Quarterly* 22(2): 242–60.

———. 1990. *Fragments of Cities: The New American Downtowns and Neighborhoods*. Columbus: Ohio State University Press.

Berman, Marshall. 1986. Take It to the Streets: Conflict and Community in Public Space. *Dissent* 33(4): 476–85.

Betsky, Aaron. 1993. All Roads Lead Downtown. *L.A. Weekly*, November 12–18, 16–19.

Blake, Peter, 1960. *The Master Builders: Le Courbusier, Mies van der Rohe, Frank Lloyd Wright*. New York: Norton.

Bluestone, Daniel M. 1991. *Constructing Chicago*. New Haven: Yale University Press.

Boddy, Trevor. 1992. Underground and Overhead: Building the Analogous City. In *Variations on a Theme Park: Scenes from the New American City and the End of Public Space*, edited by Michael Sorkin. New York: Hill and Wang.

Bowden, Martyn J. 1971. Downtown through Time: Delimitation, Expansion, and Internal Growth. *Economic Geography* 47(2): 121–35.

Boyer, M. Christine. 1983. *Dreaming the Rational City: The Myth of American City Planning*. Cambridge: MIT Press.

———. 1985. *Manhattan Manners: Architecture and Style, 1850–1900*. New York: Rizzoli.

———. 1992. Cities for Sale: Merchandising History of South Street Seaport. In *Variations on a Theme Park: Scenes from the New American City and the End of Public Space*, edited by Michael Sorkin. New York: Hill and Wang.

———. 1994. *The City of Collective Memory: Its Historical Imagery and Architectural Entertainment*. Cambridge: MIT Press.

Brackey, Harriet. 1990. Making a New Metropolis. *USA Today*, March 23.

Bradbury, Ray. 1991. The Aesthetic of Lostness. *Yestermorrow: Obvious Answers to Impossible Futures*, 45–68. Santa Barbara: J. Odell Editors/Capra Press.

Bressi, Todd W., ed. 1993. *Planning and Zoning New York City: Yesterday, Today, and Tomorrow*. New Brunswick, NJ: Center for Urban Policy Research.

Brill, Michael. 1989. Transformation, Nostalgia, and Illusion in Public Life and Public Place. In *Public Places and Spaces*, edited by Irwin Altman and Ervin Zube. New York: Plenum Press.

———. 1990. An Ontology for Exploring Urban Public Life Today. *Places* 6(1): 24–31.

Brooks, Harvey L. 1984. Seeking Equity and Efficiency: Public and Private Roles. In *Public Private Partnerships: New Opportunities for Meeting Social Needs*, edited by Harvey L. Brooks, Lance Liebman, and Corinne S. Schelling. Cambridge, MA: Ballinger.

Brooks, Jane S., and Alma H. Young. 1993. Revitalizing the Central Business District in the Face of Decline. *Town Planning Review* 64(3): 251–71.

Buck-Morss, Susan. 1989. *Dialectics of Seeing: Walter Benjamin and the Arcades Project*. Cambridge: MIT Press.

Burnham, Daniel, and Edward Bennett. 1970. Reprint. *Plan of Chicago*. Edited by Charles Moore. New York: Da Capo Press. Original edition, Chicago: Commercial Club of Chicago, 1909.

Caen, Herb. 1978. Bay Area Rapid Transit. *San Francisco Chronicle*, June 8.

California Plaza. 1981. *Disposition and Development Agreement Bunker Hill Parcels R, S, T, U & Y-1*, between the Community Redevelopment Agency of Los Angeles and Bunker Hill Associates, September 30.

Calthorpe, Peter. 1993. *The Next American Metropolis: Ecology, Communities, and the American Dream*. Princeton: Princeton Architectural Press.

Carpenter, Horace, Jr. 1978. *Shopping Center Management: Principles and Practices*. New York: International Council of Shopping Centers.

Carr, Stephen, and Dale Schissler. 1969. Recall and Memory. *Environment and Behavior* 1(2): 7–35.

Castells, Manuel. 1977a. Crisis, Planning, and the Quality of Life: Managing the New Historical Relationships between Space and Society. *Environment and Planning D: Society and Space*, 1(1): 3–21.

———. 1977b. *The Urban Question*. Cambridge: MIT Press.

Chapin, Francis Stuart. 1974. *Human Activity Patterns in the City: Things People Do in Time and in Space*. New York: Wiley.

Chidister, Mark. 1988. Reconsidering the Piazza: City Life Requires New Design Models for Public Spaces. *Landscape Architecture* 78(1): 40–43.

———. 1989. Public Places, Private Lives: Plazas and the Broader Public Landscape. *Places* 6(1): 32–37.

Citicorp Plaza. 1981. *Disposition and Development Agreement*, September.

Cleveland City Planning Commission. 1988. *Cleveland City Vision 2000 Downtown Plan*. Cleveland: Cleveland City Planning Commission.

Colquhoun, Alan. 1985. On Modern and Postmodern Space. In *Architecture, Criticism, Ideology*, edited by Joan Ockman. Princeton, NJ: Princeton Architectural Press.

Committee for Central City Planning, Inc. 1972. *Downtown Los Angeles 1972/1990: Preliminary General Development Plan*. Los Angeles: The Committee for Central City Planning, Inc.

Community Redevelopment Agency of Los Angeles. 1951. *Annual Report*. Los Angeles: Community Redevelopment Agency of Los Angeles.

———. 1953. *Annual Report*. Los Angeles: Community Redevelopment Agency of Los Angeles.

———. 1959. *The Redevelopment Plan for the Bunker Hill Urban Renewal Project*. Los Angeles: Community Redevelopment Agency of Los Angeles.

———. 1966. *Annual Report 1965–1966*. Los Angeles: Community Redevelopment Agency of Los Angeles.

———. 1968. *Design for Development: Bunker Hill, Los Angeles, California*. Los Angeles: Community Redevelopment Agency of Los Angeles.

———. 1973. *Bunker Hill Urban Renewal Development Offering, Parcel L*. Los Angeles: Community Redevelopment Agency of Los Angeles.

———. 1985. *Downtown Art in Public Places Policy*. Los Angeles: Community Redevelopment Agency of Los Angeles.

———. 1991. *Factbook Downtown Los Angeles*. Los Angeles: Community Redevelopment Agency of Los Angeles.

———. 1993. *Los Angeles Downtown Strategic Plan, Final Draft*. Los Angeles: Community Redevelopment Agency of Los Angeles, June 10.

Condit, Carl W. 1973. *Chicago, 1910–1929: Building, Planning, and Urban Technology*. Chicago: University of Chicago Press.

Cooper Marcus, Clare, and Carolyn Francis. 1990. *People Places: Design Guidelines for Urban Open Spaces*. New York: Van Nostrand Reinhold.

Crilley, Darrell. 1993. Megastructures and Urban Change: Aesthetics, Ideology, and Design. In *The Restless Urban Landscape*, edited by Paul Knox. Englewood Cliffs, NJ: Prentice Hall.

Cruikshank, Jeffrey L., and Pam Korza, eds. 1988. *Going Public: A Field Guide to Development in Art in Public Places*. Amherst: University of Massachusetts.

Cuff, Dana, Tridib Banerjee, Ken Beck, and Achva Stein. 1994. Form in Contention: Design in Development Disputes. Lusk Center for Real Estate Development, University of Southern California, Los Angeles.

Davis, Mike. 1985. Urban Renaissance and the Spirit of Postmodernism. *New Left Review*, no. 151:106–13.

———. 1987. Chinatown Part Two? The Internationalization of Downtown Los Angeles. *New Left Review*, no. 164:65–86.

———. 1990. *City of Quartz: Excavating the Future in Los Angeles*. New York: Verso.

———. 1991. The Infinite Game: Redeveloping Downtown Los Angeles. In *Out of Site: A Social Criticism of Architecture*, edited by Diane Ghirardo. Seattle: Bay Press.

Dear, Michael J. 1986. Postmodernism and Planning. *Environment and Planning D: Society and Space* 4(3): 367–84.

———. 1989. Privatization and the Rhetoric of Planning Practice. *Environment and Planning D: Society and Space* 7(4): 449–62.

Dear, Michael J., and Jennifer R. Wolch. 1987. *Landscapes of Despair: From Deinstitutionalization to Homelessness*. Princeton, NJ: Princeton University Press.

Deben, Léon, Sako Musterd, and Joan van Weesep. 1992. Urban Revitalization and the Revival of Urban Culture. *Built Environment* 18(2): 85–89.

Detroit City Plan Commission. 1970. *Detroit 1990: An Urban Design Concept for the Inner City*. Detroit: Detroit City Plan Commission.

Dowall, David. 1986. Planners and Office Overbuilding. *Journal of the American Planning Association* 52(2): 131–32.

Downtown Strategic Plan Advisory Committee. 1993. *Overview/Downtown Strategic Plan: Los Angeles*. Los Angeles: Downtown Strategic Plan Advisory Committee.

Dreier, Peter, and Bruce Ehrlich. 1991. Downtown Redevelopment and Urban Reform: The Politics of Boston's Linkage Policy. *Urban Affairs Quarterly* 26(3): 354–75.

Duncan, James. 1978. Men without Property: The Tramp's Classification and Use of Urban Space. *Antipode* 10(1): 24–34.

Dyckman, John W. 1962. The European Motherland of American Urban Romanticism. Journal of the American Institute of Planners 28 (May): 277–281.

Eco, Umberto. 1985. Innovation and Repetition: Between Modern and Postmodern Aesthetics. *Daedalus* 114(4): 161–84.

Eliade, Mircea. 1959. *The Sacred and the Profane: The Nature of Religion.* New York: Harcourt Brace & World.

Ellickson, Robert C. 1990. The Homelessness Muddle. *Public Interest*, no. 99: 45–60.

———. 1996. Controlling Chronic Misconduct in City Spaces: Of Panhandlers, Skid Rows, and Public Space Zoning. *The Yale Law Review* 105(5): 1165–1248.

Ellin, Nan. 1996. *Postmodern Urbanism.* Cambridge, MA: Blackwell.

Ethington, Philip J. 1994. *The Public City: The Political Construction of Urban Life in San Francisco, 1850–1900.* New York: Cambridge University Press.

Fainstein, Norman I., Susan Fainstein, and Alex Schwarz. 1989. Economic Shifts and Land Use in the Global City: New York, 1940–1987. In *Atop the Urban Hierarchy,* edited by Robert Beauregard. Totowa, NJ: Rowman and Littlefield.

Fainstein, Susan S. 1991. Promoting Economic Development: Urban Planning in the United States and Great Britain. *Journal of the American Planning Association* 57(1): 22–33.

———. 1994. *The City Builders: Property, Politics, and Planning in London and New York.* Cambridge, MA: Blackwell.

Fainstein, Susan S., Ian Gordon, and Michael Harloe, eds. 1992. *Divided Cities: New York and London in the Contemporary World.* Cambridge, MA: Blackwell.

Ferriss, Hugh. 1929. *The Metropolis of Tomorrow.* New York: Ives Washburn.

Fisher, Claude A. 1981. The Public and Private Worlds of City Life. *American Sociological Review* 46(3): 306–16.

Fisk, Donald M., Herbert Kiesling, and Thomas Muller. 1978. *Private Provision of Public Services: An Overview*. Washington, D.C.: Urban Institute.

Fitch, Robert. 1993. *The Assassination of New York*. New York: Verso.

Flusty, Steven. 1994. *Building Paranoia: The Proliferation of Interdictory Space and the Erosion of Social Justice*. West Hollywood: Los Angeles Forum for Architecture and Design.

Foglesong, Richard. 1986. *Planning the Capitalist City: The Colonial Era to the 1920s*. Princeton, NJ: Princeton University Press.

Ford, Larry R. 1994. *Cities and Buildings: Skyscrapers, Skid Rows, and Suburbs*. Baltimore: Johns Hopkins University Press.

Foster, Hal. 1985. *Recordings: Art, Spectacle, Cultural Politics*. Port Townsend, WA: Bay Press.

Foucault, Michel. 1984. Des espaces autres. *Architecture-Mouvement-Continuité*. Translated version appeared in *Diacritics* 16(1): 22–27.

Francis, Mark. 1988. Changing Values for Public Spaces: Addressing User Needs Is Crucial to Success. *Landscape Architecture* 78(1): 54–59.

———. 1989. Control as a Dimension of Public Space Quality. In *Public Places and Spaces*, edited by Irwin Altman and Ervin Zube. New York: Plenum Press.

Franck, Karen A., and Lynn Paxson. 1989. Women and Downtown Open Spaces. In *Public Places and Spaces*, edited Irwin Altman and Ervin Zube. New York: Plenum Press.

Frank, André Gunder. 1967. *Capitalism and Underdevelopment in Latin America*. New York: Monthly Review Press.

Frantz, Douglas. 1991. *From the Ground Up: The Business of Building in the Age of Money*. New York: Holt.

Free Speech versus Free Commerce. 1986. *The Economist* 299(7440): 35.

Freeman, Christopher. 1996. The Two-Edged Nature of Technological Change: Unemployment and Underemployment. In *Information and Communication Technologies: Visions and Realities*, edited by W. H. Dutton. Oxford: Oxford University Press.

Friedberg, Anne. 1993. *Window Shopping: Cinema and the Postmodern*. Berkeley: University of California Press.

Frieden, Bernard. 1990. Center City Transformed: Planners as Developers. *Journal of the American Planning Association* 56(4): 423–28.

Frieden, Bernard, and Lynne B. Sagalyn. 1989. *Downtown Inc.* Cambridge: MIT Press.

Fulton, William. 1987. The Profit Motive. *Planning* 53(10): 6–10.

Gans, Herbert J. 1962. *The Urban Villagers: Group and Class Life of Italian-Americans.* New York: Free Press.

Garreau, Joel. 1991. *Edge City: Life on the New Frontier.* New York: Doubleday.

Gerckens, Lawrence Conway. 1988. Historical Development of American City Planning. In *The Practice of Local Government Planning,* edited by Frank So and Judith Getzels. Washington, D.C.: International City Management Association.

Gill, Brendan. 1991. Disneyitis. *New Yorker,* April 29, 96–99.

Gilmartin, Gregory F. 1995. *Shaping the City: New York and the Municipal Art Society.* New York: Clarkson Potter.

Gindick, Tia. 1984. An Elegant Welcome Back for Pershing Square. *Los Angeles Times,* July 13.

Goffman, Erving. 1969. *Behavior in Public Places: Notes on the Social Organization of Gatherings.* New York: Free Press.

Goldberger, Paul. 1989. Why Design Can't Transform Cities? *New York Times,* June 25.

Goldfield, David R., and Blaine A. Brownell. 1990. *Urban America: A History.* 2d ed. Boston: Houghton Mifflin.

Goldin, Amy. 1974. The Esthetic Ghetto: Some Thoughts about Public Art. *Art in America,* May/June: 30–35.

Gottdiener, Mark. 1985. *The Social Production of Urban Space.* Austin: University of Texas Press.

———. 1986. Recapturing the Center: A Semiotic Analysis of the Shopping Mall. In *The City and the Sign: An Introduction to Urban Semiotics,* edited by Mark Gottdiener and Alexandros Ph. Lagopoulos. New York: Columbia University Press.

Greengard, Samuel. 1988. Let's Make a Deal! *Los Angeles Magazine,* June.

Griswold, Charles L. 1992. The Vietnam Veterans Memorial and the Washington Mall: Philosophical Thoughts on Political Iconography. In *Critical Issues in Public Art: Content, Context, and Controversy*, edited by Harriet F. Senie and Sally Webster. New York: Icon Editions.

Grönlund, Bo. 1993. Särtryck: Life and Complexity in Urban Space. *Nordisk Arkitekturforskning* 4:49–70.

Grubb and Ellis. 1992. *Los Angeles Basin Real Estate Forecast.* Los Angeles: Grubb and Ellis.

Gruen, Victor. 1964. *The Heart of Our Cities; The Urban Crisis: Diagnosis and Cure.* New York: Simon & Schuster.

Habermas, Jürgen. 1985. Modern and Postmodern Architecture. In *Critical Theory and Public Life*, edited by John Forester. Cambridge: MIT Press.

Haig, Robert M. 1927. *Major Economic Factors in Metropolitan Growth and Arrangement: A Study of Trends and Tendencies in the Economic Activities within the Region of New York and Its Environs, Regional Plan of New York and Its Environs.* New York: Regional Plan Association.

———. 1929. *The Assignment of Activities to Areas in Urban Regions, Regional Plan of New York and Its Environs.* New York: Regional Plan Association.

Halbreich, Karen. 1988. Stretching the Terrain: Sketching Twenty Years of Public Art. In *Going Public: A Field Guide to Development in Art in Public Places*, edited by Jeffrey L. Cruikshank and Pam Korza. Amherst: University of Massachusetts.

Hall, Peter. 1989. The Turbulent Eighth Decade: Challenges to American City Planning. *Journal of the American Planning Association* 55(3): 275–333.

Hanrahan, John. 1977. *Government for $ale: Contracting Out the New Patronage.* Washington, D.C.: American Federation of State, County, and Municipal Employees.

Harris, Neil. 1987. Spaced-Out at the Shopping Center. In *The Public Face of Architecture: Civic Culture and Public Spaces*, edited by Nathan Glazer and Mark Lilla. New York: Free Press.

Hartman, Chester W. 1984. *The Transformation of San Francisco.* Totowa, NJ: Rowman and Allanheld.

Harvey, David. 1988. Urban Places in the "Global Village": Reflections on the Urban Condition in Late-Twentieth-Century Capitalism. In *World Cities and the Future of the Metropoles: International Participations. International Exhibition of the XVII Triennale*, edited by Luigi Mazza. Milano: Electa.

———. 1989. *The Condition of Postmodernity: An Enquiry into the Origins of Cultural Change*. Cambridge: Blackwell.

Head, Franklin H. 1892. The Heart of Chicago. *The New England Magazine*, n.s., 6(5): 555–67.

Hebert, Ray. 1959a. Results on Central City Will Be Seen in Decade. *Los Angeles Times*, November 2.

———. 1959b. New Concept of City Envisioned. *Los Angeles Times*, November 3.

———. 1959c. Rebirth Seen for Downtown Area. *Los Angeles Times*, November 4.

Heckscher, August. 1977. *Open Spaces: The Life of American Cities*. New York: Harper & Row.

Hill, Richard C. 1983. Crisis in the Motor City: The Politics of Economic Development in Detroit. In *Restructuring the City: The Political Economy of Urban Development*, edited by Susan S. Fainstein, Norman Fainstein, Richard Hill, Dennis Judd, and Michael Peter Smith. New York: Longman.

Hines, Thomas S. 1974. *Burnham of Chicago, Architect and Planner*. New York: Oxford University Press.

Hitt, Jack, and Ronald L. Fleming, Elizabeth Plater-Zyberk, Richard Sennett, James Wines, and Emily Zimmerman. 1990. Whatever Became of the Public Square? *Harper's* 281(1682): 49–60.

Hitters, Erik. 1992. Culture and Capital in the 1900s. *Built Environment* 18(2): 111–22.

Howe, Frederick C. 1908. The Cleveland Group Plan. *Charities and the Commons*, no. 19:1548.

Hoyt, Homer. 1933. *One Hundred Years of Land Values in Chicago: The Relationship of the Growth of Chicago to the Rise in the Land Values, 1830–1933*. Chicago: University of Chicago Press.

Hubbard, William. 1984. The Meaning for Monuments. *The Public Interest*, no. 74: 17–30.

Huxtable, Ada Louise. 1968. Slab City Marches On. *New York Times*, March 3.

International Council of Shopping Centers. 1974. *The Shopping Center as a Public Forum: The Supreme Court Reconsiders.* New York: International Council of Shopping Centers.

Jackson, John B. 1980. *The Necessity for Ruins, and Other Topics.* Amherst: University of Massachusetts Press.

———. 1984a. *Discovering the Vernacular Landscape.* New Haven: Yale University Press.

———. 1984b. The American Public Space. *The Public Interest*, no. 74: 52–65.

Jackson, Kenneth. 1985. *Crabgrass Frontier: The Suburbanization of the U.S.* New York: Oxford University Press.

Jacobs, Allan. 1993. *Great Streets.* Cambridge: MIT Press.

Jacobs, Jane. 1961. *The Death and Life of Great American Cities.* New York: Vintage Books.

Jameson, Fredric. 1991. *Postmodernism, or, The Cultural Logic of Late Capitalism.* Durham: Duke University Press.

Jencks, Charles A. 1977. *The Language of Post-Modern Architecture.* New York: Rizzoli.

Jencks, Christopher. 1994. *The Homeless.* Cambridge: Harvard University Press.

The Jerde Partnership. 1992. *Process Architecture 101: Jerde Partnership: Reinventing the Communal Experience . . . A Problem of Place.* Tokyo: Process Architecture.

Jones, Mary Margaret. 1986. Percent for Art: Boardroom Decisions Blur the Boundaries. *Landscape Architecture* 76(6): 46–51.

Kantor, Paul. 1988. *The Dependent City: The Changing Political Economy of Urban America.* Glenview, IL: Scott Foresman.

Kaplan, Sam Hall. 1983. New Ideas Offered in Plan to Revitalize Pershing Square. *Los Angeles Times*, November 30.

Katz, Peter. 1994. *The New Urbanism: Towards an Architecture of Community.* New York: McGraw Hill.

Kayden, Jerold S. 1978. *Incentive Zoning in New York City: A Cost Benefit Analysis.* Cambridge, MA: Lincoln Institute of Land Policy.

Keating, W. Dennis. 1986. Linking Downtown Development to Broader Community Goals: An Analysis of Linkage Policy in Three Cities. *Journal of the American Planning Association* 52(2): 133–41.

Keating, W. Dennis, and Norman Krumholz. 1991. Downtown Plans of the 1980s: The Case for More Equity in the 1990s. *Journal of the American Planning Association* 57(2): 136–52.

King, Anthony, ed. 1996. *Re-Presenting the City: Ethnicity, Capital, and Culture in the Twenty-First-Century Metropolis*. New York: New York University Press.

King, Margaret J. 1990. Theme Park Thesis. *Museum News*, September/October: 60–62.

Koptiuch, Kristin. 1991. Third Worlding at Home. *Social Text 28* 9(3): 87–99.

Kostof, Spiro. 1992. *The City Assembled: The Elements of Urban Form through History*. Boston: Little Brown.

Kowinski, William S. 1985. *The Malling of America: An Inside Look at the Great Consumer Paradise*. New York: Morrow.

Krieger, Alex. 1995. Reinventing Public Space. *Architectural Record* 183(6): 76–77.

Kuhn, Thomas. 1970. *The Structure of Scientific Revolutions*. Chicago: University of Chicago Press.

Lash, Scott. 1990. Postmodernism as Humanism? Urban Space and Social Theory. In *Theories of Modernity and Postmodernity*, edited by Bryan S. Turner. Newbury Park, CA: Sage Publications.

Lassar, Terry J. 1989. *Carrots and Sticks: New Zoning Downtown*. Washington, D.C.: Urban Land Institute.

Law, Christopher M. 1988. *The Uncertain Future of the Urban Core*. London: Routledge.

Le Corbusier. 1927. *Towards a New Architecture*. New York: Payson & Clarke.

———. 1929. *The City of Tomorrow and Its Planning*. New York: Payson & Clarke.

Lefebvre, Henri. 1971. *Everyday Life in the Modern World*. Translated by Sacha Rabinovitch. New York: Harper & Row.

———. 1991. *The Production of Space*. Oxford: Blackwell.

Le Grand, Julian, and Roy Robinson, eds. 1984. *The Retreat of the State*. Hemel Hempstead: Harvester Wheatsheaf.

Leo, Christopher, and Robert Fenton. 1990. Mediated Enforcement and the Evolution of the State Development Corporations in Canadian City Centres. *International Journal of Urban and Regional Research* 14(2): 185–206.

Levine, Marc V. 1987. Downtown Redevelopment as an Urban Growth Strategy: A Critical Appraisal of the Baltimore Renaissance. *Journal of Urban Affairs* 9(2): 103–23.

Liebs, Chester H. 1985. *Main Street to Miracle Mile: American Roadside Architecture*. Boston: Little Brown.

Lofland, Lyn H. 1973. *A World of Strangers: Order and Action in Urban Public Space*. New York: Basic Books.

———. 1989. The Morality of Urban Public Life: The Emergence and Continuation of a Debate. *Places* 6(1): 18–23.

Los Angeles Department of City Planning. 1983. Action of the City Planning Commission, City Plan Case No. 83–193 (TDR), July 7.

Loukaitou-Sideris, Anastasia. 1988. Private Production of Public Open Space: The Downtown Los Angeles Experience. Ph.D diss., School of Urban and Regional Planning, University of Southern California.

———. 1991. Designing the Inaccessible Plaza. In *On Architecture, the City and Technology*, edited by Mark M. Angelil. Stoneham, MA: Butterworth Architecture.

———. 1993. Privatization of Public Open Space: The Los Angeles Experience. *Town Planning Review* 64(2): 139–67.

———. 1994. Reviving Transit Corridors and Transit Riding. *Access*, no. 4: 27–32.

———. 1996. Cracks in the City: Addressing the Constraints and Potentials of Urban Design. *Journal of Urban Design* 6(1): 91–103.

Loukaitou-Sideris, Anastasia, and Tridib Banerjee. 1993. The Negotiated Plaza: Design and Development of Corporate Open Space in Downtown Los Angeles and San Francisco. *Journal of Planning Education and Research* 13(1): 1–12.

Loukaitou-Sideris, Anastasia, and Gail Sansbury. 1996. Lost Streets of Bunker Hill. *California History* 74(4): 394–407, 448–49.

Lynch, Kevin. 1960. *The Image of the City*. Cambridge, MA: Technology Press.

———. 1962. *Site Planning*. 2d ed. Cambridge: MIT Press.

———. 1972. The Openness of Open Space. In *The Arts of Environment*, edited by G. Kepes. New York: Braziller.

———. 1980. *A Theory of Good City Form*. Cambridge: MIT Press.

———. 1984. The Immature Arts of City Design. *Places* 1(3): 10–21.

———. 1985. Reconsidering the Image of the City. Reprinted in *City Sense and City Design: Writing and Projects of Kevin Lynch*, edited by Tridib Banerjee and Michael Southworth. Cambridge: MIT Press, 1990.

Lynch, Kevin, Donald Appleyard, and John R. Myer. 1964. *The View from the Road*. Cambridge: MIT Press.

Lyotard, Jean-François. 1984. *The Postmodern Condition: A Report on Knowledge*. Translated by Geoffrey Bennigton and Brain Massumi. Minneapolis: University of Minnesota Press.

Marzorati, Gerald. 1992. From de Tocqueville to Perotville: The Call-In Show Has Replaced the Town Square. *New York Times*, June 28.

McCraw, T. K. 1984. The Public and Private Spheres in Historic Perspective. In *Public-Private Partnership: New Opportunities for Meeting Social Needs*, edited by Harvey Brooks, Lance Liebman, and Corinne S. Schelling. Cambridge, MA: Ballinger.

McGee, Terence G. 1982. *Proletarianization, Industrialization, and Urbanization in Asia*. Bedford Park, South Australia: Flinders University.

McNamara, Mark. 1990. Big Deal on Rodeo Drive. *Los Angeles Magazine*, September, 104–12.

Mera, Koichi. 1967. Consumer Sovereignty in Urban Design. *Town Planning Review* 37(4): 305–12.

Milgram, Stanley. 1970. The Experience of Living in Cities: A Psychological Analysis. *Science* 167 (March 13): 1461–68.

Mollenkopf, John H., and Manuel Castells. 1991. *Dual City: Restructuring New York*. New York: Russell Sage Foundation.

Morris, Anthony E. J. 1979. *History of Urban Form: Before the Industrial Revolutions*. 2d ed. London: G. Godwin.

Morton, Pat. 1994. Getting the "Master" out of the Master Plan. *The Los Angeles Forum for Architecture and Urban Design Newsletter*, no. 2.

Mozingo, Louise. 1989. Women and Downtown Open Spaces. *Places* 6(1): 42–7.

———. 1995. Public Space in the Balance. *Landscape Architecture* 85(2): 43–7.

Muller, Peter. 1986. Transportation and Urban Form: Stages in the Spatial Evolution of the American Metropolis. In *The Geography of Urban Transportation*, edited by Susan Hanson. New York: The Guilford Press.

Mumford, Lewis. 1961. *The City in History*. New York: Harcourt Brace & World.

Murphy, Raymond. E., and J. E. Vance Jr. 1954. Delimiting the CBD. *Economic Geography* 30(3): 189–222.

Murphy, Raymond E., J. E. Vance Jr., and Bart J. Epstein. 1955. Internal Structure of the CBD. *Economic Geography* 31(1): 21–46.

Museums, Theme Parks, and Heritage Experiences. 1991. *Museum Management and Curatorship* 10(4): 351–58.

Netzer, Dick. 1978. *The Subsidized Muse: Public Support for the Arts in the United States*. Cambridge: Cambridge University Press.

Newman, Morris. 1995. Los Angeles' Defensible Parks. *Landscape Architecture* 85(2): 48–51.

Newman, Oscar. 1972. *Defensible Space: Crime Prevention through Urban Design*. New York: Macmillan.

New York Times. 1987. Calcutta, New York: A Revolving Door. September 2.

New York Times. 1988. New Calcutta: At Least Help the Homeless off the Street. December 25.

New York Times. 1989. Help the Homeless off the Street: New Calcutta. May 18.

New York Times. 1990. New Calcutta. January 28.

Park, Robert E. 1915. The City: Suggestions for the Investigation of Human Behavior in the City Environment. *American Journal of Sociology*, no. 20: 577–612.

Perlman, Janice E. 1976. *The Myth of Marginality: Urban Poverty and Politics in Rio de Janeiro*. Berkeley: University of California Press.

Pershing Square. *Urban Design International* 10: 1.2–1.3.

Poole, Robert W. 1980. *Cutting Back on City Hall*. New York: Universe Books.

Portes, Alejandro, Manuel Castells, and Laura Benton, eds. 1989. *The Informal Economy: Studies in Advanced and Less Developed Countries.* Baltimore: Johns Hopkins University Press.

President's Task Force on Private Initiatives. 1983. *Investing in America.* Washington, D.C.: GPO.

Pugsley, William. 1977. *Bunker Hills: Last of the Lofty Mansions.* Corona Del Mar, CA: Trans-Anglo Books.

Raban, Jonathan. 1974. *Soft City.* New York: E. P. Dutton.

Regional Plan Association. 1929. *Regional Plan of New York and Its Environs.* Vol. 1, *The Graphic Regional Plan.* New York: Regional Plan of New York and Its Environs.

————. 1931a. *Regional Plan of New York and Its Environs.* Vol. 2, *The Building of the City.* New York: Regional Plan Association.

————. 1931b. *Regional Plan of New York and Its Environs.* Vol. 6, *Buildings: Their Uses and the Spaces about Them.* New York: Regional Plan Association.

————. 1968. *The Second Regional Plan: A Draft for Discussion.* New York: Regional Plan Association.

————. 1969. *Urban Design Manhattan.* New York: Viking Press.

Reich, Robert B. 1991. Secession of the Successful. *New York Times Magazine,* January 20, 16–17.

Reichl, Ruth. 1984. When Big-Name Chefs Get Together at Pershing Square, They Know How to Have a Good Time and Everybody Gets a Square Meal to Boot. *Los Angeles Times,* July 13.

Relph, Edward C. 1976. *Place and Placelessness.* London: Pion.

Reps, John W. 1965. *The Making of Urban America.* Princeton, NJ: Princeton University Press.

Rieff, David. 1991. *Los Angeles: Capital of the Third World.* New York: Simon and Schuster.

Riesman, David. 1961. *The Lonely Crowd: A Study of the Changing American Character.* New Haven: Yale University Press.

Robbins, George W., and L. Deming Tilton, eds. 1941. *Los Angeles: Preface to a Plan.* Los Angeles: Pacific Southwest Academy.

Robertson, Kent A. 1995. Downtown Redevelopment Strategies in the United States: An End-of-the-Century Assessment. *Journal of the American Planning Association* 61(4): 429–37.

Robinson, Eugene. 1979. Crocker to Lop 200 Feet Off Its Proposed High-Rise. *San Francisco Chronicle*, March 20.

Roseman, Curtis, and J. Diego Vigil. 1993. From Broadway to Latinoway. *Places* 8(3): 20–9.

Rossi, Peter H. 1989. *Without Shelter: Homelessness in the 1980s*. New York: Priority Press.

Ruchelman, Leonard I. 1977. *The World Trade Center: Politics and Policies of Skyscraper Development*. Syracuse, NY: Syracuse University Press.

Rybczynski, Witold. 1993. The New Downtowns. *The Atlantic Monthly* 271(5): 98–106.

Sachner, Paul M. 1986. Horton Plaza, San Diego, California. *Architectural Record* 174 (March): 128–35.

San Francisco Department of City Planning. 1979. Rincon Annex Post Office, Spear and Mission Streets; Final Case Report, September 5.

—————. 1983. *The Downtown Plan: Proposal for Citizen Review*. San Francisco: San Francisco Department of City Planning.

—————. 1985. *The Downtown Plan*. San Francisco: San Francisco Department of City Planning.

Santos, Milton. 1975. *The Shared Space: The Two Circuits of Urban Economy in the Underdeveloped Countries and their Spatial Repercussions*. London: Methuen.

Sassen, Saskia. 1991. *The Global City: New York, London, Tokyo*. Princeton, NJ: Princeton University Press.

Sassen-Koob, Saskia. 1983. *The New Labor Demand: Conditions for the Absorption of Immigrant Workers in the U.S.* New York: UNESCO.

Savas, Emanuel S. 1982. *Privatizing the Public Sector: How to Shrink Government*. Chatham, NJ: Chatham House.

Savitch, H. V. 1988. *Post-Industrial Cities: Politics and Planning in New York, Paris, and London*. Princeton, NJ: Princeton University Press.

Schuyler, David. 1986. *The New Urban Landscape: The Redefinition of City Form in Nineteenth-Century America*. Baltimore: Johns Hopkins University Press.

Schwadron, Terry, and Paul Richter. 1984. *California and the American Tax Revolt*. Berkeley: University of California Press.

Scott, Mel. 1969. *American City Planning since 1890*. Berkeley: University of California Press.

Scruton, Roger. 1984. Public Space and the American Vernacular. *The Public Interest*, no. 74: 5–16.

Senie, Harriet F. 1992. Baboons, Pet Rocks, and Bomb Threats: Public Art and Public Perception. In *Critical Issues in Public Art, Content, Context and Controversy*, edited by Senie Harriet F. and Sally Webster. New York: Harper-Collins.

Sennett, Richard. 1977. *The Fall of the Public Man*. New York: Alfred Knopf.

Sheridan, Thomas B., and David Zeltzer. 1993. Virtual Reality Check. *Technology Review* 96(7): 20–28.

Siegel, Fred. 1991. Reclaiming Our Public Spaces. In *Metropolis: Center and Symbol of Our Times*, edited by Philip Kasinitz. New York: New York University Press.

Simmel, Georg. 1950. *The Sociology of Georg Simmel*. Glencoe, IL: Free Press.

Smith, Neil, and Michelle LeFaivre. 1984. A Class Analysis of Gentrification. In *Gentrification, Displacement, and Neighborhood Revitalization*, edited by J. John Palen and Bruce London. Albany: State University of New York Press.

Smith, Wilson, ed. 1964. *Cities of Our Past and Present: A Descriptive Reader*. New York: Wiley.

Soble, Ronald L. 1984. Enlightened Self-Interest Fuels Plan to Revive Downtown's Pershing Square. *Los Angeles Times*, April 1.

Soja, Edward W. 1989. *Postmodern Geographies: The Reassertion of Space in Critical Social Theory*. New York: Verso.

Soja, Edward W., Rebecca Morales, and Goetz Wolff. 1983. Urban Restructuring: An Analysis of Social and Spatial Change in Los Angeles. *Economic Geography* 59(2): 195–230.

Sommer, Robert, and Franklin Becker. 1969. The Old Men in the Plaza Park. *Landscape Architecture* 59(2): 111–13.

Sorkin, Michael. 1994. Philistine History: Ten Scenes from the Future of Fun. *International Design*, November, 67–69.

————, ed. 1992. *Variations on a Theme Park: Scenes from the New American City and the End of Public Space*. New York: Hill and Wang.

Southworth, Michael. 1989. Theory and Practice of Contemporary Urban Design: A Review of Urban Design Plans in the United States. *Town Planning Review* 60(4): 369–402.

Southworth, Michael, and Susan Southworth. 1973. Environmental Quality in Cities and Regions. *Town Planning Review* 44(3): 231–53.

Spain, Daphne. 1992. *Gendered Spaces*. Chapel Hill: University of North Carolina Press.

Stepick, Alex. 1982. *Haitian Refugees in the U.S.* London: Minority Rights Group.

Stern, Robert A., Gregory F. Gilmartin, and Thomas Mellins. 1987. *New York 1930: Architecture and Urbanism between the Two World Wars*. New York: Rizzoli.

Stewman, Shelby, and Joel A. Tarr. 1982. Four Decades of Public-Private Partnerships in Pittsburgh. In *Public-Private Partnerships in American Cities: Seven Case Studies*, edited by R. Scott Fosler and Renee A. Berger. Lexington, MA: Lexington Books.

Sudjic, Deyan. 1992. *The 100 Mile City*. London: A. Deutsch.

Suisman, Douglas. 1993. Plaza Mexicana. *Places* 8(3): 4–19.

Suttles, Gerald D. 1968. *The Social Order of the Slum: Ethnicity and Territory in the Inner City*. Chicago: University of Chicago Press.

————. 1972. *The Social Construction of Communities*. Chicago: University of Chicago Press.

Tafuri, Manfredo. 1983. The Disenchanted Mountain: The Skyscraper and the City. In *The American City: From the Civil War to the New Deal*, edited by Giorgio Ciucci, Francesco Del Co, Mario Manieri-Elia, and Manfredo Tafuri. Cambridge: MIT Press.

Todd, John Emerson. 1982. *Frederick Law Olmsted*. Boston: Twayne.

Toffey, William E. 1985. *The Urban Form of Center City*. Philadelphia: Philadelphia City Planning Commission.

Torre, Susana. 1981. American Square. In *Precis: Architecture in the Public Realm*, edited by Deborah Dietsch and Susanna Steineken. Vol. 3. New York: Rizzoli.

Tunnard, Christopher, and Henry H. Reed. 1956. *American Skyline: The Growth and Form of Our Cities and Towns.* New York: New American Library.

Turner, Robyne S. 1992. Growth Politics and Downtown Development: The Economic Imperative in Sunbelt Cities. *Urban Affairs Quarterly* 28(1): 3–21.

Urban Advisors to the Federal Highway Administration (Lawrence Halprin, Thomas Kavanagh, Harry Powell, Michael Rapuano, Kevin Roche, Matthew Rockwell, John Simonds, and Marvin Springer). 1968. *The Freeway in the City: Principles of Planning and Design.* Washington, D.C.: GPO.

Vance, James E., Jr. 1966. Focus on Downtown: Community Planning Review. Reprinted in *Internal Structure of the City: Reading On Space and Environment,* edited by Larry Bourne. New York: Oxford University Press, 1971.

Venturi, Robert. 1966. *Complexity and Contradiction in Architecture.* New York: Museum of Modern Art.

Venturi, Robert, Denise Scott Brown, and Steve Izenour. 1977. *Learning from Las Vegas.* Cambridge: MIT Press.

Vernez Moudon, Anne, ed. 1987. *Public Streets for Public Use.* New York: Van Nostrand Reinhold.

Wallace, Amy. 1992. Like It's So L.A.! Not Really. *Los Angeles Times,* February 29.

Wallerstein, Immanuel M. 1984. *The Politics of the World Economy: The States, the Movements, and the Civilizations.* New York: Cambridge University Press.

Walzer, Michael. 1986. Public Space: Pleasures and Costs of Urbanity. *Dissent* 33(4): 470–75.

Ward, David, and Olivier Zunz, eds. 1992. *The Landscape of Modernity: Essays on New York City, 1900–1940.* New York: Russell Sage Foundation.

Warner, Sam Bass. 1972. *The Urban Wilderness: A History of the American City.* New York: Harper & Row.

———. 1987. *Private City: Philadelphia in Three Periods of Its Growth.* Philadelphia: University of Pennsylvania Press.

Webb, Michael. 1990. *The City Square.* New York: Whitney Library of Design.

Webber, Melvin. 1964. The Urban Place and the Non-Place Urban Realm. In *Explorations into the Urban Structure,* edited by Melvin Webber, John W.

Dyckman, Donald L. Foley, Albert Z. Guttenberg, William L. C. Wheaton, and Catherine Bauer Wurster. Philadelphia: University of Pennsylvania Press.

Weiss, Mark. 1992. Density and Intervention: New York's Planning Traditions. In *The Landscape of Modernity: Essays on New York City, 1900–1940*, edited by David Ward and Olivier Zunz. New York: Russell Sage Foundation.

Whiteson, Leon. 1986. The Pershing Prize. *Los Angeles Herald Examiner*, August 2.

———. 1990. Urban but Human. *Los Angeles Times*, March 22.

———. 1994. Bold New Look, Same Old Hope: New Pershing Square Declares Confidence, but Can Design Change LA's Social Habits? *Los Angeles Times*, February 13.

Whyte, William H. 1973. Please Just a Nice Place to Sit. In *More Streets for People*. New York: Italian Art and Landscape Foundation.

———. 1980. *The Social Life of Small Urban Places*. Washington D.C.: Conservation Foundation.

———. 1988. *City: Rediscovering the Center*. New York: Doubleday.

Willis, Carol. 1986. Zoning and Zeitgeist: The Skyscraper and the City in the 1920s. *Journal of the Society of Architectural Historians* 45(1): 47–59.

———. 1993. A 3D CBD: How the 1916 Zoning Law Shaped Manhattan's Central Business Districts. In *Planning and Zoning New York City*, edited by Todd W. Bressi. New Brunswick, NJ: Rutgers University Press.

———. 1995. *Form Follows Finance: Skyscrapers and Skylines in New York and Chicago*. Princeton, NJ: Princeton Architectural Press.

Wingo, Lowdon, and Jennifer R. Wolch. 1984. Urban Land Use Policy under the New Conservatism. *Urban Law and Policy*, no. 5: 315–32.

Wirth, Louis. 1938. Urbanism as a Way of Life. *American Journal of Sociology* 44(1): 3–24.

Wolch/Dear Consultants. 1992. *Homelessness and Social Services: Strategic Planning Interventions and Central City East District Planning Strategies*. Los Angeles: Community Redevelopment Agency of Los Angeles.

Wolfe, Tom. 1987. *The Bonfire of the Vanities*. New York: Bantam.

Yaro, Robert D., and Tony Hiss. 1996. *A Region at Risk: The Third Plan for the New York–New Jersey–Connecticut Metropolitan Area.* Washington, D.C.: Island Press.

Zucker, Paul. 1959. *Town and Square: From the Agora to the Village Green.* New York: Columbia University Press.

Zukin, Sharon. 1991. *Landscapes of Power: From Detroit to Disney World.* Berkeley: University of California Press.

INDEX

Access tree, 61–62
A. C. Martin Associates, 144, 208, 267, 272
Air rights, 85
Allegheny Conference, 75, 312n
Allen, Terry, 241
Angel's Flight, 135
Arco Plaza (Los Angeles), 235
Arendt, Hannah, 177, 300
Art deco, 50, 212, 225, 272
Art ordinances, 236–38, 318–19
Atlanta, 16, 236

Bacon, Edward, 59–60, 67
Baltimore, 43, 79–80, 291
Bank of America Plaza (San Francisco), 202
Barker, Michael, 125, 128, 205–6
Baroque town planning, 41
Beaux Arts, 41
Beverly Hills, 258
Biltmore Hotel, 151, 158
Blessing, Charles, 67
Boston, xxi, xxv, 5, 20, 43, 68–69, 79, 81, 85, 155, 163, 235, 291; City Hall, xxi; Commons, xxi; Redevelopment Authority (BRA), 22; West End, 68
Broadway Plaza (Los Angeles), 24
Broadway Street (Los Angeles), 160, 162, 172, 190
Broadway Street/District (New York), 5, 20
Brown, Martin, 115, 117, 202–3

Buffalo, xxiii
Bunker Hill, 24–32, 68, 87–89, 110, 133–43, 153, 162, 222, 224, 272, 282–83, 306
Bunker Hill Associates, 134, 135
Bunker Hill Steps (Los Angeles), 105, 138–41, 193, 200, 206–8, 230, 291, 302–4
Burgess, Ernest, 10
Burnham, Daniel, 40, 42–46, 281
Butler, Andrew, 201–3, 229, 231

Cadillac Fairview, 134–36, 238, 245
California Plaza (Los Angeles), 24, 83, 105, 133–38, 190, 200, 222–25, 229–30, 238, 245–47, 257, 265, 281, 302–3
California Tax Foundation, 77
Cambridge, 245
Cannizzaro, Frank, 119–20
CBD, xxv, xxvii, 3–4, 6–7, 10–12, 16–17, 20–21, 24, 38–39, 44–45, 48, 59, 68, 78–81, 104, 130, 180, 286, 310n. 6
Charles Center (Baltimore), 65, 79
Charleston, 5
Chicago, xxv, 5, 8, 10,13–14, 16, 18, 43, 79, 155, 235, 277, 293, 310n. 3; Burnham's plan, 45–46; Chamber of

Commerce, 75; Commercial Club, 45
Cincinnati, xxiii, 20
Citicorp Plaza (Los Angeles), 89–90, 92, 94 (photo), 95–97, 105, 128–33, 189, 193, 200, 210, 218–21, 230, 241, 243, 248, 264–65, 274, 301–3
City Beautiful, 16, 18, 35, 40–47, 304
City Centre Development, 265
City Practical, 47–56
City Walk (Universal City), xx, 291
Civil Society, xxvi
Civitas, xxi, xxii, 47
Cleveland, 43, 44, 79, 288
Colonial square, 35, 38–39, 176
Colorado Place (Pasadena), 258
Commercial Partners, 117
Common. See Village green
Community Development Block Grant (CDBG), 74
Comprehensive plan. See Master plans
Corbett, Harvey Willey, 50–52
Corporate Center Strategy, 78–81, 147
Cosgrove, Don, 222, 239
CRA. See Los Angeles Community Redevelopment Agency
Crocker Center (San Francisco), 105, 110–15, 189, 193, 200, 210, 215–18, 230–31, 267–71, 301–2

Dade County, 237
Dallas, 237
Deal-making, xxviii, 73, 83, 148
Denver, 66, 288
Department store, 6–7, 16, 19, 310n. 2
Design district, 69
Design guidelines, 69, 104
Design review, 109
de Tocqueville, Alexis, xxii
Detroit, 20, 61–62, 67, 79, 233
Development agreements, 104
Development rights, 103
Disneyland, 255–56
Disney World, 256
Disposition and Development Agreement (DDA), 83, 94, 109, 135–36
Downtown: circulation, 58–60, 62–63; decline, 18–20; frame, 16, 20, 24, 299; office market, xx, 16, 18; polarization, xviii, xxiii, xxviii, 16, 31, 153–54, 162, 164–69, 288, 308; promotion, xxii, 256, 275, 292; renaissance, 4, 73; skyline, xviii, 12–13, 81, 173, 278; suburbanization, 180; visual form, 68–70

Eco, Umberto, 279
Economic Development Corporation, 83
Embarcadero Center (San Francisco), 65, 122, 211
Eminent domain, 221, 306
Empire Group, 115–17, 202–3
Empire State Building, 50
Entitlement, 82, 309n. 4
Erickson, Arthur, 134–36, 138, 222–25, 239–40
Exactions, 85

Facility lease-back, 84
Feinstein, Dianne, 114

Faneuil Hall Market (Boston), 81, 291
FAR, 12, 14, 80, 84–85, 116, 126, 130, 135, 140, 142–43, 210, 269–70, 301, 314n. 25
Ferriss, Hugh, 50
Festival marketplace, 79, 81, 182
Fifth Avenue Association, 17
Figueroa at Wilshire Tower (Los Angeles), 105, 141–46, 193, 208–10, 230, 243, 271–72
First Interstate World Center (Los Angeles), 84, 138, 140, 158, 206, 272
Fort Worth, 57–58
Foucault, Michel, 316
Fried, Helene, 265–66
Futurists, 52

Gas Company Tower (Los Angeles), 138, 140, 158, 272
Gateway Center (Pittsburgh), 24, 65
Gehry, Frank, 134
Gentrification, 158
Ghirardelli Square (San Francisco), 291
Gilchrist, John, 260–63, 274
Gilhooly, David, 242
Gillam, Jim, 203
Glendale Galleria, xxi
Goffman, Erving, 177, 258
Goldberger, Paul, 154–55
Goodhue, Bertram, 138
Government Center (Boston), 69, 163
Grabhorn Park, 105, 115–18, 185, 193, 200–203, 230, 302
Grand Central Market (Los Angeles), 286
Graves, Michael, 264–67, 273, 275, 307
Great Society, 75
Gruen Associates, 134
Gruen, Victor, 20, 57–58

Haas, Richard, 245
Hahn, Ernest (Hahn Company), 259–63, 274
Halprin, Lawrence, 134–35, 207–8, 302, 304
Harborplace (Baltimore), 79, 80 (photo), 83
Hardy Holzman Pfeifer, 134
Harvard Square (Cambridge), 245
Hedman, Richard, 112, 267, 270
Height district, 48
Heller, Jeffrey, 125, 127, 206
Herman, Justin, 22
Hill Plaza (San Francisco), 157
Hollis, Douglas, 212
Homelessness, 155, 162, 167, 169–71, 183, 186, 191, 299
Honolulu, 142
Horton Park (San Diego), 260
Horton Plaza (San Diego), 200, 222, 225–30, 257, 259–64, 267, 275–76, 281, 291
Housing Act of 1949, 20–21
Hines Interests Limited Partnership, 144, 209, 271–72, 274

Impact fees, 85
Incentive zoning, 69–70, 84–85, 267, 312n. 10; in Los Angeles, 89, 108, 110, 142; in New Orleans, 80, 85; in New York City, 84–85, 104; in San Francisco, 106, 108, 110, 112
Independence Hall (Philadelphia), 60
Informal economy, 169, 171–72, 302
Inner Harbor (Baltimore), 79, 236, 291
International style, 279
Interstate highway system, 19, 56, 310
Isozaki, Arata, 236, 239

Jackson Square (New Orleans), 38
James, Henry, 6, 13
Jameson, Fredric, 279
Jerde Jon, 92, 132, 218, 220, 225, 227–29, 231, 257–58, 261–62, 275, 295
Jersey City, 68
Johnson, Scott, 212, 214, 231, 258
Joint development venture. *See* Partnership, public-private

Kamnitzer, Cotton, and Vreeland, 134
Kansas City, xxiii
Keating, Richard, 125, 127, 158, 205–6
Kennard, Robert, 134
Koch, Edward, 81

Lafayette Square (Washington, D.C.), 44
Land assembly, xxii, 84, 126
Landmarks Preservation Advisory Board, 244
Land write-down, xxii, 84, 103, 222
Larson, David, 110, 218
Latinismo style, 160, 162
Las Vegas, 246
La Ville Contemporaine, 52
Laws of the Indies, 35, 311
Le Corbusier, 29, 52, 62–63, 163
Lefebre, Henri, 178, 181, 278
Legoretta, Ricardo, 134, 160, 162, 224, 285
L'Enfant, Pierre, 43
Lindsey, John, 69
Linkage fees, 85–86, 250
Little Tokyo (Los Angeles), 89, 233
Logue, Edward, 22
Los Angeles, xix, xxi, xxv, xxviii, xxix, 5, 16, 19, 68, 70, 79, 85, 87, 89, 104, 155, 164, 168–69, 171, 183, 186, 189, 200, 206, 209–10, 218, 222, 233,

235–36, 277, 283; downtown, 128, 133, 138, 141, 147–48, 152, 155, 157–58, 190, 208, 220, 223–24, 237, 245, 247, 266, 271, 273–74, 281, 284, 287, 291, 293, 301–2, 305; open spaces, 86, 96, 98, 146, 155–56, 288, 300–301; planning, 104–5, 108–10, 146; plans, 21, 58; privatization, 86–99; workers, 16
Los Angeles Central City Association, 75, 159
Los Angeles Central City Committee, 21, 58, 310n. 8
Los Angeles Central Library, 138–39, 160, 206, 303
Los Angeles City Housing Authority, 27
Los Angeles Committee for Central City Planning, 108
Los Angeles Community Redevelopment Agency (CRA), 22, 24, 27–28, 89, 94–96, 98, 108, 110, 119, 121–22, 130–32, 134–36, 138–41, 143–44, 155, 159–60, 222, 233, 236–39, 265, 282, 311nn. 11–13
Los Angeles Cultural Affairs Department, 247
Los Angeles Downtown Strategic Plan (DSP), 110, 153, 170, 173, 282–86
Los Angeles Planning Commission, 139, 143
Los Angeles Planning Department, 119
Los Angeles Strategic Planning Task Force, 108
Lynch, Kevin, xviii, xxiv, 68–69, 300–301, 310n. 10

MacLaughlin, Herbert, 258
Macris, Dean, 126

Maguire Thomas Partners (MTP), 134–35, 138–41, 160, 186
Main Street, xx, xxi, 5–6, 148, 154, 256, 288
Mall (Washington, D.C.), 44
Mall of America, xx
Mancini, Jay, 121–22
Manhattan, 5, 20, 48, 50, 53, 67, 69, 81, 84, 312n; plan for CBD, 54, 61, 69–70
Marginality, 170–71, 173
Market Square (Pittsburgh), 38
Market Street (San Francisco), 105, 114, 120, 156, 167, 211, 267
Martin, David, 146, 208–10, 243
Marzorati, Gerald, xxii
Master plans, 56, 82
McKim, Charles, 43
Megablock. *See* Superblock
Megastructure, 28, 65–66, 64
Metropolis Project, 264–67, 273, 275, 281, 307
Metropolitan Structures, 136, 247
Miami, 155, 165, 171
Mies van der Rohe, Ludwig, 35
Minneapolis, 43, 166
Miracle Mile, 19
Mitsubishi Estate Company, 131
Mitsui Fudosan Corporation, 117, 141–44, 204, 272
MMA Plaza Associates, 131
Mobile, 37
Model Cities program, 74
Montreal, 37
Modernism, 47, 278, 280, 284; modernist city planning, 28, 283; modernist design/architecture, 24, 56–67, 97, 251, 278–82, 288, 292

Montgomery Associates, 117
Moore, Charles, 134–35
Moscone Center (San Francisco), 24, 83, 105, 157, 211
Moses, Robert, 22
Museum of Contemporary Art (MOCA) 133, 135, 222, 224–25, 236, 238–40, 246, 319–20nn. 10–11
Myers, Barton, 134–35

National Highway Trust Fund, 19
Negotiation, 81–83, 85, 89, 96, 99, 114, 118, 122, 131–32, 144
New Conservatism, 73
New Deal, 18, 75
New Orleans, 5, 37–38, 79–80, 85
New Urbanism, 173
New York City, xxi, xxiii, xxv, 5, 13, 16, 22, 39, 43, 48, 50–51, 69–70, 79, 81, 84–85, 103, 142, 155, 163, 165, 167–69, 171, 235, 277, 291, 293; Regional Plans, 52–54, 61, 67, 311; zoning ordinance, 17, 48–50, 104, 311n. 3. *See also* Manhattan
New York City Commission on Building Districts and Restrictions, 48
Noguchi, Isamu, 233, 235, 240
Noguchi Plaza (Los Angeles), 89–90, 92, 93 (photo), 97

Okamoto, Rai, 113–14, 267
Okitami, Komada, 117
Olin, Laurie, 160
Olmsted, Frederic Law, 42–43, 182, 193
One Hundred First Plaza

(San Francisco), 105, 123–28, 157, 193, 200, 204–6, 230–31
Orr, Eric, 208–9, 243
Oviat Building (Los Angeles), 158
Owner Participation Agreement (OPA), 121, 131, 144
Oxford Properties, 129, 131

Paley Park (New York), 202–3
Park Guell (Barcelona), 218
Park, Robert, 10
Partnership, public-private, xxiii, 78, 81–87, 98–99, 103–4
Peak land value intersection, 16
Pedestrian mall, 66
Pedway plan (for Los Angeles), 313n. 5
Pelli, Cesar, 134
Penn, William, 38, 60, 303
Perini Land Development Company, 121
Perloff, Harvey, 134
Pershing Square, 151–53, 157–64, 166–67, 173, 186, 189, 191, 285, 303
Pershing Square Management Association, 159
Petite, Philippe, 274
Philadelphia, xxiii, 5, 38, 43, 59, 66–67, 288
Philadelphia Center City Plan, 59, 303
Philadelphia City Planning Commission, 59
Philadelphia Redevelopment Authority, 236
Phoenix, 237
Photosweep, 315n. 3
Physical determinism, 68
Pioneer Square (Seattle), 38
Pittsburgh, 79, 80
Place d' armes, 35, 37, 176
Poetics of design, 199–200, 229, 230–31, 295

Poet's Walk (Citicorp Plaza), 241–43, 248
Portland, 66, 288
Portsmouth Plaza / Portsmouth Square (San Francisco), 5, 201
Postmodernism, 97–98, 279–81, 289, 296; postmodernity, 250; postmodern urban design, 200, 278–82, 288–93, 295, 302–4
President's Task Force on Private Initiatives, 75
Privatism/privatization, 98, 278, 286; of public services, 73–77. *See also* Public open space, privatization of
Proposition 2 (Massachusetts), 74
Proposition 13 (California), 74, 77
Proposition K (San Francisco), 106, 204
Prudential Center (Boston), 24, 65
Prudential Development Company, 96, 131, 241
Public art, 103, 233–37, 247–52, 255, 294, 301, 317n. 1, 318nn. 2–7, 319nn. 8–10
Public domain, xxvi, 235, 238, 248, 286–87, 300–301
Public good, 77, 104, 255
Public life, xxii, 175–78, 181–82
Public open space: privatization of, 86–89, 99, 146, 286–88; provision of, 96, 103–4, 146–47
Public realm, xxviii, 73, 79, 86–87, 97, 103, 109, 128, 147, 154–55, 175, 178–82, 186, 209, 220–21, 224, 229, 286–87, 291, 295, 299, 304
PWA, 18

Radial city, 10
Radial urban form, 3
Ratkovich, Wayne, 158
Reagan Administration, 73, 75
Refregier, Anton, 120, 243
Regional Plan Association (RPA), 53, 57, 311
Reich, Robert, 168
Renaissance Center (Detroit), 24, 25 (photo), 65
Rincon Annex, 120, 243–44
Rincon Center, 105, 118–23, 157, 189, 193, 200, 210–15, 230–31, 243–45, 281, 301–2
Rising, Nelson, 160
Rockefeller Center, 14, 15 (photo), 50, 258, 310n. 5, 312n. 7
Rouse Company, 79, 81

Saint-Gaudens, Augustus, 43
Saint Julian Commons (Los Angeles), 186, 189, 191, 285–86
San Diego, xxviii–xxix, 200, 210, 222, 225, 228–29, 259–60, 281, 291
San Diego Redevelopment Agency, 262
San Francisco, xxi, xxiii, xxv, xxviii–xxix, 69–70, 104, 114–15, 142, 169, 183, 186, 189, 200, 204, 214–15, 243, 247–48, 250, 267, 281, 288, 291, 294, 301–2, 305–6; downtown, 5, 118, 123, 147–48, 167, 190, 216, 287; Burnham's plan for, 45; downtown open spaces in, 107, 147, 156–57, 288, 300–301; downtown plan of, 105–6, 110, 115, 122, 125–26, 146–48, 236, 243, 303; and planning, 85, 104–6,

108, 110, 146–48, 303
San Francisco City Planning Commission, 114, 117–18
San Francisco Department of City Planning, 112, 117, 120, 125–27, 203, 267–68, 271
San Francisco Redevelopment Agency (SFRA), 22, 105, 118–20
Sant' Elia, Antonio, 52
Santa Fe, 38
Scollay Square (Boston), xxi, 163
Seattle, 69, 142, 235, 237, 250, 288
Security Pacific Plaza (Los Angeles), 89–90, 91 (photo), 97
Sennett, Richard, 176–77
Shadow impact, 126
Shepherd, Colin, 209
Shopping centers/malls, xx, xxii, 19, 31, 56–57, 66, 182, 187, 212
SITE Projects, 159
Sitte, Camillo, 199, 268
Skid row, 157, 168, 170, 299
Skid row park. See Saint Julian Commons
Skidmore, Owings, & Merrill (SOM), 110, 113, 218, 241, 270–71
Skyscraper, 12, 14
South Figueroa Plaza Associates, 131
South Street Seaport (New York), 81, 83, 291
Spanish plaza, 176
Spanish Steps, 206–7, 293
Spatial dialectics, 166, 308
Spiral Court (California Plaza), 224–25, 238, 240, 246–47
St. Louis, 37, 43
Stage set, xxviii, 257–58, 275, 296
Stella, Frank, 158

Streamline Moderne style, 120
Street vendors, 291, 299
Suburban centers, xix–xx
Suburbanization, 179–80
Superblock, 14, 23, 28, 30, 57, 200, 210, 222, 283–84, 306
Sussman, Deborah, 262

Tax abatement, 84, 86
Tax-cut movements, 74, 77
Tax district, 85
Tax-increment financing, 84, 108, 110, 309n. 1, 312n. 6
Theme parks, xxviii, 255–57, 291, 302
Theming, 265, 275, 304
Third World, 89, 154, 164–66, 168–69, 173, 307
Times Square (New York), 163–64, 166
Transfer of development rights (TDR), 142–43
Transit mall, 66
Trinity Church (New York), 13
Trump Tower (New York), 84
Two Rodeo Drive (Beverly Hills), 258

Underwood, Gilbert, 120
Union Square (San Francisco), 245
Urban Development Action Grant (UDAG), 74–75, 80
Urban Land Institute (ULI), 84
Urban renewal, xxiii, xxiv, 4, 14, 21–22, 24, 28 56, 74, 79, 158, 222, 306, 310n. 7
Urbanism, 250, 255; polarized, xviii; postmodern, xxv, xxvi, 280
User fees, 76–77

Vallance, John, 265–66
Village green, 6, 35, 37, 176
Vreeland, Tim, 134–35

Washington, D.C., xxiii,
    43–44, 235
Watercourt (California
    Plaza), 223–25, 246–47,
    265
White City. *See* World's
    Columbian Exposition

Whiteson, Leon, 160, 162,
    265, 275
Whyte, William, H., 87,
    103–4, 155, 183, 189,
    193, 202, 208, 245, 258,
    305, 313
Wilson, Pete, 259, 263, 274
Wirth, Louis, 177, 181
World Trade Center (New
    York), 24, 81

World's Columbian Exposi-
    tion, 42–44
WPA, 120

Yerba Buena (San Francisco),
    49, 54, 105, 157, 167

Zoning, 55–56, 85, 179;
    envelope, 49–50; vari-
    ance, 84, 103